Crazy is Relative

By Melissa Keller

© 2017 by Melissa Keller
TMI Publishing

Edited by Julie Mosow
Cover Design by Hugh Syme
Inside book design by Tim Gaskins
Back cover photo by Kip May Photography
Inside photo of Keller-Kuhn Family by Jaime Sweany

Library of Congress Cataloging-in-Publication Data
Keller, Melissa
Crazy is Relative: Melissa Keller/Memoir
p. cm.
ISBN 978-0-692-93446-3
1. Keller, Melissa 2. Memoir I. Title
Original Printing 2017

It's odd that we fantasize super-heroines like Wonder Woman while overlooking, in our own real families, people like Shirley. Shirley was the salty-talking, exasperating, durable mother-in-law of Melissa Keller, author of this family memoir, *Crazy is Relative*. By the time you lay down this touching, funny, vividly-recalled family history, you will marvel that any life that began so badly as Shirley's -- in an orphanage because her father ran off and her mother was committed to the state mental hospital -- and ended so miserably in sickness, infirmity and dependency– can glow as an example of love, devotion, and human worth. This book is a tribute to the everyday heroism of the women who are really hereabout, enriching our lives and proving that inspiration is contagious.

James Alexander Thom (Author of *Follow the River*)

Melissa Keller's luminous, tender, laugh-out-loud funny memoir, *Crazy is Relative*, is a nod and testament to family with all its head-scratching, heartbreaking, and absolutely glorious quirks. Melissa Keller has beautifully written a page-turner description of rolling with what life tosses at you, sometimes with grace sometimes with frustration or good humor, sometimes with an unexpected revelation that changes what you thought was true. *Crazy is Relative* captures all of this with a wry perceptiveness for all that is sublime and absurd, and then for good measure adds a cup full of faithfulness. Not faithfulness that is pious or sugar coated, but faithfulness that looks like hanging in there for love—always for love. I could not put it down.

Carrie Newcomer (Musician/Songwriter, *A Permeable Life* and *The Beautiful Not Yet*)

The smartest thing I've ever done was to marry my husband, Thomas Kuhn.

This book is dedicated to him.

There is fiction in the space between
The lines on your page of memories.
Write it down, but it doesn't mean
You're not just telling stories.
                    -Tracy Chapman

Table of Contents

Prologue

Part 1 - Rules of Engagement
1984-2000

Part 2 - Rules of Commitment
2000-2009

In Need of Assistance

Epilogue

Prologue

BEST OF INTENTIONS

My relationship with my mother-in-law, Shirley, was like one of those woven cylinder finger traps I played with in my youth, the kind that is impossible to escape if you're pulling in different directions. We were bound together by our love for her son and my husband, Thomas, and eventually, two grandchildren, but never agreed on what our connection should look like. I thought we should be the best of friends. Shirley responded by putting up a formidable wall, one of the few boundaries she'd ever established as far as I could see. I never viewed the wall as insurmountable, much to Shirley's dismay, and spent years demonstrating how much I cared, mostly because I couldn't let go of a picture of the bond I thought we should have. This image was thwarted not only by her resistance to my overtures, but by the fact that they eventually became forced, something she must have spied early on, given her impressive bullshit detector. Over time, I noted how often my inner voice that expressed love for my mother-in-law was countered by another, saying, dear God, she is deranged.

I felt guilty when such thoughts crept into my consciousness, especially as I learned over time about her growing up as an orphan. Sometimes I would remind myself that she was doing the best she could, that she meant well. It took a lot of growing up for me to see the condescension of this view. But she did provide ample material to make a case against her in my more defensive moments. How do you make sense of a grandmother teaching her preschool-aged grandchildren how to open bottles with childproof caps? Or choosing first aid books for bedtime stories? I still recall her voice as she read to my children:

Once upon a time, a little girl stuck her finger in the socket in the *wall. Now she's passed out and somebody's pokin' her with a stick. Let's find out what happens to her. And **this** little boy just split his head open like a coconut! Wonder what they say we oughta do about that.*

Like so many aspects of her life, when it came to grand-parenting, my mother-in-law blazed her own trail.

This is my story of Shirley, stitched together from bits and pieces that were divulged to me over the 25 years that I knew her, as well as from accounts that have been shared by others since her death in 2009. The chronicles of her past are told according to how and when I discovered them, which was a kind of unfolding over time, looking repeatedly at the same narrative of her childhood, but with greater understanding as various pieces were added to the puzzle of who she was and where she came from. It includes stories of the people in Shirley's life who influenced the person she became and, as such, has been a sensitive undertaking in parts. Although Shirley was aware I was writing a book about her and often asked me why I wasn't writing down something she had just said, the other characters in her story did not know about this endeavor. With this in mind, I have tried to be cautious in my choices of what to share without changing the story beyond the use of pseudonyms where they are needed.

Some of the dialogue I've written between Shirley and me is pulled from my recollection over time, but much is verbatim, based on my documentation of it over the years. Early in our relationship, I was struck by how funny or poignant our worst moments could be, so I began to write them down on whatever scrap of paper was handy. As time passed, the collection of anecdotes and conversations grew considerably.

Overall, this is a tale of my relationship with my mother-in-law, built on a foundation of miscommunication, frustration, and détente. In her final days, when Thomas and I moved her into our home, she expressed surprise that I would allow this. "I guess she really does love me," she said to Thomas, who, having observed our failure to bond for a quarter-century, laughed and said, "I think she really does."

Part 1

1984-2000

Rules of Engagement

Strange Country

1

NAOMI AND RUTH

As a young woman, I fantasized about being someone's daughter-in-law almost as much as I dreamed of being a wife. My mother was compassionate, smart, and devoted to me, so it wasn't about filling a void. Perhaps it was the Old Testament story of Naomi and Ruth that enchanted me, something I heard in Vacation Bible School in the Southern Baptist churches of my childhood. Although I no longer attended a Christian church, such Bible stories remained foundational to my education.

Whither thou goest, I will go.
Thy people shall be my people,
And thy God my God.
And where thou lodgest, I will lodge.
Where thou diest, will I die,
And there will I be buried.
         -Ruth 1:16

My heart was drawn to the poetry of those verses. Maybe I just wanted to experience such a noble choice, without my husband dying, of course, which was what had happened to Ruth's husband before she took off with her mother-in-law. I imagined that my future Naomi and I would have a profound connection from the first we met; I really did. Regarding Ruth's pledge to her mother-in-law, I never considered Naomi's perspective on the matter. I assumed she didn't object, that she wanted to be with Ruth as much as Ruth wanted to be with her. I assumed I would be the gift.

In 1982 Thomas and I met at the est® training, a two-weekend seminar from the 1970s Human Potential Movement, designed to make us more evolved, enlightened, and completely present people, something I wasn't aware I was lacking until I signed up. The training took place in Cincinnati, Ohio, where I lived and was teaching 1st-3rd grade in a Montessori school. I don't recall a lot of what happened, except that Thomas was an eager participant, often volunteering for the leader's demonstrations, and I was nodding off in my chair the majority of the time.

It took about a year and a half for us to begin dating, given that Thomas lived in Indianapolis, Indiana, where he worked as a nurse and hospital administrator, and there were few opportunities to connect. There was a time when Thomas was visiting the director of my school, whom he had befriended at the est training as well, and he took a tour of the building. He walked through my classroom during morning meeting, as I modeled careful listening to a student telling an interminable story about what he learned while reading his big sister's driver's education manual. Thomas and I held up our hands in greeting without realizing our soul mate potential in the least. But once we each showed up without dates at a mutual friend's wedding in 1984 and struck up a conversation, our relationship developed at warp speed, and we knew very quickly that we would be married. There was a level of comfort and trust neither of us had known before, as well as a sense of ways we would encourage each other to grow. Thomas wanted me to experience a parachute jump from a plane, which was a non-starter, and sensory deprivation tanks, to which I became addicted, eventually working at the Serenity Flotation Center in Indianapolis with time in the tank as my only compensation. I wanted Thomas to read books, which took a bit more time to become a daily habit.

A couple of months later, when I met Thomas's parents, Shirley and Walter, it was as their future daughter-in-law. Making a good first impression meant everything to me. In the last gasp of winter, I was on my school's spring vacation, staying with Thomas in his apartment in Indianapolis, which proved to be an eye-opening experience in itself. Thomas's first wife, Jaime, was living in the apartment next door on one side and his ex-girlfriend was in the apartment on the other side. When I asked him about that, he laughed and said, "Hey, I was here first." I had felt an instant connection with Jaime that didn't seem to have anything to do with Thomas, interestingly enough. She was kind and she carefully avoided flaunting her history with my fiancé. Their divorce from four years earlier had been amicable, as far as I could tell. Thomas's ex-girlfriend was more of a challenge for me. She was charming and funny, but very flirtatious.

Plans had been made to have dinner at Thomas's parents' house. I was to pick Thomas up at the hospital where he worked, we would go to his apartment to change clothes, and then drive to his folk's place.

As quickly as Thomas and I fell in love, we happily dropped our standards and saw each other in our least attractive states unfazed. It wasn't unusual that, when I picked him up, I had dirty hair and was dressed in a flannel shirt and ripped jeans and, I still can't believe this as I look back, no bra. My plan, of course, was to shower, blow-dry my hair, and put on make-up and a carefully chosen outfit before meeting my Naomi. So when Thomas got in the car and commented on the near blizzard conditions that had suddenly arisen, I was unprepared for his insistence that we proceed to his parents' home as we were – him in a suit and tie, me looking like roadside trash. I was vehement in my resistance, but he wouldn't let up.

"Listen to me," he said. "If we don't go now, we won't be

able to later and you're going home tomorrow. They really want to meet you and – listen to me – they won't notice how you're dressed. You look beautiful, seriously. You'll see when you meet them. They don't care what people wear. I guarantee they're in sweatpants. Trust me. It will be okay."

As each minute passed on the snowy ride to the home of my future in-laws, I knew this was a misstep. After all, I was my southern mother's daughter, raised on social courtesies like thank you notes, hostess gifts, and matching shoes and handbags. (I may not have worn shoes to match my purse, but I was familiar with the practice and could do it if I had to.) Thomas gave up reassuring me when I became sullen. The only distraction from my misery was a huge tropical scene on his parents' garage door as we pulled into the driveway. It was a picture of a palm tree on a beach and the sun setting on the water just beyond it, particularly striking in the blowing snow. "Well, look at that! That's nice!" I said, trying to find a compensatory tone of speaking, dressed as I was.

Thomas rolled his eyes. "Whoa, Miss Manners. Save it for when we're inside."

"Well, did someone paint that?"

"No, it's a kind of decal you can get. My parents have interesting taste." He stopped me before we entered the house. "Don't say anything about how old Dorothy is!" he said in a low voice. Dorothy was the wife of Thomas's brother, Joe, and as Thomas had told me, 35 years his senior.

"So you think I've suffered a head injury on top of everything else?" I hissed. The door opened and we were all smiles. Focused on my flopping breasts, I was grateful that we didn't hug.

"Hiiii," Shirley sang in what I came to know as her signature falsetto voice. "You're Melissa." Her voice dropped to its normal range. "Tom says you's keepin' your last name so I guess I better learn that, too." She took a breath. "Do you know Jaime? She didn't take Tom's name neither. I guess nobody wants to be a Kuhn. Do you know she lives next door to Tom?" I was too worried about myself to note the reference to Thomas's first wife in the first moments of our first conversation.

Thomas smiled tightly and took my coat, which I was reluctant to relinquish, given my braless situation. I said I did know Jaime and Thomas were neighbors and that I liked her very much.

"Might as well, I guess," Shirley said with a nervous laugh. "She's livin' right next door. But she's got a boyfriend, so it's probably okay."

I tried to focus on Shirley and Walter. First I looked for a way to compliment their décor. My eyes darted from the ceramic statuettes to the fake plants to the plastic on the furniture. I commented on how wonderful dinner smelled instead. We sat down right away, crowded around three sides of a tiny kitchen table pushed against the wall and covered with every condiment known to humankind. I don't remember much of the conversation or what we ate; I was so nervous. It was evident from the start that Walter had a more reserved manner, but he was smiling and clearly making an effort to welcome me by asking about my family and where I was from. An awkward moment developed when Shirley asked, "You's a schoolteacher, right?"

"Yes," I said a little too brightly while pushing a lock of dirty hair behind my ear. "I teach first, second, and third grade."

"Can you teach Joe to read? That's Tom's brother. He keeps tryin' to go to heating and cooling school, but he don't get very far because he can't read. He says he can, but he can't."

"Oh. I don't know. Is he looking for a tutor? Sometimes there are services like that at the public library."

Shirley waved her hand at me dismissively. "He's too embarrassed. Maybe you could talk to him. When you meet him."

"Oh, well, we'll see." I looked to Thomas for help and got nothing. Thus began my list of allegations against him to be discussed in the car.

Dinner was over in ten minutes with the dirty dishes stacked in the sink. We repaired to the living room where Walter pulled out a stack of photo albums. This was good; I love looking at pictures and I wanted to see what Thomas looked like as a little boy. However when Shirley joined us, I found I was unprepared for all she had to say about various family members.

"Here's Lee's first wife, Tammy. Have you met Lee? He's the oldest boy. She was a size 6 back then; now she's really fat. That's her mom, Jolene. She says she used to be a size 4, but she's always been fat since I knew her. I seen some pictures though. They've all tried to commit suicide, Tammy's mother, too. Jolene stuck a tennis ball in her mouth. Turns out it just screwed up her jaw. Lee is on his third one now; that's Marian. We're hopin' this one sticks. Joe's married just to Dorothy. We told them they could come say hi after supper, but they's probably watchin' some show. They's livin' on top of the garage. It's a lot better than when they was *in* the garage. Have you met Dorothy? Well…you'll see."

I wish I could blame what happened next on liquor, but Walter and Shirley were teetotalers and all that I had drunk was Crystal Light. The overall tension I was feeling was a factor, but mostly, I blame Thomas. As Walter showed me pictures, Thomas stood behind his parents, pulling from the stack and holding up photos of his dad in scene after scene, wearing plaid shorts, Hawaiian shirts, a Fedora, and black knee socks with sandals. I willed myself to ignore him and couldn't believe he was doing this to me, my emotions swinging from anger to the kind of hysteria that happens when holding back laughter. After a while, I felt my resolve slipping away and, in a panic, shifted my focus back to Shirley.

"Shirley?" I said. "Thomas told me your maiden name is Peacock. That sounds British."

She jumped in. "Yeah, my sister, Georgie, she went to England to study cocks and –"

Mother of God, I cannot explain what happened here. It's like I snapped. My laugh was a screeching yelp even I didn't recognize. Suddenly, I was snorting and unable to get my breath. Shirley and Walter stared and my cowardly fiancé looked down at the rug, the pictures of Walter now tucked neatly back in the pile on the table. I tried to speak and struggled for words to explain my strange behavior. Tears were streaming down my face. Every phrase was cut off by my bizarre shrieking and gasps for air.

"I'm so sorry...I don't...Thomas was..." and so it went for several minutes until everyone made noises about it getting awfully icy out there and that we should start back. I was still laughing as I waved in lieu of a proper goodbye and thank you. Walter and Shirley nodded and laughed uncomfortably and Thomas pursed his lips, leading me out the door as if I really was drunk.

As soon as we got in the car, nothing was funny. I burst into tears. "You jackass, you made me do that. That did not go well."

"Well, I thought you could handle it." Thomas began to laugh. "Look at the bright side. I don't think they're talking about whether you were wearing a bra or not."

The next time I saw Shirley, I apologized for acting so strangely. She waved it off like it never happened, which was generous. It turned out that Shirley's sister, Georgie, had been in Europe studying Cox, not cocks. As in the Cox family history. Because she had married a man whose last name was Cox.

Thomas called his mom the day after my odious introduction and later relayed the conversation to me. "She just said they didn't get what was so funny," he said.

I groaned. "This is a nightmare. What did you say?"

"I told her that you were laughing about Aunt Georgie researching cocks in Europe."

"What? Are you trying to sabotage my relationship with your parents? That was not the whole story and you know it."

He held up his hand. "Don't worry, I told her I was also making you laugh by holding up pictures of Dad in his old man clothes."

"Omigosh, do not tell me anything else. There's a lot to repair here."

In subsequent visits to Indianapolis, I met Thomas's two siblings who lived in town, along with their spouses and his sister's children. Thomas was the youngest of four children, with two older brothers, Lee and Joe, and an older sister. His sister, Brenda, the oldest and ten years Thomas's senior, and her husband, Dennis, had a manner that was reserved, but friendly. Their children were young adults, polite and careful in their way of speaking to me. I kept wondering if everyone knew about me making fun of Walter and turning family history research into something dirty. Thomas said that Brenda was a good student in high school who married as soon as she graduated. Her children were known to be smart and studious. Their relationship with Thomas seemed rather formal, which he explained was a result of Dennis and Brenda protecting them from his influence when he had shoulder-length hair and smoked pot as a teenager. From there, the group dynamic felt like a circus.

Joe and his wife, Dorothy, proved to be the main event of the big top. Joe was 32 when Thomas and I married, two years older than Thomas. Dorothy was 67, give or take, and they had been married about twelve years by that time. It was evident from the first time I met Joe that he had developmental delays, although no one seemed clear about what they were exactly. He never spoke to me directly. Sometimes, he was silent; other times, he'd talk in circles and never stop, standing in the headlights of the car and continuing a one-sided conversation as Thomas and I backed out of the driveway. Thomas would wave out the window and say, "Okay, Joe, see ya later."

Dorothy was cloying, strange, and borderline inappropriate, but sincere. She'd pat my hair and say, "You're pretty." She carried around a little dog named Baby all the time. In the middle of dinner conversations, she was known to say odd things like, "I wish I was a monkey swingin' through the jungle all day," when no one was talking about monkeys, jungles, or what they wished they could be. She had few possessions, in part due to her generosity. If a person admired a piece of jewelry she was wearing, she'd take it off and give it to them.

I was particularly scandalized by the apartment Dorothy and Joe had cobbled together above Shirley and Walter's garage. It was a tiny space with a slanted ceiling that allowed an adult to stand only by one wall, which was wallpapered by three posters of scantily clad women. A dilapidated refrigerator and stove were crammed into the corner. The apartment held two rickety chairs, two TV trays, a television, and a dirty mattress on the floor. There were lots of cigarette butts, some in a plastic ashtray, but most extinguished in empty beer cans, which were strewn on every surface, including the floor. There was a dog and a cat, pet bowls, and flea powder everywhere. The steps to the apartment were cement blocks that Joe had piled on top of each other. I noted their instability with each precarious step on that first visit.

Finding Joe and Dorothy's relationship endlessly fascinating, I was full of questions. "How did they meet?" I asked Thomas.

"Well, Joe was streaking through this bar one night –"

"You mean naked?"

"Yes, and —"

"Was he by himself? Did someone put him up to it?"

"I don't know. Maybe someone promised him a beer. Do you want to hear this story or not?"

"Yes."

"Dorothy was at the bar, and she had just lost her husband."

"You mean he died? She was a widow?"

Shirley called from the kitchen. "Yeah, he died in her arms."

I gasped. "From what?"

"Oh," she said, "a heart attack or something."

Thomas snorted. "More like an overdose of Quaaludes."

"Hey! I was tryin' to be nice."

"Anyway," Thomas continued, "Joe noticed her sitting at the bar as he ran through — "

"Noticed her. How do you notice someone when you're streaking?"

"Melissa."

"Okay, sorry, keep going."

"So he put his clothes on and came back in to talk to her."

I was dying to ask how *that* worked — you could run through a bar naked and then come back in? But I wanted to hear what came next, so I kept it to myself.

"Apparently, Dorothy liked what she saw —"

"Ugh."

"—and they started dating." He lowered his voice. "Even though she's older than Mom and Dad. That's a secret, by the way."

"Not really, but keep going," I whispered back.

"She was kind of exotic and young-looking for her mid-fifties. She had long black hair like now and she wore all these feathers and beads. They decided to get married right away."

"Wow, how old was Joe?"

"Oh, about 19 or 20."

"What did your parents say?"

"I don't remember. Anyway, Dorothy had inherited what seemed like a fortune to the two of them, around $40,000, and they decided to buy this used Winnebago and move to Florida. They moved down there, drank a lot of beer, smoked a lot of pot, and blew through the money in about six months. Then they came back to Indiana and moved into Mom and Dad's garage and that's where they've been ever since."

I imagined Dorothy sitting at the bar when Joe barreled by in the buff, her long hair dyed jet black and her aging body dressed to say she was open for business. She may have looked like a black widow, but luckily for Joe, she was kindhearted. She was different from other people and Joe may have seen this in the pandemonium of his naked dash. Or maybe he was streaking to get her attention in the first place. Regardless, they went home together that night and sealed their fate as the Harold and Maude that, against all odds, were together after more than a decade.

It would have been a gross understatement to say I wasn't in Kansas anymore. My family had stories, but not like this. I considered the possibilities. My uncle and aunt had divorced and remarried each other a couple of times, but that was about as madcap as it got, at least that I knew of. I began to reconsider the tale of Ruth promising to follow Naomi wherever she led.

2

THY CRAZY-ASS PEOPLE
SHALL BE MY CRAZY-ASS PEOPLE

More strange stories emerged as I got to know my fiancé, causing me to suspect that Thomas intentionally proposed marriage before I met his family. Lee, Thomas's other older brother, and one of his former wives had been swingers. Thomas described this catalogue that existed, with black and white pictures of naked people with black bars printed over their eyes.

"So, it was a way of, I don't know, advertising yourself?" I asked. "And Lee and his wife were in it? Did you actually ever see this catalogue?"

"Of course." He was incredibly nonchalant.

"Well?"

"Well what?"

"What did everybody look like?"

Thomas began to laugh. "You do not want to know."

"True." I paused to think. "Why would someone do this? I mean, how embarrassing. It sounds a lot weirder than those key parties in the 70s where everybody switched partners for the night. At least everyone would have been drunk."

Thomas looked at me. "So I've been told," I added. I considered the catalogue some more. "Did they read it while drinking coffee in the morning? Like reading the paper? What kind of paper was it printed on? What did it say on the cover? Did it come in the mail, like in a brown wrapper?"

"I don't know and now I'm thinking I shouldn't have told you."

"Well, I'm not doing that. Ever."

"I guess the wedding's off." And then he'd breeze out the door, clearly delighted with himself.

At times, I wished I could stop giving Thomas the satisfaction of scandalizing me with his childhood stories, along with tales that were more recent. But my enthrallment with his family always prevailed. He had been telling me about how when he and Joe were little boys, they used to play on the railroad tracks in some woods where "hobos" camped. They would take the men food from their house and hop on and off the train cars with them whenever the train was moving slowly enough, all without their parents' knowledge of their whereabouts. "Once," he said, "we got scared because the train started moving fast after we hopped it, but we were able to jump off in a place that wasn't too far for us to walk home before it got dark."

"And how old were you?" I had asked.

"I'm thinking third grade."

I had tried to explain how outrageous this was, but Thomas challenged me.

"What do you mean?" he asked. "And who put you in charge of this standard?"

"I mean our generation may have been the last to not have their childhood micromanaged, but that's really bad."

"So, your parents always knew where you were," he said.

"Well, no, and I'm not saying they did. Sometimes, they would drop us off at our church on a Saturday, when we lived in Dallas, and we would sneak off to buy candy down the street, when they thought we were playing ping pong in the activities building."

The comparison had given us pause.

That night as I climbed into bed, I sighed and said, "Your family is really weird."

"Well, maybe to you," was Thomas's retort. Then after a pause, "Okay, to me, too. And there's still a lot you don't know."

"Like what?"

"Like my cousin who married a midget who hits her. They

knocked over a bank and I think they're still in some Mexican jail."

It was too much to take in. I gasped, then suspected a gullibility test. "You're making this up."

"I am not."

"Then why aren't you doing something about it?"

"About what?"

"About getting them out of jail, asshole."

Thomas yawned. "We just aren't like that – we don't get excited like you do. At least he isn't hitting her if they're in separate cells."

"I'm asking your mother tomorrow," I threatened, as if Shirley were the source of all things true.

"Go ahead."

"I know you're lying."

"She weighs, like, three or four hundred pounds."

I punched him and said, "Shut up," as my good night. The next morning, when I called Shirley for the precise purpose of verifying Thomas's obvious fabrication, she didn't skip a beat in expressing her ire.

"That midget husband of hers; wait, maybe he's a dwarf. I get them two mixed up. He's the meanest snake I ever knowed. Sometimes, she weared these big sunglasses even inside the house. She got so big and fat, I used to think she should just roll over him at night."

My mouth opened and closed like a fish out of water. Finally, I found my words, though they came out as a whine. "Well, what are we going to do to get them out of the Mexican prison?"

"Is they still in jail? I haven't heard in a while. Somebody said she was lookin' good since she lost a bunch of weight in there. Y'know, 'cause the food's so bad. It's Mexican. They got this daughter; she's a midget, too – or maybe a half-midget and half-dwarf, I don't know – and maybe she knows somethin'. But I don't know where she's livin'. I can't think of her name neither."

I longed to find their daughter and see if they were okay. But also, I just wanted to know more about the incarceration of Big Bonnie and Little Clyde. Another image that had come to mind was a Midwestern version of Charlie in the Kingston Trio's song, "MTA," doomed to ride the train forever because he was short one nickel. And instead of having a wife handing off a sandwich through the train window each day, which was Charlie's fate, Thomas's cousin had everyone cheering for her successful weight-loss.

All these people really did exist and who knew what else I would discover? Walking into this marriage, my eyes were suddenly wide open, with the realization that my assumptions about family life would be challenged, as if I were viewing the world while standing on my head. It felt like what my students often declared as Opposite Day whenever they didn't want to accept something that had been said to them. And if I told them it wasn't Opposite Day, they took this as confirmation that it really was Opposite Day after all, fomenting profound metaphysical quandaries every time it came up.

Everything in Thomas's family was different from what I had expected. I began to focus on ways I could help with various problems, even if no one else saw them that way, establishing the foundation of many fruitless endeavors for years to come. What I didn't realize was the context in which these problems had occurred, that both Thomas's parents had come from their share of adversity, which affected their responses to crises. I simultaneously bore the naiveté and arrogance of the uninitiated.

3

TOO MANY EDITHS IN THE FIRST GRADE

Let us strive on to finish the work we are in, to bind up the nation's wounds, to care for him who shall have borne the battle, and for his widow and his orphan.

-Abraham Lincoln, Second Inaugural
Address, March 4, 1865.
- cited as "The Vision of Abraham Lincoln"
in The Home 1865-1965, p. 50

Early in our relationship, I learned from Thomas that his mother had spent much of her childhood in an orphanage called the Indiana Soldiers' and Sailors' Children's Home in Knightstown, Indiana. It had been established in the nineteenth century for Civil War veterans, then their widows and children, and eventually, for the orphans of all American war veterans. It functioned under a Superintendent and a Board of Trustees appointed by the Governor. There was a picture of Shirley and her four younger siblings that Thomas said was taken the day they went to the children's home in 1928. They were four little girls in summer dresses and a small boy in a winsome, white sailor suit. Shirley was the tallest, anchoring the group from behind with a shy smile.

"Gosh, your mom was an orphan during the Depression," I said, "just like Little Orphan Annie."

"I guess," he said with a shrug.

I sighed as I studied it. "Poor little lambs," I said. "What are the names of the others?"

"The littlest one is my Aunt Roberta," he said. Roberta stood with her thumb and two fingers in her mouth, one leg of her pantaloons gathered at her round, little knee, and one pushed up under her dress.

"She looks like she isn't even two. Oh, look, she's sucking her thumb."

"The boy is Donald. The one that is a little blurred is my Aunt Dot, and this one is Aunt Georgie. She's a bitch; wait till you meet her."

I was riveted. "Well, I do want to meet her. Are the siblings close because they grew up together without their parents?"

Thomas knitted his brow. "I don't think that's how it worked. But they know each other now."

"Why wouldn't they have known each other as kids?"

"I don't know; ask my mom."

"Were their parents dead?"

"No. My grandmother is in a nursing home and we don't know what happened to my grandfather."

"What do you mean?"

"I mean he flew the coop and no one ever heard from him again."

"How awful!" I said.

Thomas shrugged his shoulders again. "I guess so. Nobody ever talks about him, so he's never been very real to me."

"And their mother couldn't take care of them?"

"Yeah, she was in Central State Hospital in Indy."

"What was wrong with her?"

"Some kind of mental breakdown. I never knew the details."

"That is so sad," was all I could think to say.

Shirley wasn't one to talk much about her experience as an orphan. She just said she was grateful to have been given shelter and food during the Depression, and to have learned a trade as a beautician. I tried to be sensitive in these conversations, but my curiosity often got the best of me. "Did the five of you lean on each other?" I asked.

Shirley stared at me for a moment. "Lean on each other! We hardly even got to look at each other! Back then, they thought it was best to keep all of us in our different groups. We never saw each other, except sometimes during meals in the dining hall. But we wasn't allowed to talk to people at other tables. One time I snuck into the infirmary when I heard Georgie had got her appendix out. That was the first we talked to each other in years."

"Did they think separation helped kids to adjust or something? It's so wrong!" My mind flashed to my second-grade student who was spending time each morning in the preschool downstairs, helping his little sister adjust to being separated from her mother. She had been terrified at drop-off time, but Jacob's presence for the few minutes it took for her to be drawn into an activity made all the difference. And she was apart from her mother for a few hours, not a lifetime. I also thought of a song a friend had ruefully shared with me, the song her three-year-old son had been taught at his daycare center. "My mommy comes back. She always comes back. She ne-ver will forge-et me." I had reassured her that this song, clearly made up on the spot by a teacher wanting to mollify her anxious little boy, didn't mean she was a bad mother, and that of course she would never forget her own child. It didn't help that he had this tune stuck in his head and was singing it to himself all the time, including in front of her in-laws and at the pediatrician's office.

"Well, times was like that. We wasn't friendly – my sisters – till we married. They didn't push being friendly in the home. They didn't push relationships. It was different then. My first day, they changed my name."

I was dumbfounded. "What?"

"Yeah, my name is Edith Shirley. But when I got there, there was hundreds of kids and five Edith's in the first grade. So the matron said, 'We have too many Ediths; we're gonna call you

Shirley.'" She paused. "I always liked Shirley better anyhow. I got a lot of razzing though, when I was older. You know, boys are cruel. Sitting in church, they'd say, 'Shirley goodness and peacock will follow you all the days of your life.' But there was worse names than mine."

By 1928, Shirley's father, Morris Peacock, had ensured the eligibility of his five children to live in the Indiana Soldiers' and Sailors' Orphans' Home in two ways. He served in WWI and he deserted his family. It is remarkable to think that it could have been worse, that the children could have been loaded on to trains heading to rural areas farther west, resulting in the phrase, "put up for adoption," used to this day without knowledge that this was a physical action, to put a child up on a train. They would have been displayed like cattle at train stops and inspected by people responding to advertisements about orphans that needed homes, a practice that was waning, but still in existence in the late 1920s. Often, children were chosen as glorified indentured servants doing farm work or caring for younger children.

Shirley and her four younger siblings had a place to go where all their physical needs would be met. They were safe, sheltered, and fed, but no one was there to help them remember who they were, that they were part of a family; indeed, they may have had their first names changed. No one was paid to love and cherish them as only a parent could. The year after the children moved to the orphanage in Knightstown, it was renamed the Indiana Soldiers' and Sailors' Children's Home. Four out of the five children lived there until they were 18. It would be a while before I knew why Donald left earlier.

I framed the print of Shirley and her siblings going to the orphanage and found myself drawn to it many times. Shirley, 8 years old, was tall and had her hair cut in a short, dark bob, as did Georgia and Dot. Georgia peeked up at the camera, her head hung low. There were deep circles under her eyes. From crying? I asked myself. The teacher in me wondered if she had allergies. She looked shy or scared or sad, maybe a combination of all of them. Staring at the picture, I had many questions that would remain unanswered for a long time.

TURNABOUT IS FAIR PLAY

My parents were moving to the Philippines in 1984, having lived in England the previous three years for my father's work as the CEO for Procter and Gamble in Great Britain. Now he was transferring to Manila, again as a CEO. In their absence, the family gathering place had become my grandmother's apartment in Cincinnati. This was where my two older sisters, Laurie and Lynne, my younger brother, Rob, and I met once a month to talk on the phone when Mom and Dad called. I had broken an agreement to limit expensive international calls, calling mid-month to tell my parents that I had met someone whom I was going to marry. This must have been a lot to take in all at once. In hindsight, it might have been better to have let them know I was dating a man named Thomas during one of the monthly calls, then tell them later that things were going swimmingly, and eventually, that we were engaged. But being in love, it was hard to hold back, so it came out all at once. They expressed guarded enthusiasm, perhaps wringing their hands when we hung up. That's what I would do as a parent hearing such a declaration today.

Not long after my announcement, my mother was scheduled to come home for a visit while my father remained overseas. It was interesting to see the shoe on the other foot, noticing Thomas's nervousness about meeting her, and with my siblings and grandmother looking on, all of whom he had already met. Over the years my parents were gone, we had stopped picking them up at the airport en masse and usually took turns making the trip. Lynne was picking Mom up that day while the rest of us waited at my grandmother's place, a grandmother we referred to as Mom, too.

"Why do you call your grandmother, 'Mom'?" Thomas had asked.

"I don't know." I paused. "I think my oldest sister, Laurie, started that when she saw my dad calling her Mom."

"Isn't it confusing?"

I shrugged my shoulders. "Maybe sometimes. It shouldn't be a problem for you, since my parents will want you to call them Alex and Gayle." It had been a relief that I wasn't expected to call my future in-laws Mom and Dad.

We sat around, catching up with each other, and Thomas seemed to be holding his own with Rob, Laurie, Lynne's husband Mark, my grandmother, and several young nieces and nephews. He was taken aback, however, when Rob glanced at his watch and announced, "The Visa has landed." We all had various requests for money whenever my parents came home. Mom visiting without Dad, who was less likely to hand out cash without questions, was an opportunity no one wanted to miss.

My mother came through the door all smiles and charm and warmth, impressive after her long flight. I could tell Thomas was struck by her beauty the moment he saw her. At 49, she was lovely, a strawberry blonde with fair skin, and impeccably dressed. In other words, she looked nothing like me, wearing old jeans and having recently cut my dark hair very short, sticking up in front in an unintended, almost-punk style. Although she was happy to see everyone, her grandchildren in particular, it was gratifying to see her interest focused on the man who would be the newest member of the family.

"You go by Thomas?" she said. "I just love that. And how do you pronounce your last name? Is it 'kyuhn'?" I could tell she was hoping for the European pronunciation, still one syllable, but a variation on what sounded like coon.

"No," Thomas said with a smile. "It's Kuhn. Like Coon-Dog, which was my nickname in high school."

"Oh!" she said with a laugh.

After a few minutes had passed, my mother dreamily said, "Melissa Kuhn," pronounced kyuhn, her selective memory on full display. I looked at Thomas and he shook his head almost imperceptibly. Better to deal with such things later.

Maybe my mother saw Thomas's admiration of her and responded in kind. I don't know what it was exactly, but they became fast friends in that meeting and Thomas never lost his sense of awe of her in the eight years they knew each other. All our family dynamics fascinated him. Adult kids asking for money from a parent who could afford to give it. (She said yes to my need to go to the dentist, no to the pricey time management workshop I wanted to take.) Other than his mother, I don't think Thomas had ever known a middle-aged woman so keenly interested in him. He basked in her attention, actually forming a small crush that bothered me only a little. From that day forward, I knew I wouldn't have an ally in my mother when it came to bitching about my husband, if everything that I found charming began to grate. Somehow, I knew she would take his side and point out what I was doing wrong and how I could try harder, because Thomas was such a good and sensitive man. There was more good to this situation than bad, so I accepted it easily enough.

Although she had the good manners not to launch into this when they first met, it was hardly surprising that eventually, my mother posed the question, "Thomas, you would make such a wonderful doctor. Is there a reason you chose to become a nurse?" Geez, Mom, I thought, and sputtered some incoherent protest that she would ask such a thing. But Thomas's response was sincere and articulate, describing the difference between treating disease and treating people, and why being a nurse was the better choice for him. She sighed in approval. "I can just tell you are marvelous at your job." Maybe I was just jealous that my relationship with Shirley hadn't gotten off to such a good start, this being my only explanation for my grudging acceptance of something quite lovely.

Thomas didn't meet my father until a couple months before our wedding, after we had already moved in together. Given my parents' position on the impropriety of this situation, and the absence of my mother since Dad only came into town briefly for a business meeting, it felt different. Not a love fest, but cordial still. Thomas admired my father for his intelligence and wit from the first time they met. He was also intimidated and wanted to earn my dad's approval and affection, but knew it might take a bit more time than with my mom, with whom he had an immediate rapport. It wasn't until after my parents had moved back home, when my father yelled at him for walking into the sliding screen door, that Thomas knew he was being seen as one of the gang. I don't know what it was about that screen door. We all kept bumping into and bending it, and it really got my father's goat.

5

MEETING IN THE MIDDLE

As soon as the school year finished in the spring of 1984, Thomas and I found a place to live in Batesville, Indiana, which was halfway between our jobs in Indianapolis and Cincinnati. Enchanted by the thought of living in a rural area, I first found a ramshackle house for rent, outside of town, with nothing but cornfields as far as the eye could see. Thomas met me in Batesville one evening in May to see what I had been talking about. To my dismay, he thought the place was a terrible idea.

"Well, first of all, the road isn't paved, which will be a problem in the winter. Good roads are going to be important in our lives this year. And, Melissa, this place has no insulation. It'll be freezing as soon as it starts to get even a little cold."

My romantic notion of our love keeping us warm began to fade. "I guess I didn't really think about that. Don't you think it's a cool house though? And wouldn't it be a blast to have parties this summer in this field?"

He stared at me for a moment. "Who's going to come to a party in Batesville? And there's no air conditioning."

"We could get a window unit."

"I don't want to live here."

I didn't pout for very long, although I still think it would have been a nice memory to begin our lives together in that old farmhouse. Much more interesting than the apartment we settled on in the Village in the Woods complex in town. But life at home was easier there, with good roads on which to travel when the heavy snows indeed came that year and reliable air-conditioning that summer. The air-conditioning was appreciated when the farmers covered their fields with manure and I couldn't get the windows closed fast enough. On the road trip vacations of my youth, I remembered passing through towns like this, where the stink was a remarkable assault to your olfactory senses. Coming from solid suburban stock, my siblings and I would exclaim, "How could anyone live here?" In the summer of 1984, I pondered this question and was glad we didn't settle in that shack, smack dab in the middle of those fertilized fields, hardly the party atmosphere I had imagined.

Soon after we moved to our new apartment, Thomas brought Shirley into town to see it. She came up the stairs in the entryway. "Well, isn't this nice! It's big! I don't know why you need a place this big." She looked around. "I like the kitchen. Hey, you got a dishwasher."

"Yes!" I said, my relief audible.

She made her way up the stairs and looked around. "Tom says you got two bedrooms. Ain't that more expensive? Why do you need two bedrooms? Oh."

She had found the second bedroom, which was crammed with boxes and piles of my things.

"Well, what is all this doin' here? Melissa, is this all yours? What is this stuff?"

Suddenly, I felt defensive. "Oh, all kinds of things. For teaching, mostly. And things that are sentimental to me."

"It's a lot! What's all these books? Is they all for teaching?" she frowned as she studied the cover of *The Cinderella Complex*.

"Well, no."

"Why do you need so many?" She continued before I had a chance to respond. "You haven't read all them, have you? Did Tom have to carry all them in?"

"No, I did," I stammered. "Along with my friend, Mary, and my brother. And, Thomas, too."

"Seems crazy to me." Uncertain about what to say, I let her have the last word.

We didn't spend a lot of time at home in Batesville, leaving early in the mornings and getting home late each night. Some nights, we each stayed in Cincinnati or Indianapolis, me with my grandmother and Thomas with his parents, because the few hours we'd have at home didn't merit the drive back and forth. But the weekends when we were there were delightful. We knew no one, except the elderly couple whom we had befriended in the laundry room, so our time and attention were devoted only to each other. We took long walks around town, usually ending up at the Dairy Queen for supper on Saturday nights.

Often we would go for Sunday drives. One winter day when we drove past Paoli, a small town in southern Indiana, we saw at a distance through the bare trees a massive dome and drove in its direction to explore it. We arrived at the falling down relic of the West Baden Springs Hotel, one mile from the French Lick Resort, a name that provoked juvenile snickering on my part. We approached the old hotel cautiously, wondering if it really was okay to walk around freely under this immense, crumbling dome - - as a sign indicated, the largest free-standing dome in the world until the Houston Astrodome was built. We later found out that West Baden and French Lick had had their heyday in the early part of the 20th century, when millionaires and celebrities flocked to rural Indiana by train to partake of the region's restorative mineral springs, said to cure almost anything. It felt like our own personal discovery, like no one else had ever seen something so grand. After this initial, awe-inspiring experience, I hoped West Baden would be restored and carefully watched the process of this happening until its grand reopening twenty years hence.

When we described our great find to Shirley, she was unimpressed. "I been there," she said, "back when it was still open."

"You have?" I said, fascinated. "Why were you there? What was it like?"

"I don't really remember, but they took all us orphans there for a field trip. They took us down to the basement and give us cups. They made us drink that Pluto water; that's what they called that stuff. Shooo-eee, did it stink!"

"Did you drink it?" I asked, remembering the pervasive smell of rotten eggs from the sulfur water natural to the region. "I know the kids in my class wouldn't touch that stuff!" Maybe someone who would take a dare, I thought, considering all the ways one achieved status in my 1st-3rd grade classroom. But the truth was that if I had required children to drink Pluto water in 1984, I would have been faced with irate parents threatening to sue me for damages.

"Well, yeah, we were orphans. They told us to drink it, so we did. That's how it was. It stunk to high heaven, too! Later on, 'cause of the Depression, nobody had any money and it closed down and the Jewzies took it over. No, the Jewzits."

Thomas attempted to correct his mother. "The Jesuits."

"Well, that's what I said."

Thomas's and my commutes to Cincinnati and Indianapolis that year were comparable, though we enjoyed pointing out ways we each had it harder. Thomas's drive was a few minutes longer than mine, but I had to deal with a time difference and always drove into the sunrise or sunset with the sun in my eyes. This was a reach, but it was my story and I stuck with it.

New, true love was evident in many forms, including our habit of making each other breakfast shakes and egg sandwiches that could be eaten while driving to work, and even my renewed interest in brushing my hair before Thomas got home from work if I got there first. The most dramatic example of my devotion to my fiancé was the artwork that hung on the wall above our kitchen table. It was his beloved iconic poster of naked Natassja

Kinski with a massive boa constrictor strategically wrapped around her body. Classy. Soon enough, it would be relegated to the garage of our first house, then banished altogether, its destination quickly forgotten. But in 1984, love was blind and if it made Thomas happy, what did I care? In fact, I didn't even give it a moment's thought as we sat at the kitchen table, eating chicken casserole with Shirley and Walter, who had driven to Batesville one evening for dinner. Conversation was limited, as usual, with no one feeling the awkwardness of that but me. The meal ended quickly, and since nothing was on television that they wanted to watch, they were on their way in no time. About an hour after they left, we received a phone call from Shirley, who was having trouble containing her laughter.

"Walter said something funny. This is Shirley, by the way."

"What was that?" I asked.

"He said –." Gasps and guffaws interrupted her speech.

"He said," more laughs, "Oh, hold on just a minute." Finally, she recovered her composure.

"He said, 'How can Melissa stand that picture of Jaime hanging on the wall?'" At this point, I was laughing just as hard at the thought of Thomas's first wife, naked, wrapped in a snake, and greeting us each day over morning coffee.

"Well, this is expensive, so I gotta go," Shirley said, and I could still hear her high-pitched hooting as she hung up the phone.

We wasted no time calling Jaime, laughing and finally getting the words out, "Guess what Walter thinks?"

I can't recall whether anyone ever set him straight.

6

GOING TO THE CHAPEL

Thomas and I chose the Saturday before Thanksgiving of 1984 for our wedding, mostly because the few days we could each take off from work could be tagged on to an established holiday, with a plan to take a longer honeymoon the next summer; plus it would be easier for my parents to be in town then. Although I missed my mother while planning the wedding, I also recall the two of us making each other crazy whenever we were together. The choice of November 17th took place in a tense interaction while I was visiting my parents that spring, with me throwing up my hands and saying, "I don't care," and my mother saying, "Fine," with a finality that was all too familiar.

Later that day, my mother called to me. "I just realized something," she said. "November 17th is your grandparents' anniversary." Both my mother's parents were dead, her mother having passed away recently. She was grieving her loss very hard. This contributed to our interpersonal struggle because she seemed inconsolable at times and I didn't know how to comfort her. But here was a small moment of redemption. Knowing my grandparents would be honored by this choice, even if it was coincidental, seemed a very good sign. Eventually, my mother offered Thomas and me the use of her mother's wedding rings.

Since my parents lived so far away, I did most of the planning for my wedding without much help. Maybe that's why I don't recall it fondly. Thomas was open, but clueless, when it came to the details. I was fortunate to have an older sister, however, who saw early on that I was in over my head. My daily commute from Batesville took a lot of time, so I ended up planning the wedding during twenty-minute breaks in my teaching day. My sister, Lynne, was the one who went with me to a department store one night and helped me pick out items for my bridal registry. When it came to household appliances and fine dining accoutrements, my preferences were underdeveloped. The main criteria for choices were expediency and what my mother would approve of, and I was grateful for Lynne's expertise in these matters.

When the time came to plan the rehearsal and rehearsal dinner, I asked Thomas how he thought that should go. He looked at me with bewilderment. "I don't know. Whatever you think is fine with me." We stared at each other for a moment.

"Thomas," I said as gently as I knew how. "Do you know that it's traditional for the groom's family to plan the rehearsal dinner?"

He furrowed his brow. "Traditional? I've never heard of that. And I know my parents haven't either." He looked at me suspiciously. "They didn't do that when Jaime and I got married. Are you sure that's really what people do?"

"I'm sure."

"It isn't something just your family does?"

"Nope."

"Why haven't I ever heard of it then?"

"I guess you just didn't notice with other people's weddings." I paused before continuing. "They're supposed to pay for it, too."

Thomas laughed. "Okay, that isn't going to happen." Then he got serious. "So this is what your family expects?"

I shrugged my shoulders.

"We're going to have to handle it, then. My parents won't know what to do. Seriously, they've never heard of this. We'll have to pay for it, too. Will it cost very much?"

It struck me as odd that Thomas didn't know about the rehearsal dinner tradition. Conversely, I wondered whether I was the one with unusual expectations and didn't know it because I was sheltered. I asked him about his parents' wedding and, getting nowhere, decided I'd ask Shirley the next time we were over at their house.

Soon after, I started the conversation obliquely as we washed the dishes after dinner. "Shirley, how old were you and Walter when you got married?"

"Oh, I don't know. We was in our twenties."

"How did you meet?"

"Somebody set us up on a blind date."

"Oh, yeah? Where was that?"

"I don't know."

It was like pulling teeth.

"When was your wedding?"

She put the dishrag down and sighed. "We got married on Memorial Day, in 1941. I wrote it down somewhere."

I recalled Shirley's birth year of 1920. "So, you were 21?"

"I guess."

"Do you have any pictures of your wedding?"

"Well, they's one. I suppose you wanna see it."

"Would you mind?"

"No, but it wasn't nothin' fancy like your wedding's gonna be." She went into her bedroom and came out holding a 5x7 black and white photograph sitting crooked in its frame. I studied it for a moment, which made her laugh. "I told you it ain't much."

"No, it's…interesting."

That was the best descriptor I could come up with. It is an odd picture, a somber close up of Shirley and Walter holding their hands together waist high, upon which rests another hand reaching in from the side of the picture, supposedly that of the justice of the peace. In the disembodied justice's other hand is a Bible. Shirley is staring at the camera and Walter straight ahead at no one, his chin slightly tucked. They look like they're being sentenced to life in prison. They are certainly young. Walter has his hair slicked back and is wearing a pinstripe suit and tie. Shirley has on a white skirt and blouse with capped sleeves that come to just above her elbow. She isn't wearing any jewelry, but has a white flower corsage pinned below her left shoulder. Her dark hair is pretty in shiny, finger waves and pin curls on top. There are two shadowy figures in the background, a dour looking woman and a man leaning against the wall with his arms folded on his chest, his slight smile the only one of the bunch. Both appear to be middle-aged.

"Who are these people?" I asked.

"Oh, some people we knew that was the witnesses. I don't remember their names."

"They look a lot older than you. Were they your friends?"

She was getting exasperated now and took the picture to study it more closely. "I don't remember. Maybe they just worked there at the courthouse and filled in for everybody that needed them."

Whether this was true or just a way to end the conversation, there was no evidence of wedding planning in this story.

My mother flew into town two weeks before the wedding. There was a happy excitement between us when I picked her up. I was relieved to have her there, but worried at the same time, wondering if I needed to tell her up front about a mistake on the invitations already printed and sent, or if she wouldn't notice right away and would therefore be sympathetic to me not catching it in time. I decided not to tell her and hope for the best. As we drove away from the airport, she noticed extra invitations sitting in a pile in the back seat and said, "I can't wait to see these!" She had a sentimental expression on her face and I thought she might even tear up when she saw how pretty they were. She began to read them aloud in her sweetest voice, but stopped abruptly and looked at me dumbfounded when she saw the words, "half past 6:30 o'clock."

There was an undercurrent of tension between us from that point forward. If only I'd used the engravers she wanted me to use for the invitations, but no, I had to let my friend do the calligraphy. The person altering my wedding gown – and my mom reminded me that I stopped looking after trying on only one dress – had dyed the extra fabric under the arms in tea to make it match the cream colored lace. I had thought it was clever. My mom thought it was weird, noting with a stoic look on her face that it wasn't a perfect match, but it would have to do. She began to go through the invitation RSVP's that had arrived and gasped when she realized I had invited the 34 children in my class and their parents – and they were coming. "Good heavens, this is a family of eight! You invited *all* of them? This wedding is going to be wildly attended," she grimly stated.

Planning her daughters' weddings may have been especially important to my mom because she never had one, having eloped with my dad when they were 18. This could have been another factor in her annoyance with me, not that it was needed. I was careless with some of my choices, which cost my parents more money. I was an unconventional bride in some ways, during a chapter of my life when I didn't wear any makeup, didn't shave, and went to work most days with my hair still wet from the shower. I was disdainful of brides who spent time on fussy things like experimenting with different hairdos and going to tanning beds. But when I got a last minute perm and Thomas, horrified, ran and hid in the bathroom when I came home, I wished I had tried out a couple of hair styles, or at least more than one wedding dress. When I stopped by the makeup counter in the nearest department store on the way to my wedding rehearsal and mentioned what I was doing in an hour, the employees gasped and surrounded me for an emergency makeover. I arrived done up with orange blusher and lipstick, thinking it might have been a good idea to spend more time on such things.

Soon after she flew in prior to the wedding, Mom started talking about what she was going to wear. "I found a dress and just hope it will coordinate with what Shirley's wearing. Has she said anything to you about it?"

"No. Why do you need to know that?"

"Well, I don't suppose it's a big deal, really. But it helps to coordinate what you wear for the pictures. I'm sure it will be fine."

I then recalled this conversation between my mother and my sisters' future mothers-in-law when they married, and how coordinated everyone looked in the wedding pictures. "Um, Mom…I doubt she's wearing a long dress."

She blinked. There was an awkward silence as she took this in. "You didn't talk with her about it?" she asked. I thought about Shirley's comments about my fancy wedding. "Well, no. And I don't think I can do that now."

She sighed and set her mouth in a way that indicated self-censorship. Then she kind of snapped to, saying, "I guess it will be fine." But the expression on her face didn't look like it was fine. I made a point of shaving that evening.

My sister Lynne and her husband generously hosted the rehearsal dinner, offering their home so that we wouldn't have to rent space in a restaurant. They turned their house inside out to fit all the tables to make it work. By then, my father had flown in for the occasion and it was the first my family met Thomas's family, everyone present except Joe and Dorothy. Watching our parents in conversation, I was reminded that Shirley and Walter were 15-20 years older than my mom and dad. They seemed like an older generation, like grandparents.

The wedding went smoothly. On my father's arm, I walked down the aisle, smiling at all the tiny legs in white stockings and patent leather shoes sticking out, belonging to the little girls from my class who were given the best view of the bride going to the altar. They had been drawing ziggurat wedding cakes for weeks.

The reception was fun with dancing and friends plying Thomas and me with drinks. Looking at the pictures later, it appeared that lots of people were plied with drinks, including my friend the photographer who was actually featured in a few pictures, much to my mother's chagrin. When it was time to throw the bouquet, some of the little boys in my class followed me to the balcony. They shouted in alarm when I turned around and almost tossed the flowers over my shoulder and into the chandelier, a save for which I told them I would be forever grateful.

In the formal pictures of our wedding, our families' attire wasn't coordinated, to say the least, but this didn't matter much to Thomas and me. Everyone got along well and we were happily married. I'm glad I didn't expect our parents to become fast friends, even though I didn't realize what a rare development that would be. After the wedding, the four of them would not gather again until years later when Thomas and I brought our first baby home.

Part of the Tribe

7

CAN'T BUY ME LOVE

Early in our relationship, I focused on earning Shirley's acceptance. She didn't know what to make of me and the feeling was mutual. I was confused whenever Shirley told a story because she used only pronouns when talking about multiple people. Figuring out what was being said felt like so much work. Often, Shirley would say something and I'd panic that I didn't understand the word, even after asking her to repeat it. Like when she talked about her pineys, as in, "Did you see my pineys out there?" When I'd finally say, "What's a piney?" she'd describe the flower I have always known as a peony. And I couldn't say, "Oh, you mean peonies," for fear of offending her. So I'd just act like I didn't know that flower and then she'd look at me as if I were seriously uneducated. This is how it went with many of our interactions.

I tried gifts. Little tchotchkes or trinkets to show my affection. This was an area in which I'd taken pride in other relationships, successfully showing the person that I was attentive to their needs and interests. Not so much with Shirley, though. One day, I overheard her saying to Walter, "Melissa give me this rock to be a doorstop. She said it's a g-node and she found it in the woods. She says it looks different on the inside." Undeterred by Walter's lack of response, she continued. "All I know is it's ugly on the outside, but I guess it keeps the door open." And so it stuck around, ever the reminder of my inability to win her approval.

Our first Christmas after Thomas and I were married and I was officially part of the family, I carefully selected the gift of a robe I thought Shirley would like. The robe she had worn was old and tattered, the color faded. The new robe had a pastel, floral print, not too busy or bold. I had felt confident about this choice, but the moment she opened the box, I could tell she wasn't taken with it. Without masking her emotions for the sake of decorum, she furrowed her brow and thanked me tentatively. After we finished opening gifts and everyone was mingling, I could see her making the rounds to each family member and hear her comments about my gift. She thought she was keeping it down, I suppose, something between a murmur and a hushed voice, which was actually pretty loud.

"Melissa got me this robe, but I don't know."

"I know Melissa was trying to be nice when she got me this robe."

"I don't think the robe Melissa got is my style. I like a zipper."

"This robe from Melissa is pretty thin material. Feel of it."

"I like most of them colors, but not this green. I never liked this kind of green."

"It gets really cold in the winter here."

Finally, I said, "Shirley, please let me take it back and get you something else."

She feigned surprise. "Well you don't have to do that. It's a nice robe."

"I'd like to."

"Okay, if that's what you want. It's a very nice robe."

Clearly, we considered each other a piece of work.

In our first years together, Thomas and I had to adjust to each other's different sets of expectations around birthdays and Christmas. The need became apparent when Thomas's birthday occurred a few months after we moved in together. He had never had birthday parties as a child and didn't have any expectations, but I wanted to surprise him with gifts. I bought a bunch of inexpensive items along with a couple of nicer presents, wrapped them with bright paper and bows, and stacked them up high on the kitchen table after he left for work. I knew he'd be home before me because I had to work late, so I put a sign on top of the pile, saying, "DO NOT OPEN UNTIL I GET BACK." Like anyone would need such directions, I told myself, but I wanted to be clear.

I was excited to see his reaction when I finally got home and ran into the kitchen ready for the big festivities. Upon seeing the opened gifts on the table, my magnanimous feelings drained away. Thomas was smiling broadly and gave me a big hug. "I can't believe you did this, honey. This was really special."

I didn't hug him back. "Why are they opened?" I demanded.

"Was I supposed to wait for you? I didn't know."

"What about the note I left?"

Thomas put his hand up and hurried to show me the tiny gift that had been on top of the pile. "I waited! I didn't open it!"

"You thought the note only referred to the present on top?"

"Well, yeah."

"And you sat here all by yourself in silence and opened these presents?"

"Yeah…I thought that's what you wanted me to do."

"You are a strange little man."

Although I tried interrogating Thomas about what his childhood Christmas holidays and birthdays were like, he didn't seem to remember much to share. "Oh, I'm sure there was something. But not parties. My parents didn't do that."

"So, maybe a special dinner at home?"

"I don't recall any. But I'm thinking about all the years my mom worked the evening shift and we never ate as a family."

I asked Shirley about Christmas gifts when she was growing up in the orphanage.

"You got a piece of paper and you could ask for three things," she said. "If they wasn't too expensive, you might get all three. But usually, the American Legion would pick one of your three choices and the governess would hide them in her closet. My sister Dot told me she knew this because sometimes she cleaned her governess's room. She was the snoop of the family. Anyway, on Christmas morning, you got up and ate breakfast and Santa Claus would come. They was oranges and candy. And lots of popcorn."

"What kind of things would you ask for?"

"Oh, I don't know. Probably something to wear when I was older. At the Home, everyone had three outfits and sometimes you got tired of 'em."

"What about birthdays?" I asked.

"Well, there weren't no presents. I guess you could say there was a little party in your cottage. The kids got together and had popcorn and fruit drinks."

"Was it fun?"

"I don't remember."

Once when Thomas's Aunt Dot was visiting Shirley, Dot said, "I think I remember getting some presents from our father. Not for birthdays ever, but sometimes for Christmas."

Shirley had rolled her eyes. "I don't remember that."

Dot stuck to her story. "I think it happened a couple of times."

"Then they was probably from his sister, Jean."

Dot thought about this. "I guess you're right because Aunt Jean brought them. She probably just said they were from him."

"Well, no matter," Shirley said. "It was the Depression. We didn't really expect anything."

Over time, Thomas observed my family's celebrations and began to get the hang of how we did things. At Christmas time, we would never all tear into our gifts at once, which was his experience growing up. We took turns with everyone watching each present unwrapped and giving it the proper acknowledgement in the form my mother taught us, which was to say, "That's a nice one." My mother tried to keep us mindful of days gone by when children were thrilled to receive a piece of fruit for Christmas by always putting an apple and orange in our stockings. Thus began one of our traditions each year, which was the march to the refrigerator the moment we took our stockings down, dumping the fruit back into the crisper drawer.

Typical of most newlyweds, I didn't notice the amount of ritual in my family around holiday events until I contrasted it with the ways of my in-laws. There had been theme birthday parties when I was growing up. The one I remember most vividly was a so-called hobo party with all the children carrying a packed lunch in a knapsack on a stick, quite politically incorrect by the mid-80s when Thomas and I were married. My mother liked theme parties and when she and my dad had moved back to the US, she resumed her announcements of what she'd come up with on a semi-regular basis. Sometimes she couldn't get anyone to cooperate and gave up, like when she wanted to have a CPR birthday party at which Thomas would train all the attendees in life-saving. For my 30th birthday in 1988, she decreed that we were all to come dressed up as farmers. I whined about this, but was reminded that it was also my sisters' birthday celebration since the three of us were born in the same week, so I wasn't in the best position to say how it should be. But I tried. "Mom, Thomas and I don't want to dress up as farmers."

"Well, everyone else is. Your sisters have put together some darling outfits for the children. I found these cute, little clay pigs at an antique shop and I'm going to pass them out. The people with the best costumes will get first choice."

When we arrived unadorned, she was prepared with kerchiefs, which she tied around our necks and pronounced us ready to go. We did not win first choice of the clay pigs. This was how it was with my mother, smiling and saying, "Isn't this fun?" even when facing moping adult kids like me. I look back at this and admire her tenacity almost as much as her enthusiasm. I suppose we could all use more of that.

8

WALTER

Although our attachment was tentative as mother- and daughter-in-law, it was easy to appreciate Shirley's sense of humor early on, particularly in contrast to Walter's. Walter was always polite to me and, over the years, there were even a couple of tender moments, but we never laughed about anything together. After a while, he was able to tease me about things *he* thought were hilarious, like the enormous loom inherited from a friend before she moved out west. It was taking up space in our family room, accumulating dust, always a reminder of the weaving I said I was going to learn how to do. "How's the weaving coming?" he'd ask every damn time he entered the room, and he'd laugh and laugh. This went on until I gave up and passed the loom on to the Indianapolis School for the Blind, filling the space it had occupied with a large computer table.

There wasn't any animosity between Walter and me, but we never established much of a connection. Conversations between the two of us were rare and spare.

"What kind of heat do you have at your school?" he'd say.

"Well," I'd answer. "I'm sure I should know that. It's an old building and there are these radiators."

"Probably steam," he'd say. Then an awkward silence would follow and one of us would find a reason to leave the room.

One day, I was over at Shirley and Walter's house and walked through the family room unannounced. Had I known the commotion I was about to cause, I would have made some noise first. Walter had been surreptitiously watching *Lilias, Yoga, and You*, an exercise program that had been around as far back as I could remember, still led by the now middle-aged Lilias, lithe and limber as ever, her dark hair in a signature side braid. When I appeared, he scrambled for the remote in such a way that made me say, "Oh! I'm so sorry!" I quickly exited the room. We never spoke of it.

Perhaps the biggest influence on my feelings about Walter was stories Thomas told me about harsh punishments for mild transgressions of his youth. I could never get out of my head the image of Walter smashing Thomas's guitar at a party when, as a teenager, he snuck out of the house at night to play with his band. Or when Walter whipped him with a belt when he was a little boy caught showing the girl next door a sanitary napkin found in a package on his mother's dresser, both of them trying to figure out what you did with it. Walter was there to punish Thomas for examining a feminine hygiene product, but dangerously absent when Thomas and Joe tried to explode his live shotgun shells outside by pounding them with shovels, or hitting his 22-gauge bullets with rocks, at the ages of 5 and 7.

Walter had abstained from alcohol since he became a Christian in his twenties. Stories of his strictness made me wonder about his intolerance of childish behaviors, the black and white judgments in the name of what was holy and unholy. When Thomas was a boy, he was not allowed to see "Flipper" at the movie theater because this was an evil place, but it was fine to watch the same movie at home when it was shown on television. All of this resulted in a profound emotional distance in Walter's relationship with Thomas, and with Shirley, too, as I later discovered.

By this time, I had arrived at a crossroads on my own religious journey. I had grown up going to church at least every Sunday, and three times a week all the years I was active in the youth group. My best friends were from our huge church in Dallas, and then in Cincinnati where we moved when I was a teenager. Church camp adventures were rife with a heady mix of spirituality and suppressed sexuality, spurred on by segregated swimming for boys and girls, and the girls being required to wrap our skinny legs in towels when walking back to our cabins. I loved my church experiences, unlike Thomas, who always felt forced to attend his family's small fundamentalist church, and skipped out whenever possible. In my family, baptisms and public rededications of one's life to Christ were venerated, hallowed moments, although what I mostly remember was celebrating by going to our favorite Mexican restaurant, El Fenix, instead of Luby's cafeteria, which was our normal spot. If one of my siblings responded to an altar call, the other three of us would exchange meaningful looks. The organist may have been playing the hymn "Just as I Am," but we were thinking "La Cucaracha." Those formative years would always be precious to me, but in my young adulthood, I became interested in other ancient traditions of worship, arriving at a belief in the great unknown, and that if there was salvation, it was universal. While I focused on new insights into what I held sacred, Thomas was still affected by all the church lessons he'd been taught that were rigid, punitive, and unforgiving. From what I could tell, these lessons came from the church of Walter more than anything else.

At the beginning of our marriage, Thomas made a decision to let go of the hard past with his father, due in part to his participation in the est training, where we had met. He demonstrated this change by hugging him every time he saw him. At first, Walter was taken off guard and brusque in his response. But Thomas was unfazed by this reception and just kept greeting him with hugs until it was no longer strange. It was inspiring to watch, but I never quite forgave my father-in-law for the past I'd only heard tell of, showing my limited capacity for understanding compared to that of my husband's, a consistent pattern throughout our years together. Over time, I realized that Walter had given his four children more than he'd received growing up. I didn't understand such things in my twenties, however, when I was full of righteous indignation and sat in judgment of the judgmental.

If ever there was a model of good cop-bad cop parenting, albeit unintended, it was Shirley and Walter. Walter was strict and uncommunicative, and Shirley, unable or unwilling to stand up to him, would commit sabotage in various forms, not telling him about Joe's marijuana plants being grown in his own back yard, along with Thomas's minor offenses committed throughout his youth. I saw her extreme passive aggression as nothing short of fascinating. I couldn't imagine how much the enabler versus enforcer dynamic would be replicated in Thomas's and my future parenting partnership, and damn it all if I didn't end up being Walter.

9

MOVING INTO THE FOLD

After almost a year of commuting in opposite directions, a year that included me chaperoning a group of 11-year-olds on a month-long trip to Norway, not to mention the planning of our wedding, Thomas and I were exhausted. It was time to decide where we wanted to live. Batesville had been a mere stop along the way to our permanent home. One of the kindest stories I can tell about my husband, and there are many, is about his selflessness in this decision. He was doing very well at Methodist Hospital, running their occupational health program, which was a lot of responsibility for a young man. He loved his work, but knew how committed I was to my friends, family, and my school in Cincinnati. His salary was more than twice mine – which was only 10,000 dollars, but still – but he didn't hesitate when he said, "I'll look for a job in Cincinnati. This will be okay."

When it became apparent he wasn't going to have difficulty finding work in Ohio, Thomas tendered his resignation to the hospital. The next day, he came home and told me that he had been asked to meet with Dr. Frank Lloyd, the hospital president whom he revered, and that he had asked him to reconsider. We were both awed by this attention from such an important guy. Sitting in a Laundromat in town, Thomas told me about the conversation.

"It was strange. I guess I didn't think anyone would see me leaving as that big a deal."

"Well, what did he say?"

Thomas hesitated. I could tell he was deciding how to answer this question, which made me suspicious. "Seriously, what did he say?"

Thomas sighed. "He said he heard I was resigning because

my wife works in Cincinnati." He laughed. "You aren't going to believe this, but he said they'd help find you a job. When I said all your friends are in Cincinnati, he even said they could help with that, too."

"No way."

"He really said that."

"That does not sound like a compliment. I think I'm offended."

As we sat in silence, the realization that we should move to Indianapolis started to dawn on us both. I began to weep. "My only friend in Indianapolis is your ex-wife."

Thomas laughed and rubbed my shoulders. "I know. I think it will be okay, though. Dr. Lloyd is going to find you some new friends."

"Shut up."

After sniffling for a couple of minutes, I tried to look on the bright side of the situation. "I do like the idea of living near your parents. If we lived in Ohio, I'd never get to know them as well. Maybe we could start a family tradition of having them over for brunch every Sunday after church."

"Yeah, we're not gonna do that," he said.

As it turned out, if I could only have one friend in town when we moved to Indianapolis, Thomas's first wife, Jaime, was the best anyone could ask for. The ease of her relationship with Thomas fascinated me. I even thought, well, if the marriage doesn't work out, I hope I can be that nice. When they had decided to divorce, they went to the library together and checked out a book on the process. They decided to split their property down the middle, even items you wouldn't normally split up. Sometimes when Jaime was visiting, I'd hand her something, like a butter dish from the dishware she and Thomas had divided. Frowning, she'd say, "Do you think Thomas will mind?" and I'd reply, "I don't think Thomas will know, but he wouldn't mind if he did." When I checked this out with him, my hunch was confirmed. I knew my relationship with Jaime was unusual, which made me appreciate it even more. I also credited her with this harmony, noting how careful she was when talking about Thomas, although we did have some good laughs when discussing the eccentricities of his family.

Jaime introduced me to wonderful people and took me to the art museum in Indianapolis, which was especially fun because she was a talented artist herself. And she showed me good places to shop, something I appreciated after Thomas took me to Burlington Coat Factory in our part of town and seemed confused that I might be looking for something else.

We moved to Indianapolis in the summer of 1985. After renting half a duplex for a year, we bought a modest ranch about a mile from Shirley and Walter's house. It was a great little house, well built, for a good price. It took months to get around to most of the boxes because I was always on the go with my job as a Montessori teacher trainer for the Indianapolis Public Schools, a job I got on my own without the help of the president of Methodist Hospital. Thomas and I were at a stage in our lives when we could get away with working long hours as we established our careers. This was mostly because we didn't have children, who would eventually impose a more healthy and balanced structure to our days, but also because we were fairly full of ourselves and didn't know better.

One day, Shirley phoned and got straight to the point of her call. "Melissa? This is Shirley. Look, Dorothy needs a job. She says she wants to clean your house."

It was never a dull moment with my mother-in-law.

"What? What do you mean?"

Her tone was immediately impatient. "Can you not hear me? I said Dorothy wants to be a house cleaner because Joe and her needs the money. I told her you would probably like that, sees how you don't have no time for it."

I wasn't sure where to begin with my reaction. It seemed like I'd been insulted. I was sure that Shirley was trying to bulldoze me.

"Oh my goodness, Shirley, I just noticed the time and I am *late* to something at work. I have to go right now. Why don't you talk to Thomas about this and we'll get back to you."

"Tom? You mean I have to say all this over again? Ain't you gonna see him?"

I responded through gritted teeth. "Sure. I'll tell him about it tonight and he'll check in about the details."

"Details? Whaddaya mean, details?" she asked.

"Well, like what Dorothy needs and what she has in mind."

"I already told you that."

"I mean, how often she would want to come and how much she would charge." Right away, I regretted opening this door before a decision had been made.

"She can come once a week and you can pay her whatever you think. Maybe twenty dollars. She cleans good, you'll see."

"Well, like I said, I'll talk to Thomas about it later, but I have to go now. Thanks for thinking of us." Hanging up the phone, I repeated my last words in a mocking tone. "Thanks for thinking of us." Shirley was probably saying the same thing in the same way. I shook my head, thinking, what's the matter with you, Melissa? Thank you, Shirley, for deciding we need and can afford a house cleaner, and that it's going to be Dorothy, of all people.

"Well, we don't have a good reason to say no," Thomas said that evening.

"How about not wanting a family member poking around in our stuff?" I replied.

"It's just Dorothy. She won't even notice anything that seems weird. Besides, what are you thinking she might find? Do you have a stash of sex toys you haven't told me about?"

"Not at the moment, but maybe I will in the future. My near future. Just for me. By myself."

From Thomas's perspective, the assumption that Dorothy would become our house cleaner wasn't a boundary breach. He had an uncommon closeness to his mother, including unusual experiences that probably stemmed from Thomas's vocation as a nurse as much as anything else. I had tried to tell him that most men didn't do things like pierce their mother's ears, to which he had no response. This was the dynamic in play when he seemed indifferent to what was looking like a considerable intrusion to me.

Seeing the handwriting on the wall, I decided to make an attitude adjustment. The truth was that Dorothy was one of the sweetest people I knew, that she was unassuming, that she needed money, and that she wanted to work for it.

Every time Dorothy came over, she thanked me profusely and she did a great job. I never got used to her tendency to jump out from corners and say, "Boo!" causing me to shriek as I left the house for work, but no housekeeper was perfect. Sometimes, Shirley would come with her and clean too, or just sit around and drink coffee, adding to my vexation over the whole set up. "Melissa," she'd say at the end of the day. "I went through all them restaurant boxes in your refrigerator and threw out the bad food. Don't worry, I made sure it smelled bad first. Then I saw all the marks on your fridge from taping pictures up there. I took a razor blade from your medicine cabinet to get all them black marks off. Is you still gonna put pictures up like that? Are you listening to me?" Trying to picture what she had seen in our medicine cabinet, I stammered some response.

The hardest part in the couple of years Dorothy worked for us was adjusting my identity as someone who hired people to clean my house, in this case a woman in her sixties, when I was still in my twenties. Despite the increasing sizes of their houses over the years, my mother had always cleaned her own house until they lived in the Philippines, where the hiring of servants was at the economic center of the culture, where servants had servants. I imagined my sisters made fun of me being la-dee-dah now. One night when we were together at my parents' home playing *Tripoli*, I felt sorry for my sister Laurie who was low on poker chips and about to lose the game. Believing she would prefer compensation for honest labor over a handout, I offered to pay her to straighten up my huge, messy pile of chips. My mother murmured, "Whenever she gets a little extra money, she hires someone to clean up." This got a good laugh around the table, but still stung. I figured an explanation of the situation would only add to the merriment, however, and decided it wasn't worth the effort.

10

THE GROWN-UPS WHO WERE IN CHARGE

Early in our marriage, I asked Thomas why his grandmother had been committed to Central State Hospital in Indianapolis and the children had been taken to an orphanage. His uncertainty turned out to be characteristic of the family's oblivion on a larger scale. There was a lack of clarity about their most recent ancestors. I mused about this over the years, supposing that family stories would be lost when you were separated from relatives who could tell you about your past. No photo albums, no mementoes, no clues about where you came from, all resulting in the absence of collective memory most of us take for granted. My siblings and I might debate the details of stories from our family lore; indeed, the argument was part of what made us a family. But we agreed about the basics of where we came from and who our ancestors were. As far as I could tell, such debates were replaced by a great void in Shirley's family. However, a few salient details were shared with me in the first years of my marriage.

Shirley's mother, Fay Hammitt Peacock, was married to Morris Peacock, who appears to have been a feckless ne'er-do-well by all accounts. When he left her with five young children and no means of caring for them, she had a kind of breakdown, resulting in her commitment to Central State Hospital for the Insane as it was so called in 1928, where she remained for most of the rest of her life.

Morris was arrested for child abandonment in 1927. He was sentenced to the Indiana State Reformatory in Pendleton, 25 miles northeast of Indianapolis, for 1-3 years, according to his prison record. Notably, this was the same time that the notorious bank robber, John Dillinger, was there. Sometimes I wondered if they shared laundry detail or encountered each other in the prison yard.

Shirley used to say, "He was there because he deserted his family – they used to do that, throw you in jail for that. I always thought it was funny. How is a man supposed to get a job and make money to support his family if he's in jail?"

Given Morris's eventual escape from prison, aided by his sister, Jean, as the story goes, and disappearance from their lives, this turned out to be a moot point. Shirley's view was pragmatic. "Course, there was a lot of men that done this. I just figured he wanted something else to do. He wanted a different life. He didn't wanna be tied down with five kids – five little babies."

Shirley recalled being taken by her Aunt Jean to visit her father before he broke out of the place. "She took me to the prison, Pendleton, to see my father. It was just me because I was the oldest. I went back there where he was and I remember walking by all them bars. The men were all yellin' stuff, but it wasn't bad stuff 'cause I was only just a kid. I don't even remember what he looked like." Shirley sighed. "He got away. And that was the last I ever heard or seen of him – to this day." Then she laughed. "I may have half- brothers or sisters I know nothin' about!"

At some point, it struck me that Morris's actions had resulted in the family of seven being dispersed into three state institutions: a prison, a psychiatric hospital, and an orphanage, all within a 50-mile radius. I wondered if Fay was really mentally ill, or just poor and female at a time when both government support and medical insight were in short supply. In six and a half years, she had been pregnant five times. Although this may not have been unusual for the 1920s, it was beyond my imagination. Who was there to help her, I wondered.

Shirley told me a story about their lives before they were separated from their mother. "Y'know, back then, there wasn't any welfare, and if the neighbors didn't pick up and help you, you were sent to a children's home. One time, some neighbor come by with a bushel of potatoes. Well, you know how kids are. We took 'em and started throwin' 'em at each other, like a fun game. We were havin' a ball! When my mother come out and see what was going on, she just screamed. I guess that was all she had to feed us."

When it came down to the final decision about where Shirley and her siblings would go once Fay was committed, their misfortune was that their Aunt Jean was their closest relative with decision-making power. She signed a document saying none of the children could be adopted, sealing their fate as orphans with the stroke of her pen. Their mother was institutionalized. Their father's whereabouts were unknown. Their maternal grandparents and uncle were deceased. They had a step-grandmother on Fay's side of the family, but she was of no help. In fact, when their grandfather died, his second wife, Edith, appears to have disconnected herself from his family, ending the financial assistance her husband had provided for his daughter and grandchildren. Shirley's sister, Dot, told me their grandfather was doing well financially when he died, that he owned an ice cream parlor and another thriving business. But when he was gone, his second wife kept everything. Dot shrugged her shoulders and said, "She took it all."

Each of the five children's orphanage enrollment records, something I saw many years after Thomas and I were married, said the same thing at the bottom of the form. Under the category, "Remarks," were the statements, "Father sentenced to Pendleton Reformatory for desertion (escaped). Mother insane."

It doesn't seem that Shirley's father's sister, Jean, wanted to be tied down either, and worse, she recognized opportunities to capitalize on her brother's children's plight. As the oldest, Shirley was the first to be discharged from the orphanage in 1938 and went to live with her aunt when she was 18, according to her records, at 26th and Clifford Streets in Indianapolis. It appears Jean was the only relative that would claim her when the people at the Soldiers' and Sailors' Children's Home made an effort to connect their charges with an older adult when they were released. No one at the orphanage knew Jean was a prostitute. Shirley used to laugh about this, saying, "Well, she told all those men to keep their hands off me! There was a guy named Max that wore spats on his shoes to decorate them. He was snazzy with his straw hat and them shoes. I kind of liked him, but he was too old for me."

Jean also charged Shirley considerable rent. "It was a two-bit flea-bag joint and she rented out rooms. She used to tell people it was a nice hotel and say, 'Isn't that right, Shirley?' and I'd nod my head. She was just a big liar."

Georgia was the next to be discharged in 1940. By this time, the people at the Home were wise to Jean's vocation and found somewhere else for her to go. But when Dot left the orphanage in 1941, she moved in with her aunt as Shirley had. Dot told me Jean must have convinced the administrators at the Home that she had changed her ways by then and she said she never saw any of the business activity Shirley witnessed. "Don't get me wrong," Dot had said. "She liked men – a lot," but she never saw her accepting money for various trysts. The rent Dot paid her aunt was steep, as it had been with Shirley. "It would have been cheaper to rent my own apartment," Dot shared, "but I stayed with her for two and a half years. It was a place on North New Jersey Street." When I asked her why she stayed so long when she could have saved money on her own, she nodded and sighed. "Well, she was someone I knew. We got along pretty well, too."

Donald, the fourth child of the five, was discharged from the orphanage in 1940, before his older sister, Dot. The records indicate that he did not graduate from the high school, but left at the "request of aunt." Both Shirley and Dot filled in the details here. Jean adopted Donald and changed his last name to her second married name. He had joined the Navy and she wanted an allotment of his wages. "She tried to get Don to sign a big life insurance policy," Dot said. "But the Navy caught on and stopped it."

"What happened to Jean?" I once asked.

Shirley waved her hand. "Well, she was livin' alone when she died. Heart attack. She was married two times but she never had kids. Somebody said she changed, started goin' to church and she worked in a dining room taking reservations; she could sit down there. She had this big burn on her arm from fallin' on a radiator when she was drunk. The radiator wasn't so hot, but she was stuck behind it a long time 'til someone got her out."

Shirley's mother, Fay, was still alive when Thomas and I married in 1984. She had been living in a nursing home since her transfer from Central State in the early 1970s. I met her two or three times. She was tiny and meek, as fragile as a sparrow, sitting quietly on the couch with a shy smile on her face. Her posture was slightly stooped, causing her to have to look up when making eye contact, her eyes luminous and wary. Thomas said that before Shirley retired, she always brought her mother home on Friday afternoons, her one day off each week, and styled her hair. Sometimes her clothes needed to be repaired, since she often burned holes in them with her cigarettes, so Shirley would mend them or replace them with two-dollar suits she bought at Good Will.

Fay died in 1986, a few months after Thomas and I moved to Indianapolis. I never had a real conversation with her. I wish I had. In my brief glimpse of Shirley's and Fay's relationship, it seemed like Shirley was parenting a mother who had not been

70

able to raise her. It also appeared she was the only one of Fay's five children who was consistently there for her. In the years to come, I would wonder about this. My mother-in-law could be so bewildering to me, so difficult, and yet she found a way to repair a relationship that most people would consider irreparable. It would take a long time for me to fathom the magnitude of her caregiving.

11

GEORGIE

As it turned out, Thomas's Aunt Georgie really was a bitch, just like he said. I'd heard stories of how mean she could be, how she embarrassed anyone out with her in public by making waitresses cry or chiding people who were overweight for taking up two spaces on a bus. But it was interesting to see her demeanor for myself. The few times I was around her, I enjoyed the emotional detachment of an in-law and found myself watching her like one would observe a character projected on a movie screen. Yikes, that was rude, I'd think, and I wondered if she was always like that or if it was because life had dealt her a bad hand. The other sisters were friendly people, but the chip on Georgie's shoulder was impossible to miss.

When I met Georgie, she had come with Shirley to see the house Thomas and I purchased in Indianapolis in 1985. My mother was visiting at the time. As an amateur interior decorator whose main projects had been her homes along with her children's, she took pride in decisions I had made on a limited budget of money and time in the first six months we lived there. Had this not been my first experience with Thomas's aunt, I would have foreseen the inevitable clash between my mom and Georgie before it happened.

We started off all smiles when Shirley and Georgie arrived, with Mom giving Shirley a hug and taking Georgie's hand as she said, "so nice to meet you." Shirley and I almost hugged each other in this process, but awkwardly stopped short of it, then laughed and said, "Well, we see each other all the time." We were both aware that Mom and Georgie were watching this. "I'll hug you anyway," I said. Shirley laughed again, this time more forced, and said, "Well, okay!" We hugged and the strangeness of the situation felt even worse. I thought about how much I did not enjoy being a girl in scenes like this, even as the Rodgers and Hammerstein tune played in my head.

Mom and I offered coffee to our guests and the grand tour of Thomas's and my humble abode began. My mother was in her element, even though I was leading the group through the few rooms that made up our small ranch house. She'd point out the few little flourishes and accessories that had been my idea. She began to tense up, however, in response to Georgie's comments. Actually, we all did.

"How old is this carpet? It's looking dingy like the last people smoked." I supposed Georgie would have known since she was a smoker.

"Your bedroom is small. Good thing you just have a double bed because a queen would take up too much room. I'll bet you couldn't even get a king through the door. Shirley and I grew up in a place where everyone's beds were only one foot apart, if you can believe that."

"Hasn't she done a great job with this room?" Mom said. "I just think these curtains," her doing, "add a lot of interest and go well with the pillows," also hers. "The fabric is actually Ralph Lauren – from a sale table at Calico Corners," her find.

Georgie snorted. "Yeah, and the dog cage adds a great touch."

Mom pursed her lips. She hadn't been happy with the dog cage either, but Thomas and I wanted our dog Skippy, with us at night while we were training him to stay in a crate. She was also miffed when I said I wasn't going to limit the books on my bedside table to those with covers that matched the room's color scheme, that I preferred to keep books I was actually reading there. So Georgie was criticizing a model that my mother did not consider her best effort, in the form of her daughter's first house, and I could see she was simultaneously conflicted and offended.

Shirley looked helpless as Georgie continued her relentless critique. "Why didn't you use the bigger room in front? *That's* the master bedroom, not this one. And this one is separated from the kitchen only by this teeny bathroom. Whose idea was it to set the bathroom up that way? And chocolate brown tile! In such a little space! *That* didn't help."

I saw Mom start to point out the pocket doors, then she seemed to think better of the idea, getting that look on her face like she had decided to soldier forth with dignity. It was the guest bedroom with the orange and green plaid wallpaper that brought everything to a point.

Georgie gasped as she walked in. "Well, this is hideous!" she exclaimed.

Hearing this proclamation, I laughed out loud. Mom put her hands on her hips and glared at her. Shirley fidgeted and looked at the floor.

"You aren't going to keep this wallpaper, are you? It's terrible!"

"Well, no, we'll strip it and paint the walls when we get a chance," I said.

Mom interjected, her diction clipped and purposeful. "Well. I think she's certainly made the best of it for now. She's very busy with her job. Look at how the pictures on the wall and the bedspread tone down the plaid. That's a pre-Raphaelite print on the wall, you know." She raised her chin. "That Melissa bought at a special exhibit at the Tate Museum. In London. And I just love the frame she picked out – all on her own."

This turned out to be a fascinating exchange unfolding on my imagined movie screen. When they finally left, my mother walked around sputtering. "Well, I never."

"I know!" I exclaimed. "She's just like Thomas said!" But I was laughing and Mom was not.

"I hope you don't have to be around her often. Did you

see how Shirley just puts up with her?"

"Well, according to Thomas, they all do."

"I can't even imagine someone as nice as Thomas in the same family with that woman."

I hugged my mom. "Thanks for sticking up for me. I doubt I'll see her very much. She and Shirley aren't close."

"Good." She hesitated for just a moment. "Do you think Skippy's cage still needs to be in your bedroom? Surely he'd be okay in another room by now." She paused, but then continued like she just couldn't help herself. "He's just a dog, Melissa. And that cage is an eyesore." I raised my eyebrows and she backed off, giving up on my decoration blunder, for now.

It was true that I encountered Georgie few times over the years. The last time I saw her before her death in 1997, she was moving slowly with an oxygen tank, not letting the nasal cannula get in the way of her litany of complaints and criticisms. Sometimes I thought about how easy it was for me not to care what Georgie thought or said the day she came to visit. I knew it was because my mother was offended for me, a luxury Georgie never knew.

12

JOE WINS THE LOTTERY

I continued to be enthralled by Joe and Dorothy in my early years of marriage. I stopped going up to their ramshackle domicile above the garage, however, mostly because I didn't want to think about the squalor of it. It was easier just to see them hanging out in the backyard or wave to Dorothy who sat at their one window above me as I passed by. I loved hearing her throaty, dramatic voice each time she greeted me, "Helloooo, Melissa." One time, when my dad was in Indianapolis for a business meeting, we went over to Walter and Shirley's house for a visit. He was with me when we passed beneath the window and stopped at her greeting from the makeshift second floor. He mumbled to me, "So, she really exists." And I liked that it wasn't a made up story, that we really did have our very own Mrs. Rochester up in the attic, just like in *Jane Eyre*, and that in strange territory such as this, I was the one who knew her way around.

The first little dog, Baby, had died, and was replaced by another mangy mess, naturally named Baby also, which I began to call Baby Two. Dorothy was mostly content to sit with Baby Two in her lap and look out the window, but on hot summer days, she ventured out to garden tomatoes – in a white bikini. It was disturbing to see a woman in her sixties dressed like this, but I noticed that it was getting harder to scandalize me with such goings-on. It would take something bigger to get my attention at this point.

One evening in July, Shirley and I sat in lawn chairs in the back yard after supper at Shirley and Walter's house. I closed my eyes and breathed in the sweet summer evening, feeling more at ease with Thomas's family after our first year of marriage. Dorothy was washing the dishes, no matter how much encouragement she had been given to leave them until later and join us outside. I sat with Shirley, watching Thomas toss a football with Joe. Walter was in his happiest place, which was his garage, wrench in hand, working on an old car.

Shirley's eyes widened suddenly and she leaned forward. "We forgot to get Dorothy's lottery ticket today."

I furrowed my brow. "Who forgot to get Dorothy's lottery ticket?"

"Me and Dorothy!"

"Why is Dorothy buying lottery tickets?"

There was a pause, as Shirley glanced to see if Joe was out of earshot. Her voice was conspiratorial. "She needs to win a lot of money. Joe thinks she's gonna have some money soon."

"Why does he think that?"

"Because she told him."

I could barely contain my exasperation. "Why did she tell him that?"

"Well," she paused again and lowered her voice. "Dorothy thinks he's goin' for other girls and she doesn't want him to leave her."

"Whoa," I whispered back. "That's pretty crazy."

"Y'know, it really is," was all she said, no explanation or defense provided.

I sat up and focused my full attention. "What exactly did she tell him?"

"She says she's gettin' money from some uncle that died."

"And her uncle hasn't really died?"

Shirley rolled her eyes. "She doesn't have a uncle!"

I shifted my gaze back to the house where Dorothy was toiling, then to Joe tossing the ball in the yard. Although my mind moved in several directions, I landed on the place that was most familiar. These people needed help and I was the only one around with common sense. "So, Joe really believes this is happening?"

"Yes! And he knows the date, too."

"She provided a date?"

Shirley laughed. "September the 21st, just ask him. He can't remember when Christmas comes every year, but he knows September the 21st. And he's makin' plans, too."

"What kind of plans?"

"Things he wants to buy. Like a car. And a stereo and a new TV. It's kep' him occupied. I guess he ain't lookin' at other girls now."

It all began to come together in my mind. "And that's why Dorothy's buying lottery tickets?"

"Yeah. I take her to the store every day."

"And you think this might solve the problem?"

She eyed me warily. "Well, you never know."

I took a deep breath. "In this case, I think you do. Shirley, Dorothy is not going to win the lottery." I had never felt like such a grown-up in my whole life.

Shirley didn't argue. "Well, what are we supposed to do?"

"I don't know, but not that. What does Walter say?"

She waved her hand at me. "He doesn't say nothin'. He's no help."

Upon hearing this yarn after we returned home, Thomas shook his head. "Christ."

"I know," I said. "I'm worried about what Joe might do when he finds out. Remember when he got mad and threw that 2x4 in your parents' direction a couple of months ago? Do you think he might hit her? You're going to need to be there when Dorothy tells him."

"I wonder if she has to tell him. Maybe he'll forget."

I stared back at him.

"Okay, I'll check on it with Mom and Dad."

This dilemma brought up my questions about Joe's challenges again. What exactly was his disability? No one seemed to know. Shirley told me that she noticed he was different as a child. "He couldn't do things the other kids did, even Tom, and he was littler. He couldn't skip to save his life. And when he tried roller skating, he'd get all red in the face and just give up."

"Did you take him to a doctor?" I asked.

"We did and the doctor just said he was slow." Her eyes darted up at me. "That's what he said. They gave him some test."

"Was it an IQ test? Like the Wechsler?" I asked. "Sometimes it's called WISC."

Shirley frowned. "I don't remember what it was called. Seems like the doctor mostly just talked to him."

Thomas had commented about this later. "Mom and Dad didn't know about things like getting a second opinion. Whatever the doctor said, they just accepted. Joe was placed in one of those special ed classes in school where all the kids had a bunch of different problems." I was aware of this history in my field. Whether you had a cognitive, learning, physical, or emotional disability didn't matter. The teacher was supposed to know how to teach and support children with epilepsy, speech impediments, muscular dystrophy, behavioral disorders, Down Syndrome, and more, all in the same classroom, not an optimal situation for meeting children's needs. Thomas admitted how embarrassed he was as a kid when Joe's class would be moving through the hallway and his friends made fun of them. He wasn't proud of his reaction, but it was a fact of his upbringing. When I looked at pictures from his childhood, it was often just Joe and Thomas. Lee and Brenda were older and off doing other things during those years. I asked Thomas if his decision to become a nurse had anything to do with taking care of his big brother throughout their youth. He just said, "Maybe. I'm not sure."

Shirley and Dorothy continued to buy lottery tickets and, as the day approached, I became anxious and took out my frustration on Thomas. "Why haven't you handled this?" I demanded, and he would promise to get to it.

The showdown was avoided, typical of my conflict-avoidant in-laws. Joe came over one evening in a new truck, happy as a clam.

"What's this?" Thomas and I asked.

Joe beamed. "It's my new truck. Mom and Dad got it for me. And a TV and a stereo, too, barely used."

Thomas looked at me then back at his brother. "What's the big occasion? It isn't your birthday, is it?"

Joe hooted at the joke. "No, it's not my birthday. But Dorothy isn't gettin' no money, so Mom and Dad got me them things."

Before long, he was on his way back home, leaving Thomas and me staring in silence. "Wow," I said. Thomas didn't respond. "We are not going to raise our kids this way," I added for good measure.

He mocked me, saying, "Okay, if you insist." But I knew this was a battle that would be revisited, that Thomas had learned from the best how to avoid direct communication about anything uncomfortable. Maybe it would happen on a smaller scale, but it would be a predictable alternative to a good old-fashioned family blow out, something I began to realize I was never going to see among my in-laws.

13

JUST LIKE RICH PEOPLE

Every fall, there was an alumnae reunion at the orphanage where Shirley and her siblings grew up. Shirley's sister, Dot, always attended and urged Shirley to come, too. Shirley's response to this annual invitation was cautious and most of the time, she chose not to attend. There were a few years, however, when she decided to go because Thomas and I wanted to go, too. Upon arrival, we could count on seeing Dot in the center of the crowd, laughing and talking with old friends.

"Come here, Melissa!" she'd say. "I want you to meet my friends."

Once, I saw this group of women chant a cheer from the Home's high school football games.

Rooty-toot-toot!
Rooty-toot-toot!
We're the girls from the institute!
We don't smoke and we don't chew
And we don't play with teams that do!

Then they each pretended to take a drag on a cigarette in unison and laughed as they held on to each other. "We were really smoking!" Dot said, "and cigarettes were forbidden. Course, we didn't really inhale. Remember that governess we caught smoking?" She looked at me to explain. "We angled the transom window above her door to reflect what she was doing in there. Then we spied on her."

Everyone had a good laugh at this recollection. It reminded one of the women of another story. "This one here," she told me as she pointed to Dot, "was someone to look out for. Once when she was cleaning the governess's room — she was such an old fuss-budget — Dot loosened a light bulb in its socket so that it shocked her when she investigated what was wrong with it."

Dot laughed and shrugged her shoulders like an innocent. "She deserved it," she said. "She was one of the mean ones you learned to avoid."

"Except you, apparently," I said with a smile.

"And," her friend continued, "there was the time Dot and Annabelle demonstrated the seamed stockings!" The women laughed even harder at the memory. One noticed my confusion and filled me in.

"That was when we were junior leaders in 4H – "

"We were called the Thread Trails," Dot said.

Nodding her head, the woman continued. "So there was a new style of stockings with seams –"

"Before the nylon stockings with no seams," Dot interjected again.

"And Dot and Annabelle got up there on the stage and demonstrated putting them on and keeping the seams straight. If you could have seen how shocked the audience was!"

"Who was the audience?" I asked.

"Oh, these old biddies that would come in from the community to see what we were up to in 4H at the Home. Really, it was scandalous!"

Dot beamed.

Throughout such exchanges, Shirley stood to the side and didn't have much to say to anyone, even with us there for support. It appeared that she and her sister had dramatically different feelings about their lives there.

Dot would say, "It was like we were in a private school in the middle of the Depression. I didn't know that people were starving. Y'know the crash happened after we moved to the Home, so we didn't know any different. We had everything. We did things like go to the movies and we had our own skating rink where we skated every Saturday. People were trying to enlist in the service so they could eat. And we would do things like go to dances. We even had our own private church. We had all the food we wanted."

There was a mantra repeated in all the conversations I observed during the reunions. "We were given three square meals a day and taught a trade." Dot would also chat with people about funny memories of teachers and matrons, but Shirley timidly stuck with the party line. She'd shrug her shoulders whenever anyone tried to talk with her and say, "We had good food, even though we didn't know it back then. And they made sure we all left with a trade." She didn't share stories with anyone but us, and only when we pressed her. She relayed them in a matter-of-fact way, in stark contrast to the carefree gaiety characterizing Dot's recollections.

The campus was impressive, 50 acres dotted with 51 buildings, including several grand Romanesque Revival mansions, very dignified and imposing. When Shirley and Dot lived there, there were 30 buildings, including a hospital, chapel, school, and cottages for the residents. At the reunion, the hundred or so people gathered were smiling and hugging, making it easy to pick up on their camaraderie and imagine this as a meeting of long lost college chums. Like homecoming at a prestigious, old university, rather than a return to the last stop for children when their homes had fallen apart.

One year, Thomas, Shirley, and I sat on a bench under a massive oak tree, perfect for climbing, on the picturesque lawn in front of the main administration building, its gentle slope green and manicured in the early fall. The effect of the place was bucolic, quiet, and even soothing, but that was the perception of the unacquainted, like me. It was a crisp autumn day and the sun shining through the golden leaves made me feel nostalgic. I asked

Shirley, "Is this where you played?"

"Once or twice a year when the photographers came," she said.

"Oh. Why couldn't you play here?"

"They didn't want us messing up the lawn."

"So, where did you play?"

"I'll show you." At this, we followed her around the back of the main building, where a small, cracked rectangle of pavement was enclosed on three sides by the building's three wings. As an elementary school teacher the first time I saw it, I could gauge how many children could safely occupy a space like this at a time. I asked, "Would you come out in small groups?"

"I guess we came out with our classes 'cause I never saw Don or my sisters out here."

"Was there play equipment?"

"No."

"What would you do?"

"Stand and wait 'til we could go back in."

And thus, each story was presented. Shirley shared only when asked and never embellished her responses. "You had to be in school 8:00 to 3:30 and you had to be in church on Sundays," she said. "You felt stupid asking questions. You didn't have any extra help. They kept you pretty busy, but I spent a lot of time just walking."

Once confined to the orphanage, Shirley stood on the margins of childhood. If her objective was to be invisible as a way of staying out of trouble, she succeeded. While Dot had played the game full out, it appeared that Shirley spent her time running down the clock.

I wondered why Shirley and Dot had such different experiences and memories of their years in the orphanage. Was it just because their personalities were dissimilar? Were their experiences leading up to their placement in the Home different?

84

I thought the difference could be explained in part by their ages when they arrived, and their arrival dates, which were at slightly different times. Records showed that Dot and the two youngest siblings, Donald and Roberta, came in July of 1928, but the two oldest, Shirley and Georgia, didn't come until November of that year.

"So much for that picture of all five of them being taken the day they went to the orphanage," I said to Thomas when this information was discovered.

"I don't want to hear it," he said. "That's what everyone in the family has always said and I like that story." I patted him on the shoulder, then reconsidered. "I guess it could have been taken before the younger three kids left."

Dot said the reason for the different arrival times was that Shirley and Georgia had eye infections that needed to be cleared up before they could move in, but no one else, including Shirley, remembered this. In fact, Shirley rolled her eyes and said, "She's always making things up."

Dot remembered being four years old when admitted to the orphanage, although the records indicate she was five. "I remember I was scared and I wet my pants in the car," she said, "so they took 'em off and I didn't have any pants on when I first got there. Years later, one of the governesses said to me, 'You didn't even have any pants when you came here.' Like I could help that! I was just a little kid! All I knew was my big sisters were there and then they weren't. And nobody told me what happened to them. I knew my daddy had left, but I didn't know what happened to my mother. I asked, 'where is my mother?' but nobody would tell me. Don and Roberta were just babies, so I didn't have anyone to talk to. When Shirley and Georgie got there, I was so excited to see them when my group marched into the dining room. We waved at each other."

I kept trying to imagine what that would feel like to a child, how terrifying it must have been, and reached the conclusion that I probably couldn't fathom it. To be taken from your home and family, from your mother, with no explanation or reassurance or comfort. And would it be harder for the younger or older children to make sense of and accept their new circumstances? I could see the argument on both sides of that debate.

Dot's story continued to unfold whenever she shared her memories. "I started wetting the bed when I first got there and this one governess made me sit in a bowl of water in the bathroom as a punishment. Another one was nice, though. She held me on her lap sometimes. But she didn't stay very long. Probably got engaged. You couldn't stay if you were married back then."

Shirley had a memory of her first day at the Home, too. "I remember standing in the dispensary and thinking, what are we gonna do? That's all I thought about it. I didn't know where my mother was. I didn't know where my father was. And I was 6 and a half. I remember the smells: some alcohol and some bleach and Lysol and something else I can't describe. But I don't really remember a lot of the details. Life just went on."

"But wouldn't you have been older than that?" I asked. "You went there in 1928, which would make you eight."

Shirley knitted her brow, then shrugged her shoulders. "I guess." She paused again. "But I thought I was 6 and a half."

In 1928, Shirley and her siblings joined 523 other children at the Soldiers' and Sailors' Orphans' Home in Knightstown, before its name was changed from Orphans' Home to Children's Home. The reported breakdown of their eligibility in the form of their parents' military service, although it adds up to less than 523, was as follows:

Civil War veterans	21
Philippines Insurrection veterans	14
Regular Army veterans	110
World War [I] veterans	302

World War I was referred to as the World War. In the ten years Shirley was there, the enrollment dramatically increased due to unemployed parents' inability to care for their children during the Great Depression, exceeding 1000 in 1935. By the time she graduated in 1938, the enrollment was 838. There were no more children of Civil War veterans, the record reflecting the following assortment of the children's parents' service:

Philippines Insurrection veterans	3
Spanish American War veterans	30
Regular Army veterans	54
World War [I] veterans	751

By the early 1940s, the enrollment at the orphanage declined due to better economic times and the rise of the foster care system in the US.

When considering the bread lines of the thirties, Shirley expressed gratitude for the food and shelter she had been provided, and never acted like she had expected more than that. Dot wore the rose-colored glasses and proclaimed theirs to be a life in tall cotton. "There was a lake in front of our cottage with swans. Swans! Just like rich people. In the winter, kids would ice skate on it. I asked for some beginner skates and got them. We were also furnished with roller skates to skate on sidewalks, too. We skated all the time."

14

WHAT WE GAINED

When we moved to Indianapolis in 1985, Thomas and I began trying to get pregnant. I thought this would be an effortless feat, but to my surprise, it was not. After all those years of cramps that had me doubled over while others really did play tennis just like in the Midol commercials, I guess I thought I would get a break in this department. I figured cramps meant you were ovulating and generalized this to mean all systems were go. Plus my sisters' pregnancies had come easily enough, and as my mother used to say about her four pregnancies before the age of 24, "Well, you were all accidents." So, no one knew what to say when time kept passing by and it wasn't happening for Thomas and me.

This was Shirley's reaction: "I was talkin' about this to my friend at church – I didn't think you'd mind. Anyway, she said her son has some problem with his seed. I told her Tom doesn't have a problem with his seed. He had the test. Some other girl at church has a daughter who was havin' problems like yours, but hers was because her husband is, well, she said he was too big." Taking in my embarrassed laughter and realizing she was digging herself into a hole, she stopped here, for once, and refrained from discussing it with me in the future, getting status reports from Thomas. I told Thomas this worked for me. He said, "Do you think I want to talk to my mother about my seed and size?" I reminded him of how much more involving the whole fertility thing was for me and this was something he would just have to deal with.

Shirley did comfort me one day, saying I didn't need to worry about Tom getting too old, now that he was in his thirties. "Men's can have babies when they're old," she said. "Maybe Tom will be like Bing Crosby. He had babies when he was 80. It's different with girls, though."

"Is she saying my ovaries are too old?" I asked Thomas. "I'm still in my twenties!"

"Who knows what she's saying," Tom replied. "I'll talk to her."

Shirley did become more careful when studying group pictures and asking if various women were pregnant, based on their protruding stomachs. At times, the person in question was me, having experienced a flat abdomen for about fifteen minutes in my early adolescence.

My mother's comments were sensitive and kind, but no more helpful. She said in a knowing voice, "I don't think you need to worry, sweetheart. I have known you your whole life and watched you develop and grow up. I think I'd know if you had a problem." I forgave this questionable statement because I knew she didn't know what else to say, and then I promised to tell Thomas to switch to boxer shorts after Mom read up on why they were better than briefs in this situation. For his seed, so to speak. My parents' moral and financial support throughout this process was considerable and I was grateful they were back in the US now, living nearby in Cincinnati.

After four years of infertility treatments that included multiple surgeries, expensive drugs that impeded normal cognitive function, new vocabulary words like "hysterosalpingogram," and the heartbreak of too many Christmas mornings without a child, Thomas and I changed paths, starting a new journey to adopt. I think Thomas mostly was relieved that I had given up on what he considered to be dangerous surgeries. In his years as a nurse, he had seen how risky any surgery could be and wrung his hands each time we decided I would have a gamete intra-fallopian transfer, optimistically referred to as GIFT, along with other types of operations.

For my first surgery, which was a laparoscopy to check out the problem, Thomas fretted non-stop about who the anesthesiologist would be. He made sure someone named Dr. Longfellow was scheduled to provide anesthesia because he had a good reputation. Thomas even made me promise that I would stop the procedure before it began if it turned out someone else was there in his place. When I was wheeled into the surgical prep room and I asked if Dr. Longfellow was my anesthesiologist, the nurses were puzzled, saying they didn't even know of a doctor named Longfellow. "Well, what's the doctor's name?" I asked. "Dr. Hemingway," they said. Without qualms, I told them to carry on.

I was also relieved to put a halt to the blood draws that were constantly being taken, never being an easy stick. I learned to walk in to my appointments requesting a butterfly needle, which was smaller and more effective for getting into my veins. Sometimes as many as twenty vials of blood were required, which was especially awful if it needed to happen on a Sunday, based on my menstrual cycle, and the more experienced phlebotomist wasn't at work. One person who was new and aware of how hard it was to draw my blood stepped out of the room briefly when she saw me one Sunday morning, so I wouldn't see her crying. I tried, to no avail, to get her to let Thomas do it. "He's really good at this," I said. "He'll get into the vein immediately and he's sitting right here." The technician continued to dig around under my skin with the needle, her eyes welling up again. "We're not allowed to let anyone else do this."

I ignored Thomas shaking his head and gesturing to me to cut it out. "But he's an RN," I said.

"I'd get in trouble," she said miserably.

I leaned in for emphasis. "We won't tell." This was a scene I didn't want to keep repeating.

Following our decision to adopt, we threw out the syringes, thermometers, and other paraphernalia we had used over the years. It was good to move forward in our quest to start a family, although hardly easy. There was the home study, the paper work, the finding of an adoption attorney and service, the money, and the monumental task of connecting with a birthmother and showing her we would be worthy of her trust to raise her child. Still, this decision felt right from the moment we made it and we knew this was how we were meant to be a family. In the future, I would tell our children how glad I was that I never got pregnant, that I probably would have liked our biological kids okay, but they wouldn't be them and we wouldn't be us, and that was that.

I left my job in the Indianapolis Public Schools in the late 80s to go to graduate school at Indiana University, pursuing a doctoral degree in education. Going to school full time and working as an Associate Instructor teaching courses to cover my tuition, I commuted an hour each way throughout the week between Indianapolis and Bloomington, which was difficult in light of my infertility appointments and treatments, all prior to our decision to adopt. There were times when I would arrive in Bloomington, sit down at my desk, then receive a call that I needed to go to the fertility clinic right away, based on the results of a blood test. This was a 90-minute drive. I would sigh, stand up, and go, after finding someone to cover my classes. Thomas and I became part of a new community through my work, with old and new friends from both towns aware of our desire to adopt a child.

As advised by our attorney who specialized in adoptions, we placed an advertisement in the classified section of several newspapers in the region and established a second phone line, our very own hotline. We also wrote what was called a "Dear Birthmother" letter, to be sent to various recommended places, spelling out all the reasons we would be great parents. We worked hard to compose an ad and letter that balanced sensitivity to a birthmother's dilemma with evidence that we were the answer. This was our ad placed in the classifieds section of the *Kokomo Tribune*, filled with code words with particular meanings:

Let's help each other. We understand this is a difficult time for you and admire your courage to look for alternatives for your baby's welfare [We're nice people. We'd never speak badly of you.]. We are a professional couple [We make a good living and education is important to us.], have been married five years [We are stable.], and have completed a home study [We've been officially checked out.]. We are eagerly seeking the adoption of an infant to love and raise as our own. Please call us and see if we are the family you want your child to be a part of. Call collect if out of town. [And we included our phone number.]

Our ad was listed first in the column of ten similar petitions, something we had been told would be helpful. I was touched by everyone else's carefully crafted requests for consideration, so many of us with open arms. Instead of the old system in which children were forced to be on display for the choosing, as was the case in the orphanages or on the orphan trains, the adults were required to publicly present themselves for inspection, hoping they would be deemed a match. Strangely enough, I was reminded of the catalogues of couples pictured in the nude and interested in swinging, the ones Thomas's brother and his wife had participated in. This was different, of course, but much of the time, I felt naked, just the same.

Our attorney had encouraged us to make our intentions known among our family members, friends, and colleagues beyond our immediate social circle, saying you never knew who might have an important connection to a baby in need of a family. We did as suggested and paid the price of responding to questions about our progress more often than we would have liked. And people had their opinions. Some asked if we had considered adopting an older child. Or a child of a different race. Or a child with a disability. We did our best to dodge these questions and refrained from asking our pregnant friends if they were hoping for a child with a disability, too. It was acceptable for pregnant couples to say, we just want a healthy child, less so if you were adopting.

When I thought about the vulnerability required by this process of adults seeking approval of birthparents, I had to admit it was better than the old way, that it made more sense for adults to face such obstacles to find their family, something no child should have to confront. But older children hoping to be adopted would never be spared this anxiety. They were still going to be judged one way or another after the prospective adoptive parents passed muster. I asked Shirley if she ever saw potential parents engaging with children at the orphanage. She frowned and said she couldn't remember. "I probably wouldn't have seen it though, since Jean had signed that paper saying we couldn't be adopted. And far as I know, no one ever wanted me." I froze when she said this, unable to comprehend how that would feel, how it would affect the person you became.

Whenever the so-called adoption phone rang, Thomas and I would gasp then gesture to each other as if the caller could hear us before we picked up. If both of us were there, I was the one to answer, the belief being that birthmothers would feel more at ease with a female. A couple of times, Thomas and I were in the middle of an argument when the hotline beckoned. Like magic, an automatic truce would materialize as I spoke glowingly of my husband, keeping mum about my annoyance that he'd left his dirty dishes in front of the TV again. Thomas likened our conversations to a dating service. "Who are we?" he'd quip when debriefing each call with me. "Well, who do you want us to be?"

Some calls from birthmothers were strange and we were at the mercy of every caller. Some gave away as little information as possible about themselves, which was understandable, given the monumental choice they were facing, along with the fear of exposure. A couple birthmothers said too much, implicating birthfathers who were quite famous, as they put it, not that they could name them, but they emphasized how shocked we'd be if they told us. One birthmother asked me how I could consider myself a woman if I couldn't conceive. A few were seeking money and faced disappointment, since the Indiana adoption laws in the late 80s strictly forbade the provision of any gifts or contributions from the adoptive parents to the birthparents. The story we had been told was that even a locket presented to a birthmother after her child was born had been used to invalidate the adoption later on. A birthmother who sought money for her healthcare, her rent, transportation, or maternity clothes would do well to move to another state in which these things were allowed.

Mostly, the calls didn't lead to next steps. Our attorney assured us that this was normal, that many women making these inquiries decided to keep their babies. Although we worried about how our words on the phone sounded to women exploring their options, we never despaired, knowing this was only one of several strategies we were employing to make this crucial connection.

The toughest challenge I faced was making a decision about whether to follow our attorney's urgent advice to share our desire to adopt with my college students. "You work in a hospital and a university," he said to Thomas and me. "These are perfect places to find birthmothers." It felt awful. It felt exploitive. It felt incredibly unprofessional. At first I said I wouldn't do it, but over time, I began to wonder if this was what it would take. I decided to tell my friend, Carol, one of the most polite and appropriate persons I knew. I was embarrassed to share the idea and confess that I was thinking about it, but when I asked what she would do if it were her, she said emphatically, "I wouldn't hesitate for a single minute." I simultaneously felt such love for my friend and terror that I was going to do this. Thomas and I created small pieces of paper with our attorney's name and phone number typed on them to pass out. I told the chair of my department of my intentions and got his blessing. Then one day soon after, I announced at the end of class that I had something personal to share and didn't want to use class time to do it. So class was dismissed and I'd talk with anyone who wished to stay. Thirty students sat stock still in their desks. No one was going anywhere. Of course. I took a deep breath and stumbled through a description of the adoption plan my husband and I sought to make, requesting that if they knew of anyone looking for adoptive parents, to please give them my attorney's contact information. Then I repeated this performance for another class, again with full attendance, no one wanting to miss out on the big mystery.

There were unexpected results, none of them desirable. Students started stopping by my office to tell me of people they thought might be pregnant and that they would try to convince them to make an adoption plan. Practically hyperventilating, I would plead for them to cease and desist, emphasizing what a personal choice this was, but then another small group of students would stop by with similar information. I had unwittingly created pregnancy sleuths on the lookout for anyone looking green at the gills or a little bigger around the middle, which could describe a lot of coeds for reasons having more to do with two-for-one beer nights than being in the family way. Soon enough, the excitement died down, but not my feelings of uncertainty about the whole process.

Despite these dubious adventures, Thomas and I knew our child was waiting for us and that we would not stop until we found him or her. Like an actual pregnancy, it took nine months before we held our son, Benjamin Alex, in our arms when he was three days old. Ben was born in Pocatello, Idaho, which was far from the region where we had advertised, but there had been a cross-country connection made by someone in Idaho, who knew someone from Indiana, who knew our attorney. Ben's birthmother, Robin, was brave, humble, and beautiful. She handed the baby to me at the hospital, an almost indescribable moment in our lives, rife with bitter sweetness -- loss, gratitude, trust, and love at first sight. Thomas and I treasured the first quiet days together in our hotel room in Pocatello as we waited for permission to leave the state. Soon we would be surrounded by family and friends eager to welcome Ben to the world, but our first days together were an important time for just the three of us. A time for him to get to know our voices. A time for making attachments.

The thing about adoption is that parents aren't able to prepare like they would for a biological child. It's almost considered bad luck or, at least, tempting fate, since birthparents have the right to change their minds after the baby's birth. For this reason, many adopted children have slept in a hastily emptied sock drawer for their first crib, regardless of the parents' ability to provide fully appointed nurseries. This was my position in almost all forms of preparation. We were so focused on the process of finding our child that we didn't think much about what we'd do when it finally happened. Carol, who had encouraged me to do whatever I could to start a family, even if it meant talking to my students about it, bought me Penelope Leach's *Your Baby and Child* to read on the plane to Salt Lake City. This was after I asked her, "How often are you supposed to feed them?" her response being, "You really don't know anything, do you?"

My other excuse for not studying up was that I was counting on Thomas to lead the way. He had worked with infants in Riley Children's Hospital in Indianapolis, so I figured he would know what to do. During our cross country flight, I was disabused of this notion. "Melissa," he said, "I have taken care of really sick babies. I have no idea what to do with healthy ones." Great, I thought, cracking open the book with the familiar feeling that this should have been done sooner, counting on my tendency to be a fast learner under pressure.

When we got home, Shirley and Walter were there to greet us. I saw a side of them that was new to me. They talked in high-pitched baby voices and gestured to get Ben's attention. Never had I seen Walter so animated. Thomas and I were less important, the mere caretakers of the little prince, which was as it should have been. Shirley did turn her attention to me to say, "Well, now everyone's gonna think you look good, y'know, for just havin' a baby. Not like you didn't look good before, but now you look better. 'Cause of you know." I laughed that this was the best she could come up with, but it turned out to be true. Never in my life was I complimented by strangers in public places for looking fit, except for the times I carried around my adopted children as newborns.

When it came to knowing not to call the birthparents the real mom and dad and other such references, Shirley was astute. I believe this had nothing to do with political correctness, but rather a perspective that came from growing up without parents, biological or adopted. She knew the real parents were the ones who were there for you each and every day of your life.

15

A NEW FAMILY PORTRAIT

Ben's birth brought Shirley and Walter's retirement to life. He was not their first grandchild, but the first after they no longer spent their days and nights at the Kroger commercial bakery and Ford factory. They had nothing but time for him, which was fun to watch. My mother, also smitten but from out of town, was a little jealous. She would ask on the phone what Shirley and Walter were doing with him.

"Well, today," I said, "they filled up this metal washtub and put him in it. He loved that."

"Okay, I'm getting a metal washtub this week, for next time you bring him to visit," she said.

"And they let him bang on this electric keyboard for a while, which was a big success."

"Got it," she replied. "I'm trying to keep up." She had changed her grandmother moniker years before from Grandmama, accent on the third syllable to make it sound French, to Poppy, after observing how quickly the grandchildren learned to say my father's nickname, which was Pop.

It was a sweet time, with Ben surrounded by Grandma and Grandpa, Pop and Poppy, aunts and uncles, and cousins of all ages. He was an easy baby, too. Beautiful blue eyes, smart and charming. The first smile he bestowed upon me was during a late night feeding – all milky gums and bobbing head, his mouth wide open for a full minute as we displayed our delight like mirror reflections.

I wish I had known how to sit still and love every moment, but this wasn't my strong suit. I was still commuting one hour from Indianapolis to Bloomington and finishing my doctoral coursework. There are pictures of friends and colleagues in the

School of Education holding Ben napping on their shoulders while I taught classes. For a while, the wife of one of my professors babysat Ben two mornings a week, so he would come with me to Bloomington and we'd arrive at her house around 8am. She always had a roaring fire in the fireplace on those frosty mornings, and I would linger at the scene before leaving for campus, wondering why I wasn't content to provide this care at home each day. But Ben was a baby on the go and seemed to handle the situation well.

Sometimes Shirley and Walter took care of Ben while Thomas and I were at work. Shirley would take on challenges like his cradle cap, which she called "cradle crap." I never knew whether she was making a joke; I was just grateful for her help. I know I took advantage of the fact that they were always home and available to babysit. Walter and Shirley were happy to help, but kept me at arm's length back then, treating me like a spinning top as I ran in and out of their house to deliver or pick up Ben. This was when Shirley began to extoll Thomas's virtues as a father, the implication that I wasn't appreciating him enough painfully clear.

"Tom's the best father I ever knowed. I never knowed a man that changed diapers! Walter never touched a single one. Is you still using cloth ones at home? We bought him some Pampers and he likes 'em better. They don't leak."

At moments like this, I was tempted to say, "That's great for Walter, but what about Ben?" but refrained from going there. It was true that I was ready to call it quits with the cloth diapers, following the more rapid relinquishment of homemade baby wipes soaked in witch hazel, which were abandoned after one week to be precise. I was finding the reality of raising a child to be very different from the fantasy I had built during the years I yearned to begin. I knew how lucky I was to have Thomas as a parenting partner. He was so much more than the guy who changed diapers; he was simply a natural, much better than I at letting everything around him fall into disarray while tending to Ben, who became a daddy's boy right away.

When Ben was 18 months old, I took a demanding job as an elementary school principal in the Indianapolis Public Schools and postponed completing my doctorate. My professors warned me that I wouldn't have time to write a dissertation, but I didn't see a problem with taking a bit more time, working on my research on the weekends, perhaps the most naïve assumption I'd ever made. As if this wasn't crazy enough, a former student from Indiana University needed a place to live for a year, so she rented our spare bedroom. Thomas's niece, Casey, who had recently graduated from college, became Ben's full-time babysitter in our home. She and our renter both had nice boyfriends that were around a lot – so ours was a happening place with the baby at the center of everyone's attention.

Casey was a hoot as a caretaker. She loved Ben and was really good with him. I trusted her to give him excellent care. However, I found her less trustworthy in areas that were minor, but irksome. I'd lay out clothes for him to wear and find that she had chosen some other outfit more to her liking, maybe one they would have found at the mall that day, where she had his portrait taken on a whim. I'd prepare food for him to eat with accompanying instructions, but would come home to discover take-out boxes from Olive Garden in the refrigerator and Ben with intense garlic breath. After a while, I considered saying something to her, but then discovered she had painted his finger and toe nails, which I found charming, so I let it go.

Looking back, I know that Thomas and I were good parents when Ben was a baby and toddler, despite our daily doubts that we were doing anything right. We didn't know that having doubts was part of good parenting. Typically enough, we weren't always good at taking care of ourselves, however, sometimes sleepwalking through our days and wondering what had kept us so busy before we had a child. In spite of our weariness, we had fun, so much more than we could have imagined before Ben was born. Life was full. I was reminded of the saying, "the glass isn't half full or half empty; it's just a really big glass."

16

WHAT WE LOST

My mother had been diagnosed with endometrial cancer the year before Ben's birth, but after a hysterectomy, followed by chemotherapy and radiation treatment, was in remission. We had dared to see this as a discrete, dark chapter, a bullet dodged, and had moved forward with optimism. Following her treatments, life was back to normal very quickly. Before I began my job as a school principal in 1991, Mom came to Indianapolis to do whatever she could to help me get ready. This included what she considered the high priority of decorating my tiny office at the school. She brought me a beautiful painting of school children, which she had purchased in China, with the intention of hanging it there. When I told her my office was too small for it and that I'd rather hang the painting at our house, she was only mildly annoyed. I am touched to think about all the worries that she must have kept to herself. Like what was I doing taking on a job like this with an 18-month-old child? And almost as important to my orderly mother, how in the world was I ever going to clean out my mess of a basement now? What she told me instead was that she was proud of me, and she became my champion. She moved in for a week, taking care of Ben and organizing everything in sight. She took every item of clothing out of my closet, clucked her tongue that I didn't even know what all I had crammed in there, and stood at an ironing board for days, getting together outfits for me to wear. At some point, she gasped over a realization that had just come to her. "Melissa. How are you going to handle it when they need to be ironed again?" I didn't have a good answer to this question. She took me shopping to buy a new suit, dress, and shoes. "It looks great," she said about the dress when we were in the dressing room, "but there isn't room for you to gain a single pound in it."

"That won't be a problem," was my breezy response, based on an assumption that I wouldn't have much time to eat and would likely lose weight, a preposterous notion in hindsight.

By the fall of that year, her cancer was back. Mom, Dad, and Thomas drove to a cancer center in Pittsburgh for a second opinion, but returned with little hope that she was going to be able to survive the disease which had now spread to multiple organs. She was 57 years old.

Time began to slow down. Priorities were instantly clarified, despite the demands I was trying to meet as a new school administrator. One night in late November, following a difficult doctor appointment Mom told me about on the phone, I typed a letter to the staff saying that I would not be there for Grandparents Day the next day because I needed to be with my family in Ohio. I left work, having made arrangements with Thomas, and drove to Cincinnati that evening. As I drove in the dark, quiet night, I was haunted by an image of a cyclone that snatched a single person from our group at random, and that we would cling to her, but fail to stop her from being taken. The sinister feeling reminded me of Shirley Jackson's short story, "The Lottery," which was assigned reading in 9th grade and one of my first experiences with arbitrary injustice, albeit vicarious. Now I couldn't shake the dread that began to form. When I got to my parents' house late that night, I entered silently, wondering if they had gone to bed, but saw the light on in the family room. I tiptoed down the hall and found my parents, stretched out on the couch together, sleeping in each other's arms. In this moment, I knew my life would be forever changed.

My mother accepted her looming demise with grace and gratitude. Rather than praying for miracle cures, she recognized her life as the miracle, saying, "I have lived 57 amazing years. I am a fortunate woman." She talked about the beautiful, historic cemetery where she and Dad had decided she would be buried. Her parents and only sibling, a brother, had died before her. As a devout Christian, she was comforted by her belief that she would see all of them soon. When playing with Ben and her other grandchildren, or looking at their pictures, she would fight back tears, refusing to let her despair take center stage. The following spring, when her oncologist estimated that she had 5-6 months to live, based largely on how good she looked, my father shook his head afterward, quietly saying, "The doctor has no idea how long it took her to prepare for this appointment." To the end, my mother took great pride in her appearance. Within a week of that appointment, she was hospitalized and my family gathered when it was evident this would be her last admittance.

Once during this last stay in the hospital, when Mom awoke after a long sleep and we were alone in the room, I shared with her one of my most tender memories. As young children learning to swim, my mother had dressed us in brightly colored bathing suits in order to find us in the crowd as she kept watch. She had never learned to swim, due to the polio scare of her youth, and worried about whether we were safe from drowning out there. I remember being about seven or eight when she and I had a conversation about what to do if something happened and I couldn't reach the surface of the water for air. I reminded her of this as I sat next to her hospital bed, hoping it would provide comfort while she contemplated her passage from this life. "You told me not to be afraid. You said it was okay to be still and close my eyes and wait for help, and that help would come."

She pushed herself up into a sitting position in the bed. "Well, that's not true. I would never have told you that. I would have said to do whatever you could to get to the surface. I don't know where you come up with these things." I laughed, of course, but I still believe it happened. And I still trust that help will come when I need it most, because this is what my mother told me when I was a little girl.

She was gone three weeks after the oncologist's 5-6 month prediction. My sisters, brother, father, and I, having sat vigil for some time, left the hospital together, now a family of five where there once were six. The cyclone was just too strong.

In the days after my mother died, Ben toddled around my parents' house, saying, "Where's Poppy?" and studied our tears with curiosity. He turned two the next month, reminding me that his time with my mother was too short, and that my time with my mother was too short, and fueling feelings that seemed unbearable. Although Thomas had known my mother only eight years, his despair at her death felt like he had lost a parent, too.

My mother's death and funeral served as a turning point in my relationship with Shirley and Walter. Perhaps my parents' jetsetter image had kept my in-laws from seeing the side of them that came from a Southern Baptist tradition in their home in Texas. Attending the funeral and singing old-fashioned hymns like, "In the Garden," helped Shirley and Walter see my parents beyond the surface, and to see me differently by association. Walter commented more than once, "That was a Godly service." And Shirley began to hug me. Her tone of voice when talking to me changed to something warm and sympathetic, and she often ended what she said by calling me "honey." My sadness and vulnerability provided a kind of breakthrough for the two of us and, for a while, Shirley really did seem like a loving mother-in-law to me. Not forever, but for a while. Life went on, as my mother had said it would, and returning to work two weeks after her death, I was swept into the chaos of it and didn't take time to fully grieve until I quit the job years later.

17

IN MEMORIAM

After my mother died in 1992, I was fascinated by old family pictures and often pored through them looking for something, though I was never quite sure what. I started framing old portraits or photographs I particularly liked. Some made me chuckle, recalling my mother bringing them over soon after Ben was born to show me how astounding it was that he looked just like various family members. Of course, it wasn't unusual to compare each grandchild to pictures of ancestors, but there was added meaning to these appraisals. It was my mother's transition from seeing Ben as someone who looked like us to simply being us. Around the third time she did this, I laughed and said, "Mom. What are you doing?"

"Oh, I know. But don't you think his looks are remarkably similar to my dad's side of the family?"

"I suppose someone could think that, but really, it's time to stop." Looking back, I don't know why it was time to stop. It wasn't doing any harm and it made her happy.

I began to create a composite of family pictures on the living room wall in the year after her death. When the grouping looked imbalanced with my ancestors' portraits and none of Thomas's family, I tried to remedy this situation by asking Shirley for pictures of Thomas's grandparents to frame and display. The next day, she handed me a couple of Polaroid snapshots that indicated a clear miscommunication. They were tiny, bland, and unappealing, the faded colors making the figures look wishy-washy at best. The picture of Walter's parents, Oscar and Marie Kuhn, showed them sitting on the plastic-covered couch, wearing matching frowns. You could see up Marie's dress, revealing her stockings rolled down to just above her knees. The photograph of

Shirley's mother wasn't much better, sitting on the same couch with a red handbag that was half her size next to her. At least she was smiling, but her glasses reflected the camera flash and you couldn't see her eyes. Imagining how the snapshots would look next to my family's framed portraits, I was reminded of my mother's worries about uncoordinated family pictures at Thomas's and my wedding. It made me smile.

I considered a basic teaching lesson, which was to show someone what you mean whenever you can, rather than relying on a verbal description only. So I brought over examples of old portraits and asked Shirley if they had any pictures like this. She directed me to some boxes of pictures spanning great amounts of time and told me to have at it. I found a couple of very old portrait photographs in one of the stacks that looked like they belonged together. The backgrounds were identical, their clothing looked to be from the same period, circa late 19th century, and their grim expressions were a clear match. "Shirley, who are these people?" I asked as I held the two portraits up for her to see.

She stared for a moment. "Well, they could be Walter's family. That's all I know."

Walter's birthday was coming up and I was reasonably certain Thomas had not gotten him a gift.

"Would you mind if I framed them for Walter?" I asked Shirley.

"What do I care? Do what you want."

Inspired by this enthusiastic encouragement, I chose a beautiful frame and had a mat with two ovals cut to hold the pair of unsmiling sepia-toned images. Thomas appreciated this effort in his own way. "Wow, those look great. Who are these people?"

"Your father's ancestors. I can't believe your family doesn't take better care of stuff like this. I think your dad will really like it, don't you?"

There was a pause. "Well...I guess. It isn't really his thing."

I was annoyed. "It doesn't have to be his thing to appreciate preserving the past, Thomas. I spent some money on this. Geez."

Patting me on the shoulder, Thomas ended the conversation. "You're right. They look great. Good job." This was his increasingly rote response to such risky situations.

I held my head high as Walter opened his birthday gift from us. He stared at it for a moment, then smiled. "Well, look at that."

"It came out well, don't you think? Who are they?" I said, eager for validation in front of Shirley and Thomas.

"Well," and he paused. "I'm not sure, but I don't think they knew each other."

"What? They weren't married?"

"No… She looks like my mother's side of the family. But I've never seen this picture of him before. My cousin, John Wesley Kuhn, left some pictures here once that wasn't ours and it turned out some of them was his wife's family. Maybe it's from them. But that's okay. It looks pretty good."

When we got home, I grumbled to Thomas, "And that's why it's important to mark the back of pictures."

Thomas laughed. "You're just worried that someone's going to frame your picture with Joe's someday." The two portraits were displayed on the wall in the living room in their shared frame and there they remained until the house was sold years later, a constant reminder of another futile attempt to bring some order to Thomas's family history. No one ever determined who the subjects were.

It was at this time, one year after my mother's death, that a new configuration of my own family of origin took place. My father fell in love with and married a longtime family friend, resulting in new siblings, cousins, aunts, uncles, and a new home base, only a half mile from our parents' previous home. My sisters, brother, and I were overjoyed that Dad had married Joan, someone we had known and loved for twenty years. Joan had been a close friend to my mother and had watched us grow up since she, her late husband, and my parents had taken turns driving their kids to church youth group meetings each week, before we had drivers' licenses. I would always be sad that my children wouldn't know my mother, but grateful that Joan was such a generous grandmother to them and that her love story with my father, who was so happy again, would be enduring.

18

FIRST FRIENDS

Ben continued to spend lots of time with Grandma and Grandpa, often coming home with little gems to share, including occasional racial and ethnic slurs that required deprogramming. He also chanted old-fashioned rhymes like, "Hey, Joe, whaddaya know? I just got back from Kokomo!" and "Teeter totter, bread and water, wash your face with dirty water!" This was almost as hilarious to him as, "Mama-mia, Papa-pia, baby's got the diarrhea," which he had already learned from Thomas. His favorite TV shows were now "Hee Haw" and "The Lawrence Welk Show," and he could name all the characters for both. Sometimes he would tell me that his hearing just wasn't what it used to be.

At home, Ben was most interested in what our dog, Skippy, was up to, and vice versa. Although they had had a sweet relationship from the start, we had begun to see potential problems as soon as Ben started to toddle around the house. It wasn't Skippy's fault. He had nuzzled Ben as a baby and looked like he was guarding him while he slept sometimes. But what could he do when a great big toddler had cornered him and was merrily bopping him on the head with a hard plastic toy? The first time Skippy bit Ben, it was a shallow bite on the face, actually a nip, a warning to back off, baby. It scared me as much as it did Ben and I was angry at our beloved dog, who cowered and whimpered, sniffing around us as Ben cried in response to the surprise attack. I took Ben to the doctor and was ambivalent about his advice to just take out a wrapped Popsicle when things like this happen and hold it up to the wound to keep it from swelling. And to keep the dog. He was one of those patronizing professionals that never called you by name. His words, something like this: "Don't get rid of the dog, Mom! He didn't mean to bite him." What the hell? was what I thought, but decided that Skippy was on probation for life and that if he did anything like this again, he had to go.

This decision resulted in Skippy's eventual involuntary transfer to Joe and Dorothy's place above Shirley and Walter's garage after the next inevitable incident. The irony was that our cat, Emily, got to stay, when she was the bully of the neighborhood, taking down songbirds even when we attached a bell to her collar. She scratched the living daylights out of Thomas and me, but somehow knew to keep her claws off that little boy, and could escape his attempts to dominate in ways Skippy never could. I was sad, but resolute in my ruling, and told Ben we would see Skippy whenever we wanted in Grandma and Grandpa's back yard, but not at our house.

Joe and Dorothy loved Skippy and he loved them, of course, but I will always feel guilty about that move to crazy town. There were no scary children to run from, but the tiny space was still overflowing with beer cans, cigarette butts, and mountains of flea powder. Because of the second hand smoke, not to mention the flea powder everyone was inhaling, I limited how often Ben could go for brief visits, which made him unhappy because he loved hanging out there. Thomas and I could see evidence of Dorothy and Joe's influence when Ben began to answer the phone in Dorothy's low, throaty voice, "Helloooo," and he tried putting his feet on the table as he did at their place, just like his uncle. Regarding their smoky apartment, Ben said he thought it smelled fancy.

Dorothy had become paranoid about fleas, which explained the preponderance of flea powder in her cramped habitat. "Fleas is smart," she'd say. "They train 'em in the circus." Interpreting my look of consternation as agreement, she'd continue. "They watch you, y'know. They're watchin' me and we got to get rid of all of 'em."

Skippy had his own problems with fleas. He was allergic to flea bites and lost a lot of the fur on his hind quarters every year in certain seasons. Dorothy had allergies, too, but she was allergic to the flea powder, rather than the fleas. At one point, when her face swelled and she could barely open her eyes, Shirley shared without sympathy what had happened. "Joe knows the only hair color she can use is Nice 'n Easy, but he's so cheap. I think he done picked up something that ain't supposed to be used on hair. I think it was Rit. Thinks he knows everything. Then Dorothy got scared and dumped a bunch of flea powder in her hair and now she's as scary lookin' as she can be. She done swelled up like a grapefruit with her eyes all bugged out. I can't even look at her. But I took her to the hospital and they said just give her Benadryl and she'll be okay."

Dorothy took Benadryl and the crisis was over in a day or so, but I worried that she needed help with her fear of fleas. I tried to talk to Shirley and Thomas about finding a counselor for her, but no one seemed to think the recent episode warranted any kind of therapy. I had gotten used to this reaction and eventually gave up on the matter, especially after her fears died down as mysteriously as they had appeared in the first place. Dorothy's bouts of instability would have proven more perilous if she and Joe were living independently or had others depending on them. But under the sheltering protection of her in-laws, I knew Dorothy was reasonably safe and let go of my insistence that we find her additional help. The short term was under control, but I wondered what would happen if Walter and Shirley died before Dorothy or if they reached a point when they couldn't care for themselves, much less their elderly daughter-in-law. But no one wanted to talk about that either.

Although Ben would never replace Skippy as his very first

friend, when he was almost three, he cultivated relationships with two imaginary friends he named Sonny and Buddy, who often accompanied him to Grandma's house. He loved them deeply, sometimes gesturing grandly and shouting with gusto, "Let's go, soccer players!" Then he would gallop across the lawn while Shirley prepared snacks for three. I saw great opportunity in Ben's invention of Sonny and Buddy and exploited their existence flagrantly. "Wow," I'd announce. "Sonny and Buddy are already in the tub!" and Ben would strip down in a flash. Or "Sonny and Buddy are already buckled up in their car seats!" Whenever I wanted Ben to do something, all I had to do was invoke the names of Sonny and Buddy and it was done.

It worked like a charm for a while, but I noted, only in hindsight, my son's eventual hesitation when responding to the constant litany of Sonny and Buddy's many assets. Theirs was an example no one could match. The day came when it was pointed out that I'd overdone a good thing. Shirley was over at the house at lunchtime on a Saturday. As we sat down to eat, Thomas and Ben solemnly told me, "We hate Sonny and Buddy now," and that they had to run them out of town. "On a rail," Ben said. He sighed as he described their transformation into kids who just weren't any fun anymore. Thomas and Shirley gave me accusing looks and I was ashamed.

"What if we gave them another chance?" I said. "Told them to just act like regular guys?" But Ben shook his head. He had made his decision. They were dead to him.

While Ben was napping, Thomas laughed, but gave me a hard time. "I told you to lay off. You ruined our kid's imaginary friendships. It's like you killed Sonny and Buddy!"

Shirley chimed in. "Yeah! They was nice little boys at the start."

There was a pause after this odd comment. Thomas looked at Shirley, saying, "Mom? Is there something you want to tell us?"

Thomas seemed to enjoy his position as the normal one, somewhere between his delusional mother and controlling wife. I sulked and wished my mom were there to defend me. If I had had imaginary friends as a young child, she would have had no qualms about using them to make life a little easier. I was the third of four children in a six year span, for heaven's sake. I imagined her saying, "Life is short; this isn't something to worry about."

Watching Ben as he slept, I considered the potential of reinventing his imaginary pals as bad boys who needed Ben to be the role model. I even wondered if I could get away with suggesting that Sonny and Buddy had taught him the three swear words he had recently recited to me in hushed tones: shut up, fuck, and nanny-nanny-boo-boo; the source of the f-word shocker we had proclaimed to be a complete and total mystery. Instead, I decided we should invite the little boy who lived on the next block to come over and play. And if Sonny and Buddy ever returned in the future, I vowed to spoil their appetites with cookies before supper.

19

UNANSWERED QUESTIONS

Shirley and her sister, Dot, rarely saw each other, although they lived in the same city. They became acquainted in their adulthood and occasionally got their families together, but they were never close friends. Still, they sent each other birthday cards each year. One year, Dot sent Shirley a Hallmark card with a cartoon of a person holding a large bouquet of red roses on the cover. I laughed when I saw it, and Shirley said, "What's so funny?"

"Nothing really," I said. "It's just funny that it spells out 'You're Old' with the flowers."

"It does not!" Shirley said as she grabbed it from me for closer scrutiny. Her eyes widened. "Well, I didn't see that!" She called Dot and found out she hadn't seen the message in the flowers either. Dot was livid.

"She's threatening to sue Hallmark," Shirley told me as she hung up the phone. "Or at least get her money back. She told me to send it back to her. I said okay, but I'm not gonna." I was struck by the difference between the two in that moment alone. Shirley had a quiet, behind-the-scenes kind of energy when it came to dealing with little things like this. She tended to dismiss minor problems and avoided explaining why by agreeing to what was asked of her with no intention of following through. Dot was fiery. She filled her life with matters of great import, simply by declaring them as such.

Now, in 1992, they were sitting on Shirley's couch and talking about truly important matters, more than sixty years after they were moved to the orphanage. "There was no point in asking what happened," Shirley said. "They wasn't going to tell you." Dot shrugged her shoulders when she heard this. "I just thought she was dead," she said about their mother. "Then when I was about eight or nine years old, I was going through the dumpster after they cleaned out the office at the Home."

"Um," I said, "why were you doing that?"

Both Dot and Shirley started to laugh. "Because I was a snoop!" Dot said. "Y'know, after I left the Home, I worked for an insurance company, where I'd sit in the back and read everybody's files. Back then, if you wanted insurance, they asked your neighbors about you and you wouldn't believe everything people had to say about each other." She laughed again. "They told me I was the best file clerk they ever had!" Dot returned to her story. "Anyway, I found a document in the dumpster that said our father had gone to prison and our mother was in a mental hospital."

"What did you think?" I asked.

"Well, I was shocked, I guess. I was just a kid; I didn't really know what to think."

I shook my head. "Did you tell anyone?"

Dot thought about this. "I might have told my friends. I don't really remember. But I guess I didn't tell my sisters and Donald because I never saw them."

"She didn't tell me," Shirley said. "I didn't know about that until Dot told me when we were both out of there."

Dot laughed. "There was all kinds of things we were supposed to figure out on our own! They sure didn't tell us about sex! One time, Georgie told me she thought she was pregnant because a boy put his tongue in her mouth."

"Did anyone go on dates?" I asked. Dot nodded her head. "Well, there were dates and there were dates. Georgie wasn't on a date anyone would have approved of when she was making out with that boy. They met in one of the tunnels on the campus. There was something called 'date night' once a week for the older girls to entertain their boyfriends in their cottages, but those were always planned out ahead of time and supervision was strict."

"Did either of you have someone over for date nights?" I asked. Not surprisingly, Shirley said she didn't remember, but Dot said she did a couple of times. "It was boring, so I didn't have anybody over except a couple of times. Those old matrons watched you closely. It cramped everyone's style."

"So, who told you about sex?" I asked. Dot laughed, "Well, it sure wasn't one of the adults! All they told us about sex was that boys had something in their pants that had a mind of its own!" Now we were all laughing. "And to just holler, no!" Shirley added.

"I think God doesn't want you to know about that part of marriage until it's too late," Dot said. "That's why He made those rules." Shirley laughed in agreement as she went into the kitchen to start a pot of coffee. After she left, Dot sighed. "Dot? Are you okay?" I asked. Something had shifted and her eyes were tearing up. She shook her head. "I left the Home with my virginity. That belonged to me and I didn't have nothin' else." I didn't know what to say and a quiet minute passed before Shirley returned with the coffee.

Dot continued as if nothing had changed. Like Shirley's story about her name being changed from Edith when she first arrived at the orphanage, she had a story about hers. She was named Dora Fay at birth, Fay being her mother's name and Dora the name of her paternal grandmother, Dora Martin Peacock. "My mother named me after her mother-in-law, but when I was still a baby, they had a falling out and she changed my name to Dorothy, and I changed it to Dot when I was older. So I thought that was my name! I didn't find out until I graduated from the Home that my name wasn't Dorothy. That's when I saw my birth certificate. I liked Dorothy and Dot better than Dora anyway."

The three of us paused to consider this, then Dot said,

"What were we talking about? Oh! Anyway, the first time I saw our mom after going to the Home wasn't too long after I found that paper," she said. "They brought her to the Home. I had thought she was dead for a long time, so I was scared to death."

"Were you there for that visit, Shirley?" I asked.

"I suppose so...I don't really remember it," Shirley said. "She wouldn't have stayed very long. They didn't let you stay very long. You could visit twice a year just for the day, but most years, she didn't come."

Dot had a faraway look in her eyes. "I remember she said, 'I'd just love to cook you a meal.'" There was a pause. "Well, there was no point in crying about it," Shirley said. "Whatever came, I just accepted it."

"Did anyone ever tell you why your mother went to Central State?" I asked. Shirley frowned. "I don't know. She just couldn't take care of us and it was too much."

"And no one was there to help her?"

"I guess not. Her father died. Her brother, too – shot hisself," Shirley said.

"What?"

"Well, that's what I heard. I don't really know," she continued.

"Did she have a mother?"

"Just a step-mother. Her mother was dead. And her step-mother didn't help her none."

In subsequent years, I pieced together more of Fay's story from various sources. Fay Hammitt was born December 26, 1896. She had one sibling, a younger brother named Fred, born in 1898. Their mother died of tuberculosis in 1903, at which time their father, George Hammitt, took Fay and Fred to an orphanage, then to live with their grandparents in Red Key, Indiana, until he remarried in 1905 and retrieved them to live with him in Lafayette, Indiana. His second wife, Edith Murphy Hammitt, helped raise Fay and Fred, but the story was that Edith favored Fred.

In 1918, Fay's brother, who was newlywed, died of a gunshot wound to the head at the age of 20. The circumstances leading to this remained a mystery. Regardless of whether it was the result of an accident, suicide, or even homicide, Fay, who was working as an assembler at a manufacturing company, was devastated by the loss of her only sibling. She married Morris Peacock four months later, in 1919.

Morris was ending his tour of duty as a WWI soldier at the time of their wedding. He was jailed for petty theft soon after he came home. Upon his release, he worked as a mechanic, then a firefighter. In both cases, he was hired with the help of his father-in-law's influence. Shirley came along in 1920. Once I asked Shirley if she had been named after her mother's stepmother, Edith. Shirley seemed startled by the question. "I don't know. I never really thought about it. Maybe I was."

"If so, I wonder why your mother named you after someone she didn't get along with," something I'd heard about from Dot in particular.

"Well, she was always trying to please her dad, I think. Maybe she thought it would help with her stepmother. She wanted people to like her."

There is a picture of George and Edith posing with the first grandchild, Baby Edith Shirley, sitting on Edith's lap. Shirley looks like a lively baby with dark hair and eyes, arms in the air, and a spirited expression on her face. There's an animated energy in the composition of this photograph. Even George's wife, Edith, who looks rather prim with her hair in a severe bun and wearing wire rim glasses, has a hint of a smile on her face. "Were there ever any pictures of you as a baby or young child with either of your parents?" I asked.

"If there are, I never seen 'em," Shirley said. "I guess he started treatin' her bad after I was born. She told me he hit her when I was a few months old and she was askin' for money. And then Georgie was born the next year, Georgia Jean."

"And she must have been named after your mother's dad, right? And her middle name after Morris's sister?" Again, Shirley seemed surprised. "Huh. I guess so! I wonder if Georgie knows that." She shook her head. "Our father just came home long enough to get my mother pregnant, then he'd be off with another woman."

Fay's circumstances may have been grim, but it appears she was getting by with the help of her father, who supported her financially. There is a story about him buying her a house in her name only, but Morris made her sign over the deed at gunpoint years later, before leaving town with his mistress.

Shirley spoke of her grandfather fondly, but in general terms, likely due to the brevity of their relationship. "I remember seeing him. He used to bounce me around on his knee. But I don't remember ever seeing his wife, my mother's stepmother. He called one of us Scoots. I think it was Dot, because she never crawled, just scooted around on her rear end to get around. Dot says he always had extra cash, but I don't know how she'd know that. She was just a baby. I think he had these properties." George's fatal heart attack in 1924 was a devastating blow to Fay's security. He was 54 years old. Her fourth child, Morris Donald, who would be called Donald, was born two months later.

Henceforward, much of Fay's story is speculation. Family lore has it that Fay's stepmother, Edith, refused to share George's estate with her, essentially cutting off the financial support on which she was dependent. Morris no longer lived at home and spent most of his time with his mistress, remembered only as

Mrs. St. John. In December of 1925, Fay's fifth child, Roberta, was born. Somehow, Fay got by on minimal income. But eventually, the children were taken away and she was institutionalized.

Chosen Battles

20

CHRISTMAS TAKEOVER

When Ben was three years old, it was our turn to host the Kuhns for a family Christmas celebration. I made the mistake of agreeing to do this on Christmas Eve, not thinking about how this would take away from Ben's experience of the night before Christmas. It was a sizable crowd at our house and the last guests left at midnight. There sat our little boy, asleep on the couch with a piece of melted fudge in each hand. The night had been so loud and chaotic and, while Thomas and I were busy with hosting, everyone was happy to hold Ben. He didn't show signs of being overtired and it would have been hard to get him to sleep amid the commotion, but I dropped the ball by not insisting that he go to bed at a decent hour.

Scooping Ben up off the couch, I made a decision. Never again on Christmas Eve would we host or attend this gathering, at least not as long as we had young children. But I wasn't sure how to make this happen, given that I was one of many in the group. I consulted my friend, Anna Lisa, about this and she had the answer.

"It's simple. You become the host every year. That way you can decide when you want to get together and everyone has to follow your schedule."

"Is that what you do?"

"Of course," she said.

I had hosted several holiday meals for Thomas's family at this point and had adjusted my expectations as a result. I was a plucky newlywed the first time I prepared Thanksgiving dinner, cooking for 15 in-laws in 1985. Low on experience and high on delusions of grandeur, I attempted to impress them all. In hindsight, nothing said irony like the *Bon Appetit* Thanksgiving menu for the Kuhns, not to mention the fact that I was in my twenties and a chef only by way of fantasy. I was overwhelmed early on. On top of all the other problems I'd experience in my preparations, the turkey didn't have the bag that held the giblets. I called my mother, taking for granted that she would always be there when I needed her. "Our turkey doesn't have a bag," I said.

"Yes, it does. All turkeys have a bag."

"Thomas and I crammed our hands in both ends. And it was gross, Mom. We felt all around and our turkey doesn't have a bag."

In the tiny pause that followed, I could imagine her look of exasperation, like when I would address Thomas's refrigerator blindness, saying, it's there if you just look. "It's there if you just look, honey," she said. "Y'know, these calls are expensive." And so our conversations went every few minutes when I'd call and say, "Still no bag."

The bag appeared miraculously as we carved the turkey. Shirley commented on its surprise arrival. "Well, I don't know how you made gravy without the giblets. The best part of the dinner is the gravy, so I hope it's okay."

I don't know what anyone thought of the gravy or anything else for that meal. They had finished and were ready for pie and football on the television in record time. When I came back from the kitchen, after trying to clear the main dishes, I found Shirley walking around with one of the pies, plopping slices on everyone's messy dinner plates. "I don't know why we need to dirty up more plates, do you?" she said.

I called my mother that night, crying as I described what I saw as a lack of civility. She basked in the glow of our family's favorable comparison. For the moment, I had forgotten about the down side of sitting too long at a holiday table, drinking too much and engaging in political debates that looked like blood sport, which was my family's holiday ritual on some occasions. There was one Thanksgiving meal of my youth when I had left the table mid-meal in anger, which made my grandmother cry.

I told Thomas I had learned my lesson and certainly wouldn't be knocking myself out like that again. He seemed relieved, even happy. Little did I know about pacing oneself for the long haul when it came to such events.

Eight years later, Anna Lisa's advice about future Christmas family celebrations worked like a charm. Everyone seemed happy to let us continue as the hosts and, for me, picking the date was worth the extra work. Over the next couple of years, I figured out how to host the crowd in a way that wasn't so taxing. For the Christmas of 1993, we would be dining on lasagna that I could make ahead of time, garlic bread, salad, and a couple of pies, finis. The hitch was that Shirley wanted a ham. She couldn't say so directly, so she chose to blame it on Walter. She left phone messages.

"Melissa? Hi. Y'know, Walter doesn't like lasagna."

Next message: "He really likes ham. This is Shirley, by the way."

And the next: "He likes mashed potatoes, too. I'm just sayin'."

I dug in my heels in a way that shocked and thrilled, not realizing that Shirley and I were laying the groundwork for sniping at each other around the holidays from then on. I suspected Walter had not said any of the things Shirley claimed, or maybe he had, but never thought Shirley would talk to me about it. Having no idea what I was about to unleash, I decided to check it out as I sat in their kitchen a couple of weeks before

Christmas.

"Walter?" I said. "It sounds like you would like to have ham for our Christmas get together."

Walter looked at Shirley, who began to yell, "I was just kiddin'. I didn't say that." Walter waved his hands, saying amid Shirley's protestations, "You should make whatever you want. I don't need a ham." He walked in and out of the kitchen, seemingly trying to get his breath, while Shirley took up the hand waving, too, and repeated what she had said before. They kept shouting to not worry about it, which felt like cognitive dissonance.

Holy shit, I thought. I guess we're having ham.

I compromised by having ham sandwiches and potato salad. The next year, I was back to lasagna and didn't hear any complaints. I knew it wasn't a favorite, but didn't see anyone stepping up to make something else. One night of the year, everyone could suffer through it. Besides, it wasn't like it was Christmas Eve, not with me in charge.

21

SHIRLEY'S CANCER

Shirley was diagnosed with breast cancer a couple of years after my mother's death. The treatment prescribed was radiation and surgery to remove the tumor and a number of lymph nodes. Walter took her to all her appointments. If she felt ill, we didn't know. Resolutely self-sufficient, she didn't talk about it very much.

When I recall this time period, I wonder where I was and why I don't remember more about it. She was diagnosed with cancer of both breasts, but not at the same time. After treatment for one side, she had to go through the whole process again for the other side. Thomas paid close attention to her care, but there was never a feeling of anxiety or despair among family members as far as I could see. Her eventual remission was what we had expected all along. Her treatment lasted about a year. It was remarkably different from my mother's experience, or my experience with my mother.

My only memory of showing some kind of support was when I took Shirley a book to read in the hospital after her surgery. She was an avid reader, which I had found interesting. Thomas said this was a fairly new pastime since her retirement, a way for her to avoid watching television all day. I asked her once if she had liked to read as a child and she said, "Not really." But now she loved to read, and I thought any book with a compelling story would be a nice distraction from the boredom of her hospital stay. If I had been paying better attention, I would have noticed that she limited her choices of reading material to daily Bible verses and bodice-ripper romances, which I could have picked up for her at any drug store. She once said to me, "I just love a good Harlem romance." Somehow, I doubted that.

What I brought her was *The Handmaid's Tale*, by Margaret Atwood. If ever there was a bleak narrative about a dismal future for American society, this was it, ahead of its time in its dystopian vision. The plot told the story of a futuristic American government overthrown by a totalitarian Christian theocracy, which subjugated women and took away their basic rights through electronic financial records. Women were forced to be concubines for men whose wives were unable to reproduce. I thought it was fascinating and couldn't imagine why anyone wouldn't feel the same way. I don't know what I was thinking. It never entered my mind that Shirley might want to read something a little more uplifting during this trying time. *Chicken Soup for the Soul* would have been a better choice, but the first of this series was yet to be published. It didn't occur to me that she would be offended by the portrayal of Christian conservatism either. I was taken aback by her hostility when I visited her in the hospital after she had read it. She glared at me.

"Melissa. Where did you get this book?"

"Oh! Did you like it? I thought it was amazing!"

She waved the book in my face. "Well, it's garbage. I don't know why you brought me this. It's a terrible story."

I was floored and stumbled around with my response. "Oh, gosh, I'm sorry, Shirley. You didn't like it?"

"No, I did not!" She took a breath and searched for words to describe her disgust. "Is this what you think is going to happen in the world?"

"Well, I certainly hope not. I just thought it was interesting and Margaret Atwood is one of my favorite writers."

"Well, that don't matter when you write terrible stories like this. I don't want it anymore," she said, holding the book out to me.

"I'm really sorry, Shirley," I said, as I tucked the book into my bag. It was hard to restrain my more defensive reactions. I noticed she was worn out by her exercised response and I said I'd come back soon.

"Not with a terrible book like that, I hope!"

In as much as there weren't tears shed over Shirley's diagnosis, there wasn't a celebration of her recovery and remission either. I wonder what that felt like. It appeared to be her preference, but I'll never know if this was how she really felt. It seemed it didn't matter whether an experience was positive or negative, major or minor, Shirley treated her daily life as if it was unremarkable, nothing to write home about. I look back at this time and wonder if she thought she didn't deserve such consideration, having grown up without anyone paying attention to her needs.

One remaining side effect of Shirley's cancer was pain and weakness in her left arm, the result of scraping the lymph nodes on that side. She would experience swelling and discomfort from dysfunction of the lymph system for the rest of her life, something that became increasingly problematic as she aged.

22

THE MAGIC KINGDOM

"Fairy tale dreams come true," according to the commercials I saw on Sunday nights on *Walt Disney's Wonderful World of Color* television show, watched in black and white by my siblings and me. I didn't know I should feel deprived of the experience when I didn't make it to the Magic Kingdom in my childhood, nor do I feel deprived in hindsight. But memories of the family vacations of my youth, all road trips in a station wagon with suitcases loaded on top, have taken on legendary qualities over time. My parents must have put a lot of planning into these excursions. I wonder what it felt like when they observed what we loved the most, which was the Magic Fingers device on the hotel beds, for which we'd pool our quarters to make the mattress shake for about thirty seconds. On the way to and from our destinations, my brother, Rob, and I, always relegated to the back of the station wagon as the younger children, long before seatbelts were required, could rough house on the surface where the seats were folded down and make faces at people in cars behind us. We especially liked one of us sitting directly behind the other as we faced the back window, arms poking through to make it look like one person with four arms waving to the hapless passengers stuck behind us in traffic. All of this was mostly fun, except for occasional crises, for example, when Rob stashed orange peanut butter crackers he purchased at a gas station, with my support even though I knew they were strictly verboten for him. He ate them right away and vomited once we were back on the road -- on my behind, when I was doing a backward somersault. My parents screamed at Rob to hold me in this position until they could pull off the highway, then lifted me out, upside down, and pulled off my pants by the side of the road, in full view of cars whizzing by. I think I was ten. It took a while to get over that. But mostly, I remember the safety of containment in the car with my family, sometimes driving late into the night, my father telling stories of heroes and historic battles. Enveloped in darkness, we'd sing folk songs like "Water" and "Stewball," and songs about martyrs such as Scotland's Roddy McCorley going to die "on the Bridge of Toome today." I couldn't tell you the destinations of many of our vacations. My memories focus on how we got there.

My experience was a far cry from that of the children of the orphanage where Shirley grew up. Shirley's summer vacations were the result of a Home program promising "many happy days and weeks to children who would not otherwise have a vacation," sponsored by the American Legion, the American Legion Auxiliary, and the United Spanish War veterans. Many happy days. This is hard to picture. Perhaps it beat the alternative of never leaving the orphanage, but surely most would not choose to be on display as the orphan child for one week with strangers. How would it end? Would everyone say, "See ya next year"? Or, "Don't forget to write"? Would children return feeling happy about their summer vacation or depressed over what they would never have? As a child who lived in five cities in fourteen years due to my father's career moves, I was less tied to a place than I was to people, my family. Shirley was tied to the Home, and I'm guessing it was a relief to return each year after sojourning in the land of nuclear families, a land where she was always the outsider.

Shirley shared only two memories of vacations in strangers' homes. One involved the children of the family, two boys, taking her to the barn, locking her in, and frightening her half to death. "They cut off a chicken's head. It was flippin' and floppin' all around. I never seen such a thing. I thought it was their pet! Then one time I spent a week with some people. I didn't really get how sharing their bathroom worked, so one time I go in, he was standin' there and I seen the man's thing." She slapped her thigh and laughed. "I screamed and ran down the street. He put on his pants and chased me so I wouldn't make a big thing about it. It was nothin' to it. Nothin' to it. I'da testified in a court of law – nothin' to it. They had to catch me and bring me back. But they was nice about it, I guess."

"How old would you have been?" I asked.

"I don't know, maybe ten."

That's all she shared. They weren't vacations; they weren't fun. It was just what they did.

Dot told a different story, typically enough. "There was a summer camp every year sponsored by the American Legion. We spent the day wading in streams and we didn't have any main meals, just sandwiches and such. It was wonderful, lots of fun."

Dot also spoke of one of the families who hosted her on a vacation. "They paid me to help with the children – not as a servant – more like a family member. I remember the mom and the dad were really in love. After I graduated, they wanted me and even said they would send me to college. But they lived in Marion and I really wanted to be in Indianapolis."

Never talking about fun summer camps or families who treated her like one of their own, the family vacation was a foreign concept to Shirley, but photographs show that she caught on as a young parent. However, her first family vacation was spoiled by her Aunt Jean. After Shirley lived a short while with Jean, it seemed she wasn't easy to shake.

There's a picture of Shirley holding her daughter, Brenda, as a toddler in 1945, standing with Jean, everyone smiling for the camera. In the background is a train, one car printed with the words, "MANITOU AND PIKES PEAK RY." Perhaps this was some kind of landmark Walter wanted to document for future memories. The two women are dressed very differently. Shirley, in her mid-twenties at the time, is stylish and neat in a white cardigan and slacks. Jean looks like she might be an actual employee of the Manitou and Pikes Peak Railway, stepping down from the train for a photo opportunity. She's wearing baggy dungarees, a loose fitting short sleeve shirt, untucked and wrinkled, and a cap with its brim pushed back. She's smiling broadly. When looking at the photograph, Shirley didn't recall the landmark, but she remembered the trip.

"Walter and me was moving back to Indiana after we'd been in California while he was in the service. Well, he was in Guam, but we lived in California. Anyway, we just wanted to take a leisurely drive back home with the baby, like a family vacation. Next thing we know, Jean took a train out to San Diego and said she didn't have money for getting home. She insisted that we drive her back. What could we say? I didn't like her, never wrote her, but there she was, with no money. We had to pay for her hotel rooms. She smoked constantly in the back seat, even set the back seat on fire, and Brenda was a baby back there! It was terrible with her swearin' and smokin' the whole time. It took us a month to get home. That was a long month. I was mad the whole time."

Another picture, circa 1960, shows Shirley with her three sons and her mother-in-law standing in front of a small tent, with supplies stacked in piles and a lone TV tray off to the side. The wide, expansive sky in the background makes me think this must have been the Kuhn family road trip out west, the one Thomas remembers mostly because he sat on a cactus. Again, Shirley is smiling for the camera, presumably held by Walter. She is wearing a smart black and white checkered sleeveless dress, for camping, and has one hand on Joe's shoulder. The boys are unsmiling and it's hard to tell whether they are sullen or just trying to look cool. And then there's "little, fat Marie," as Shirley liked to call Walter's mother, wearing a sleeveless housedress, white ankle socks, and a scowl to match that of the boys. Thomas laughs when he looks at pictures like this one.

"Yeah, Joe, Lee, and I would pull the tent pole when our grandmother was in there, so the tent would collapse on her. It was a lot like the movie, *Vacation*. The places where we almost stayed were real dives. It was much better to just pitch the tent."

Staring at this picture, I have wished I asked Shirley what *that* was like. I would have had to ask this question delicately, since what I really want to know is how she shared a tent with her mother-in-law, along with her daughter and three sons and Walter. It looked like hell to me, but I only have one vacation memory with Shirley to which I could compare it.

When I think of the 1993 trip to Disney World that Thomas, Ben, and I took with Walter and Shirley, I mostly remember everyone staking out their spot in the van and Shirley talking incessantly. Walter and Thomas sat in the front seat of the van, taking turns driving in amiable silence, and Shirley and Ben cozied up in the very back to read books and play. This left me with the luxurious position of having the middle seat to myself, where I could stretch my legs and read, as I recall, another Margaret Atwood book, *The Robber Bride*, which I refrained from sharing with Shirley. Shirley had brought odd books to read aloud to Ben, including the first aid book I kept in my kitchen, where she could go from page to page, making up stories of little children suffering from compound fractures, chemical burns, choking, and snakebite.

Occasionally, three-year-old Ben would pronounce, "Grandma, you're talking too much. It's time to be quiet for a while." Shirley wouldn't skip a beat, echoing in a sing-song voice, "I'm talking too much? What do you mean? Did you hear that? He says I'm talking too much! Well, okay I'll be quiet for a spell. What do you want to do while I'm being quiet? What should we think about? What do you want to talk about when we're done being quiet?" I couldn't decide whether the high pitch of her voice sounded more like a hyena laughing or a coyote howling in an echo chamber, or maybe this is how a meeting of the two would seem. I buried my face in my book, grateful for my middle-seat position.

We took this trip at a younger age for Ben than we would have liked because Walter had been diagnosed with lymphoma and was pretty sure he was going to die before long. He really wanted to go to Disney World and so we did. It wasn't a disaster, but it wasn't magical either. Walter was impatient with Ben's fear of scary rides, and he sulked when we stood in long lines for the "Under the Sea Journey of the Little Mermaid" and the "Many Adventures of Winnie the Pooh." Shirley's loud narration of every moment never let up, resulting in times when I wanted to weep from the exhaustion of it. We all came down with a fever, starting with Ben, causing each of us to stay in our cabin in bed for at least one day of the week. By the time we were heading home, everyone was crabby and Ben seemed less enthusiastic about sharing the back seat with Grandma again. We stopped at Cracker Barrel, my least favorite road stop for lunch. Walter and Shirley sniped at each other.

"Walter," she yelled across the store attached to the restaurant, "They's about to call our name. You have to come on."

Walter's irritation was thinly veiled, his tone edgy. "Well, I know that. I'm lookin' at something here."

"Okay, but you better get over here. They's gonna call our name and everybody's got to be here!"

Thomas and I eyed each other accusingly, but kept our mouths shut, since when it came down to it, we didn't have solid accusations to level at each other. Ben was oblivious to all our expressed annoyances and I was too tired to consider whether that was significant.

We were seated at a table with white lattice work separating us from another family whose table was lined up with ours. Walter told Shirley not to talk so loud, which he should have known by then was the least effective way of dealing with this problem. In the middle of her long, shrill expression of confusion regarding what everyone was talking about, Walter politely turned away from us to emit a particularly explosive and messy sneeze, the product of which shot through the lattice work at the family sitting next to us. There was a shocked silence between our two groups. The nearest family members at the other table were covered with a wet sheen on their hair and faces. Walter pushed his glasses up his nose, pulled out his ratty handkerchief to mop his face, and it was clear that he wasn't going to say anything. Thomas jumped in, saying, "We're so very sorry," to the father and one of the children in the midst of their silent wipe-down, his facial expression indicating his embarrassment for his traveling companion and parent. As if we hadn't behaved badly enough, Shirley and I began to laugh in that dangerous and silent way, followed by Thomas, and Ben joined in when he picked up that something funny had happened. We ate quickly and exited barely restrained, feeling energized for the trip home. Thomas and I were a team again, making faces at each other about the craziness of the trip, and I didn't even give him a hard time when Walter lived for seven more years.

23

THE GUN

Over the years that Ben spent a lot of time at his grandparents' house, I constantly weighed the importance of various conflicts with Shirley as a way of choosing my battles. For example, the language and grammar she modeled weren't such a big deal, as in pronouncing Hawaii "Hawai-yah," which Ben actually began to correct whenever he heard her. "It's Cincinnat-EE, Grandma, not Cincinnat-AH." But I would take on Shirley giving him candy before dinner, even when I knew it was a losing battle. I barely contained my anger when I found out she had a stash of pacifiers for Ben to enjoy at her house, even though she knew I was trying to wean him from using them. And safety concerns could never be overlooked. Years later, when Ben was five, he came home one evening saying Grandma was going to pull out his loose tooth by tying it with a string to the back of the car. I dreamed that night that she had accidentally put the car in reverse when executing this task, and made a point of talking to Shirley about his tooth the next day.

Shirley, who was in her early seventies when Ben was little, probably held her tongue about problems she had with me, too, but also, like me, couldn't keep her opinions to herself when Ben was at the center of whatever she felt strongly about. Regarding my desire for him to become a strong but sensitive young man, she would have none of it. By the time he was two years old, she began pestering me to get him a toy gun.

"I don't want to do that, Shirley. It doesn't seem like a good thing to introduce."

"Why not? He's a boy, ain't he? Boys like guns."

"That may be true, but I don't want to encourage it and I'm asking you, again, to respect our wishes and not get him one.

If he wants to pretend like he's shooting, there are plenty of things he can use around here, like the banana he's eating right now."

"That's not the same. I think he needs a gun." She raised her voice. "Do you think a toy gun will turn him into a murderer someday?"

"No," I sighed, "but I'd rather not teach him that shooting people is cool, just the same. Will you please just not get him a gun?"

"Well, okay, but I don't see why not."

When Ben was three, he whispered in my ear as I tucked him into bed one night. "Grandma and I have a secret."

"Really?" I whispered back. "Do you want to tell it to me?"

Ben nodded solemnly. Then he cupped his little hands around my ear and whispered, "We have a gun."

"Oh," I whispered back.

"It's in a box. Under Grandma's bed. She said not to tell you and she did this." Ben put his finger to his lips.

"What do you think about keeping secrets from Mommy?"

"Lo-know." This was how Ben used to say, I don't know.

"You're a good boy, buddy, and don't worry about the secret. Grandma and I will figure this out."

The next day, while Ben was playing in Shirley and Walter's back yard, I marched into their bedroom. Shirley was close at my heels, breathlessly calling, "What's the matter?" She began to shriek when she saw me get down on the floor and pull the Rockport shoebox out from under the bed. I lifted the lid to reveal a heavy, black, very realistic-looking toy gun.

"He wanted it! He said so!"

I sat on the bed, savoring the upper hand. "I asked you not to get this. And you told him not to tell me."

"It don't mean nothin'. It don't. We was just playin'."

"One of us is getting rid of this, Shirley. I don't want Ben to have it."

She knew the jig was up. "Walter'll take care of it." Like it was a real gun. "We was just havin' fun. Now I have to tell Ben I done lost it."

"You don't have to do that. I'll tell him that I didn't want him to have it."

"Ben," she called out the window. "I lost the gun!"

Ben whipped around and shot us both with his thumb and forefinger. "Pow, pow, pow," he cried, followed by a high-pitched ricochet sound he had recently perfected.

"See?" Shirley said. "He liked it!"

Shirley would have relished knowing that twenty years later, Ben would be studying criminal justice at school. For Christmas that year, his girlfriend would give him a 12-gauge shotgun that would never fit in Grandma's shoebox. I look back at the story of his toy gun and consider what was really going on. It was beyond my position on gun control. Mostly, it was about Shirley control, a fine oxymoron if ever there was one. She had had many years of practice going behind Walter's back to let her kids do what they wanted or have what she thought they should have; now she'd moved on to the next generation. I wondered at the time if she went behind everyone's backs when there was disagreement or just Walter's and mine. And I knew that she saw me as Walter, the parent who needed to believe he was in charge when this couldn't have been further from the truth. It was all very worrisome, but not enough to take a stand about her care of Ben. It would have taken a lot more to decide to curtail their time together. Their bond was resolute by then, and I would have had to admit how much I had come to depend on her help. She was always there to care for my child, even if she wasn't doing it for me. Even if I hadn't been so dependent on her childcare, it never would have occurred to me to threaten keeping Ben away.

I still don't know whether I should have let the toy gun become such a point of conflict between us. Perhaps Shirley and I had reached a point where we were going to fight about something, and as it turned out, the gun was just a trigger.

24

A BUSHEL AND A PECK

I resigned from my job as a school principal in the summer of 1994 because Thomas and I wanted to adopt a second child and saw no way for this to happen without more available time. The adoption process was more arduous than the first time around, which had already been formidable. Now the laws in Indiana had changed to allow adoptive parents to financially support birthmothers. This leveled the playing field between states as desirable places for women to make adoption plans, but established the now legal expectation to fund the expenses of a birthmother, all without a guarantee that there would be a baby to adopt at the end of the journey. Plus, the whole process had become more competitive. Our original *Dear Birthmother* letter had been printed on plain white paper. Now we were told that we'd need something more visual, something that would distinguish our request from all the others. We hired a friend to create a bright and colorful illustration for the margins of our letter, hoping it would do the trick.

This time around, Thomas was the busy one. In 1995, I was working half-time as an assistant principal with an agreement that I would leave as soon as our child was born. Thomas, now 41, was finishing a master's degree and learning a new job. I liked to refer to it as his midlife crisis when he put on his steel-toe boots each morning and went to work for Conrail as a medical director. He returned to hospital work after a couple of years, but was a railroad man while we were trying to adopt again. Ben, who was now five, loved to sing, "I've Been Working on the Railroad," and he asked us again and again who Dinah was and why she was blowing a horn.

Ben needed a sibling. He often asked when he would

become a big brother and once even said in a give-it-to-me-straight tone of voice, "We're not going to get that baby, are we?" He was an only child, living on a block populated mostly by senior citizens and spending lots of time with doting grandparents. Outside of preschool, most of his interactions were with adults who thought he could do no wrong. I was worried about spoiling him and always on the lookout for what Shirley was scheming against my wishes. One of our more significant clashes centered on her wanting to buy Ben an electric child-sized car. I thought it was ridiculous to buy a five-year-old a motor vehicle that cost hundreds of dollars while he was practicing riding a bicycle and dreaming of the day when the training wheels would come off. Once again, Thomas was caught between his mother and me, but he really wanted Ben to have the car. "I won't have it," I said as the argument escalated.

"It's not that big a deal," Thomas said when it was just the two of us discussing it. "They don't go very fast, and he'd keep it at Mom and Dad's to ride in the back yard. Mom said she'd pay for it." Thankfully, Ben didn't add to the pressure. He told me that he really wanted one of those cars, but he was easily distracted by what I deemed more developmentally appropriate pursuits like playing ball and drawing with chalk on our driveway. This was a battle among the adults.

Somehow, it became a matter of right and wrong in my mind. Children shouldn't have such things, I'd insist, and my parenting theme became, "I will not raise a brat." Ben was a conscientious and good-natured child, so most of my worrying was moot. The world's three cardinal sins as he saw it were smoking, littering, and riding a motorcycle without a helmet, and he would gasp dramatically whenever he saw someone committing one of these offenses. He even called a couple of his adult cousins who were smokers to make sure they knew about the patch. But I was focused on making sure he didn't develop a sense of entitlement, whereas Thomas and Shirley could only see the delight he'd experience with this new toy.

Over the years, I noticed this key distinction in Thomas's and my parenting style, based on the differences in how we were raised. I came from parents who centered their attention on the future as much as the present, if not more so. My father's career success had been built over time through hard work, careful planning, and sacrifice on his part and my mother's. When we moved to a more affluent neighborhood in Ohio as teenagers, we weren't given cars on our 16th birthdays like all the other kids on the block, and we took pride in that fact. We were taught about the importance of doing without in the present in order to have what we wanted later. Among my siblings, I wasn't known for my discipline in such matters, but the lessons had been ingrained nevertheless; the future was more important than the present. This was a less familiar way of life for Thomas, who could focus on the here and now in a way I found enviable. Regarding our little family, I would say to him, "We're building something here, every peanut butter sandwich, every bedtime story," and most of the time, I needed him to reassure me we weren't behind schedule. Another aspect of our life philosophies which affected our parenting styles was how we viewed messes, both literal and figurative. I was always looking ahead with an eye toward prevention; Thomas lived less cautiously, saying if we make a mess, we clean it up. He was the don't-worry-be-happy guy, Tigger to my Rabbit. As an only child, Ben was caught in the cross-hairs of our different perspectives that sometimes looked like disputes, along with the added dynamic of his grandmother's convictions. He needed a sibling to shake things up. A little brother or sister that would help us put fights about electronic toys in perspective. Indeed, when Ben became a big brother, the topic of whether to buy him a car or not was quickly forgotten.

The path to finding our daughter seemed even more capricious than our first time around. We connected with a birthmother named Janis, and thought we were making an adoption plan with her. We funded her expenses through our attorney for five months. Although it was a tenuous agreement, we tried not to focus on others' expressed concerns that Janis lived only a mile away from us, that this would be her seventh biological child, and she hadn't raised nor had she made an adoption plan for any of the first six. When we asked Janis where her other children were, she gave vague answers about various relatives and friends that were raising them. The birthfather was in and out of her life, as well as in and out of jail. Thomas and I tried to keep a positive attitude, but worried constantly about the health of the child she was carrying. We suspected that Janis was using drugs and we tried to confirm or disconfirm our doubts in subtle ways, recognizing the sensitivity of the inquiry and how much was riding on our relationship with her. This fear finally came to a head two weeks before the baby was due when we insisted that she take a drug test. Janis responded with indignation that we would ask such a thing, and summarily dropped us without acknowledging the thousands of dollars we had spent taking care of her needs. Thomas and I were heartbroken. Although we had never seen the baby, and I hadn't carried him in my womb, we had hung our hopes and wishes and dreams on him being our little boy. It felt like we had lost our child. We quietly grieved, protective of Ben's obliviousness that there had been a baby and that he was lost to us. Our feelings of desolation were eventually diminished by an acknowledgement that this had never been a good situation, and that we had been blinded by our desire for it to work. However, we agonized about what would happen to the baby now that we knew Janis was a con artist. She found another vulnerable couple to give her money in the last weeks of her pregnancy, then dropped them as well when she delivered. Her explanation for keeping her son was that the birthfather had bought a crib, according to our attorney. It took a long time for me to let go of my anguish for this child whom we had come to see as our own, a child we would never know.

Our attorney's assistant, Christine, was instrumental in finding our little girl in January of 1996. She had observed all that had happened with Janis and sympathized with us as we began the process anew. Although she was committed to fairness when presenting choices of adoptive parents to a birthmother who had made contact with the firm, I got the impression that Christine had expressed extra enthusiasm about Thomas, Ben, and me, resulting in us, once again, being given this long anticipated privilege and gift. We received a call the day our daughter, whom we named Alison Claire, was born in Indianapolis, and went to the hospital to pick her up the next day. It was all very exciting. I dropped Ben off at school that morning without telling him about the baby, as Thomas and I had agreed, knowing it would be easier to have him there and unaware of what we were doing until it was time to go to the hospital. It was hard not to tell him and I found myself laughing with abandon as we drove to school. I even sang the commercial song, "Save big money at Menards!" with Ben as we passed the big hardware store, something Ben sang every day on the way to school, but always as a solo. A couple hours later, Thomas and I stopped en route to the hospital to pick up a car seat and swing by Ben's school to get him out early and share the big surprise. When Ben got into the car and heard the news, he said, "I know I always said I wanted a little brother, but I didn't mean that! I really wanted a little sister!" And the modified wish came true. Alison was tiny, only five pounds. At first glance, I thought she was a doll in the nurse's arms. We swaddled her and brought her home in a heavy snowfall that January of 1996, ecstatic that she was finally here.

Although my mother went by her middle name, her first

name was Alison. We named our daughter after her grandmother, whose absence was keenly felt. Ben's middle name was Alex, after my father, and I had played with the idea of our baby girl's middle name being that of my mother's in the same fashion. Prior to Ben's birth, my mother loved suggesting names for a boy or girl. She was annoyed with me for naming our cat Emily, since that was one of her favorite names and now nobody would use it. Considering Emily's temperament, it would have been considered a curse. I had thought about the middle name, Gaia. My mother's middle name was Gayle and mine is Gay, so it had felt like a way of linking the three of us. But when I proposed this prior to Ben's birth, not knowing whether the baby would be a boy or girl, Mom had wrinkled her nose and said, "I think that's incorrect." It wasn't a matter of preference or opinion. Names were correct or incorrect. Years later, I observed various young couples refraining from sharing their choices of names until after the baby is born and the name is decided, thereby avoiding everyone else's judgments. It's an interesting trend.

Soon, our house looked like Pepto-Bismol had exploded all over it, so many of the gifts being pink for girls. Ben had anticipated this day almost as much as his father and I, and sang his little heart out to her, all the favorite songs we'd sung when he was a baby. "She needs to get used to our voices," he'd say as he crooned, "I love you a bushel and a peck, ya bet your pretty neck I do." I was struck by the ways that music linked us all between and across generations. Shirley sang in her squeaky soprano voice songs like "Sentimental Journey." I loved sharing what had been sung to me as a little girl, "Mockingbird Hill" having been decreed by my dad and me as our song, the one we sang whenever he gave me a bath.

Ben's involvement in Alison's affairs was constant. It was as if he had yearned for serious responsibility every day of his five and a half years and the day had finally come. He was second in command for all baby care, including bathing, diapering, and feeding. By the time Alison was introduced to baby food, he had moved up in the ranks, as he was the only one she would allow to wipe her face without putting up a fight. After the cleanup, he would reward her with a concerto played on his armpit and she would kick her feet wildly.

From the beginning, Shirley swooped in with renewed energy to coddle and entertain the baby. Alison was tiny, but very strong, with wisps of white blonde hair, deep blue eyes that followed Ben's every move, and a bow-shaped mouth that made us swoon. Like Thomas and me, Shirley was surprised by how different Alison's view of the world was compared to Ben's and that she didn't respond to the same tricks the way he did. In a very short time, Alison's willful personality became apparent, giving us a sense that, no matter how many parenting books we read, she was going to rule the roost. This delighted Shirley, perhaps because I had a new boss, all of 16 pounds and walking around at 10 months, before she had a lick of sense. Alison often crashed into furniture and sported a black eye, along with other bruises, but seemed undaunted by it all. We had to remove all the furniture in her room and put her mattress on the floor, making the nursery a padded cell in effect, because she could climb anything. The tall dresser was the last to go after I walked into her room late one night and found her standing on top of it, naked, with a rectal thermometer in her mouth. We constantly added ways to make the house safe for her as a toddler.

Once when Alison walked into the kitchen with her little cheeks puffed out, before I could investigate what she was carrying in her mouth, there was a loud crash in the playroom, which I could see from where we were standing. The children's wooden easel inexplicably had crashed to the ground in multiple pieces. I didn't know the reason for this, but I was relatively certain who had caused it. I held out my hand and she spit into it at least a dozen wing nuts and bolts, one at a time. And so it went in our household on a daily basis. Thomas and I would look at each other wide-eyed and befuddled by our daughter's tenacity and interest in everything we hadn't considered ahead of time. Regardless of how many electrical sockets we plugged, sharp corners we cushioned, and drawers and cabinets we locked, we were unsuccessful in staying a step ahead of her.

We moved to Bloomington, Indiana in 1998, wanting to raise our children in a smaller town that was still close to Shirley and Walter as they were aging. Thomas, now a nurse practitioner, continued his hospital administration work in Bloomington and taught in the School of Nursing at Indiana University while I taught classes in the School of Education at IU part time and fretted about writing my doctoral dissertation, which I had not touched while working as a school administrator. We lived in a setting different from any other I had experienced, on acres of woods without a next door neighbor in sight. I hadn't thought about how this would one day mean I'd be inundated with emails from organizations like the Goat Club when Alison joined 4H, or that I'd be doing what I could to avoid involvement in the politics between the Poultry Club and the Rabbit Club. You could say it was a short-sighted moment. All I saw were these beautiful woods, and living in the country filled me with both delight and worry about all that was unfamiliar. After Thomas was stung one day by a swarm of bees, and we saw the biggest snake I'd ever seen outside a zoo, I began to worry about a host of possible dangers, especially considering the distance to the nearest hospital emergency room. I had indoor locks put on all the doors to keep Alison from escaping into the wilderness without me. Toddler house-proofing continued to be a high priority in our lives.

When Alison began to talk, her sassy communication was another way of keeping us on our toes. The time-out bench seldom had time to grow cold. Ben was rarely, if ever, sent to time-out as a little boy. He was the kind of kid that would join me for problem-solving sessions as we sat on the floor and held hands. One threat that he wouldn't be allowed to listen to the Talking Heads on the way to preschool was pretty much all I ever needed. Alison, however, called for a whole new protocol.

On her frequent visits to Bloomington, Shirley observed my attempts at control and her gleeful reaction never ceased. She would watch me walking Alison to the time-out bench while Alison would take my hand and say, "I sawwy, Mommy, I so sawwy." When I said this was a good thing to say, but that she should still sit quietly for a few minutes on the bench, all hell would break loose in ways that made it clear she was not sorry in the least, and I would see Shirley covering the grin on her face with both hands to keep herself out of trouble. My daughter had the strangest and most creative epithets for me as she sat in time-out. She would lower her voice to a kind of growling whisper, narrow her eyes, and call me ludicrous names.

"You…wecked cah!"

"You…dinosaw!"

"You…stwawbewwy!"

"You…tiny pigwet!"

"You…fwat ti-uh!"

At times like this, I asked Shirley to leave the room and shut the door behind her to muffle her laughter. I was determined to respond less to the content of Alison's diatribe and more to the spirit in which it was delivered, but found it understandable when others focused on her hilarious word choices.

"I wonder what made her think of 'flat tire,'" Shirley would say as she looked me up and down. I guess "wrecked car" and "dinosaur" were less puzzling to her. "Being called a strawberry ain't so bad! You'll miss it when she's callin' you some real bad names someday." This made sense, but I tried to keep my response to the name-calling consistent.

Occasionally, the dynamic between Shirley and me regarding Alison's headstrong behavior was turned on its head, like when Alison went to Shirley and Walter's conservative Christian church and announced during Sunday school that we all come from the goddess. She colored a picture of Jesus surrounded by multiracial children, then added a drawing of a little, fat, smiling woman in the sky.

"Well, I don't know why she has to say things like that," Shirley said.

I shrugged my shoulders and replied, "No one's making her."

The unintended consequence of this standoff between Shirley and me was Alison remaining in her position of power. She behaved at times as if she were untouchable, likely because, at times, she was. Thomas was little help in these situations. Never great with confrontations anyway, he was too smitten to recognize her misbehavior and deal with it. She'd stand on her chair at dinner and slowly wave her arms back and forth, like she was witnessing Elton John singing "Candle in the Wind," and with Thomas, Ben, and Shirley laughing so hard, I knew my only option was to join them. Coming out of the grocery store with Alison facing me in the cart, she'd affix two bright red "I've been Krogering" stickers to my tee shirt, carefully located on my nipples, and most of the time, I would deem it a battle not worth fighting. Sometimes she would latch on to lines from songs we listened to and forever make them her own. Whenever I heard Joni Mitchell singing "Help Me," I thought of Alison giving it new meaning as she sang, "When I get that cwazy feewin', I know I'm in twouble again."

Alison's free-spirited nature was also manifest in her penchant for nudity whenever she could get away with it. Sometimes, she came to the dinner table this way and we were too exhausted to make her put on some clothes. Once when Ben asked a friend if he wanted to stay for dinner, rather than asking what we were having, the little boy looked at me warily and said, "Will Ben's little sister be naked?"

Having a second child was enlightening for me as a parent. Throughout Ben's preschool years, I silently judged the behavior of other children, deeming them impolite compared to my decorous son. I was certain he was well-mannered because he had been provided careful lessons in grace and courtesy. It never dawned on me that the children I was judging had older siblings. Not until I was the mother of the child telling dog fart jokes at the daycare center did I realize the difficulty of keeping children in a bubble when all they wanted was to emulate their older brothers or sisters. I learned to choose my battles, but found Shirley's relentless assessment of my choices challenging.

"Leave her alone," Shirley would say, right on cue when I would attempt a redirection of behavior. She admonished me often, enough that I began to question myself more than I liked. "She's the baby," she'd say, "and babies of the family get away with things."

"Did Thomas?" I asked.

She paused. "Probably. But what I'm sayin' is she's just a little baby and you expect too much."

This debate continued into Alison's preschool years, when I'd make sure Shirley hadn't allowed her to remove her underwear beneath her dress before hanging upside down on the monkey bars in a community park.

To Shirley, Alison was forever the baby, and babies were precious. Every once in a while, I remembered that Shirley had grown up around babies who weren't nurtured nearly enough. It might not have been a fully formed realization at the time, but I began to notice what a gift it was for Shirley to indulge children in ways no one had ever indulged her.

25

ROBERTA

Shirley often reminded me that, even in her own family, the littlest one had always gotten more attention. "Tom was a saucy little boy. He got away with a lot. I don't know if it was true for Roberta, but I know she could have been adopted if Aunt Jean hadn't signed the paper saying nobody could adopt us. Everyone wants babies."

I met Shirley's youngest sibling, Roberta, at some point, but I don't recall it clearly. I do remember her hugely attended funeral in Franklin, Indiana. It was as if the whole town had come to bid her farewell. Roberta, the baby of the family, less than two years old when she was moved to the orphanage, was the first loss of the group of five siblings. By all accounts, she was remarkably generous, kind, and much loved by all around her. Her family of five was known to be very close and she was devoted to her three daughters and their children.

Roberta's daughters once told me an extraordinary story about her time in the orphanage. "Mama said she wanted to learn to play the violin and the Home had these sponsors for things like that, so they got her a violin and she was takin' lessons. Well, one day, some kid told the governess that Mama had broken her toy and the governess taught her a lesson by breaking her violin."

I was shocked. "What?"

"Yeah, it was terrible. Well, turns out that same governess was dying before long – she must have been old. She got worried about goin' to heaven, so she asked them to bring Roberta to her. She was only eight years old. So Mama said they brought her to her deathbed and that old bat told her she knew she hadn't broken that other kid's toy and that she was sorry about the violin. She asked Mama to forgive her and Mama said, 'No'! She said, 'I wanted to be a musician and now I never will be. I do not forgive you.' She got into some trouble for that."

I suppose if you don't have parents to be indignant on your behalf, you have to do it for yourself.

"Did she ever learn to play the violin?" I asked. There was a pause with everyone considering the question. "I guess she didn't," one of them said.

Walter was ill, so Thomas and I drove Shirley to the funeral. I asked whether she thought her brother, Donald, whom I had never met, would be there. "Probably not," she said. "I don't even know where he is these days."

Upon arrival, I was immediately distracted by the four Lazyboy chairs in front of the coffin, fully reclined and occupied by Roberta's husband and three daughters, something I'd never seen the likes of before. Oh, dear, I thought. Many times, I've had a small problem at funerals, in the form of inappropriate humor and giggles. This has happened at services for people to whom I have been close, as well as people I don't know, like Roberta. I willed myself to stop looking at the scene up front once we were seated, but feelings of giddy panic arose, and I knew I was losing control again as the immediate family of the deceased faced the ceiling from their chairs, their feet close enough to touch the coffin, and expressed their grief without restraint. I sat between Thomas and Shirley. After being startled by several outbursts, calling to Jesus, Roberta, the Lord, and heaven above, all from their recumbent positions, I turned my face in Thomas's direction so that Shirley wouldn't witness my involuntary laughter. This seemed to work for a few minutes, but then a scratchy Dolly Parton record was added to the scene – "she's an eagle when she flies" – and Thomas began to laugh, too.

Suddenly, Shirley turned to me as if she had just had an urgent thought. "Help me remember that we have to take Roberta home. She doesn't have a ride back."

"What?" I said.

She turned up the volume of her stage whisper. "I said we need to take Roberta home."

"Roberta?"

"Yes," she said with irritation. "Oh, wait – not Roberta. Georgia. We have to take Georgie home." She began to laugh. "Not Roberta," and turned to see who might have overheard.

The bubble of hysteria began to rise and a giggle slipped out. "I think Roberta's home," I whispered. Shirley laughed, then noticed Thomas laughing and turned to me sharply. "What's so funny? Why's *he* laughing?" I shook my head, not trusting my normal restraint at this point.

"Is it all the caterwaulin'? They's always been a funny bunch." This was getting dangerous. I shrugged my shoulders and held on for dear life, like a kid in church all over again. Recognizing my desperate need to breathe, I imagined a pressure valve and knew I was going to explode if I didn't get out of there. Thomas beat me to it. He stood up abruptly, made his way to the end of the row, and smacked into the wall, knocking off a holiday wreath hanging there. Not even stopping to pick it up, he walked briskly out the door and never came back. People stared momentarily, then turned their attention back to the service.

That was it. Shirley and I looked at each other in bewilderment and both began to laugh, abandoning our self-control. I patted her on the knee and hoped she understood that I had to leave, too. I signaled that I'd be back and held my breath as I followed Thomas's path, carefully stepping over the wreath on the floor.

Thankfully, the women's bathroom nearby was empty. I bent forward and held on to the counter, taking in great gulps of oxygen and trying not to think about what had just happened so that I could calm down. I thought about dog vomit. And the nasty flood in our basement. And that time when my computer crashed and I lost a paper I had been writing all night. A couple of minutes of this and I was good to go. Splashing water on my face and smoothing my hair in the mirror, I walked out, unflappable, dignified, and composed.

Seeing Thomas in the hallway, all restraint was lost again. Oh, for heaven's sake, I thought with exasperation. We stepped into an alcove where we wouldn't be seen. "What the hell was that?" I choked out. He took a moment to calm down enough to respond. "I know; I don't know why I was laughing like that. Probably just the Barcaloungers."

"I mean the way you knocked that arrangement off the wall and kept going."

He laughed. "I had my eyes closed to try and keep from laughing."

"What? Like if I can't see them, they can't see me?"

"No, like I was sad and contemplative. Which I actually am – I'm sad because I loved Aunt Roberta. And I'm sad for her family."

"Well, it needs work. I'm going back in. Your mom's by herself in there. Are you coming?"

"I'll wait out here. It's probably almost over."

I poked him hard in the shoulder, something his mother often did which Thomas found particularly annoying. "Coward," I said.

"Gawker," was his response as I walked away.

I didn't meet Roberta's family at the funeral, surrounded as they were by other mourners. Shirley had been crowd-phobic and wanted to leave right away, so we collected Georgie and made a quick exit.

I often wondered about Roberta, the baby that could have been adopted if Aunt Jean hadn't signed papers forbidding this from happening. It was many years later that Dot told me a different story.

"It wasn't Jean's fault," she said. "Our mother told her to sign those papers because she wanted us to stay together. She didn't know they'd separate us at the Home and we might as well be raised in other families. Maybe she thought she'd get out of there and come back to get us. So Jean was just doing what our mother asked, since nobody was going to ask her what she wanted, not at the mental hospital."

Here was another profound misunderstanding that changed the course of the Peacock children's lives. It appears that once decisions were made regarding the fate of Shirley and her siblings, no one stopped to reconsider what had happened as the years went by. I've wondered who might have changed the painful circumstances of their childhood, but maybe the decision to institutionalize these five children who were daughters and a son, nieces and a nephew, grandchildren, was too shameful to reexamine.

26

MAKING IT TO THE MILLENNIUM

Several years after our trip to Disney World, Walter's lymphoma became more acute. By the late nineties, which were his mid-eighties, he was visibly slowing down, although nothing was ever said about it. He just spent more time in his recliner in front of the television. He had rediscovered a VHS tape of an aquarium, ordered from a television commercial years before. Sometimes there would be no action at all, no fish swimming by, just blue water and a gurgling sound accompanying it. That was okay with Walter. He also liked to watch a video of a fire in a fireplace. His church attendance dwindled for the first time in his adulthood, and he was noticeably absent from important events, such as Roberta's funeral.

Thomas thought his dad wasn't seeing as well and was relieved when Walter and Shirley had to go to the DMV to get Walter's driver's license renewed, knowing there would be a vision test. During the test, it was confirmed that Walter's vision had indeed deteriorated, resulting in the non-renewal of his license. He had driven there, but found out in that moment that he was legally blind and would never be behind the wheel again. Shirley drove him home.

Walter accepted this change quietly. After his chemotherapy was stopped, he continued to sit in his recliner and shrunk to a very small size, his face gaunt, his eyes almost lifeless. I kept wondering about hospice services when I saw how hard Shirley was working to care for him. We weren't much help from where we lived in Bloomington. Thomas said they had met with hospice, and they would be coming out from time to time, but it wasn't time to move Walter to a facility. I don't remember hearing about hospice care coming to their house again and never knew why. There was only Shirley shouldering it all. I asked her whether there were visitors from their church. Walter and Shirley had attended Calvary Baptist Church three times a week for decades.

Shirley shrugged her shoulders. "Nobody's came. Not even Pastor."

"Well, that makes me mad," I said. "You and Walter never missed church. I can't believe you haven't been missed. And he seems pretty depressed."

"Oh, well, he has a heart ache ever since his prostate."

Walter had had his prostate removed years before. "That's been awhile now, hasn't it?"

"Doesn't make it okay," she said. "Men's gotta get it up. Men wants sex and no gettin' around it. Men of a certain age."

"What age is that?"

"Five to ninety. Men's gotta have sex."

Several weeks later, Shirley had news. "Pastor come over the other day."

"Oh, yeah?" I said. "What took him so long?"

"He said he's been busy." She looked over, knowing we were of like minds about that.

"Was Walter glad to see him?"

"I couldn't tell. He ain't talkin' much these days."

"How long did he stay?"

Shirley laughed. "Longer than he wanted to! He sat with Walter for about 15 minutes. Then he get up to go and he says, 'You let me know if there's anything I can do.' So I said, 'You can mop the kitchen.' Then I pointed to the mop and the bucket."

"What?"

"I know!" she said. "Ain't that the limit?"

"What happened?"

"He mopped the floor and I watched. You should have seen it." She laughed. "He was wearing a suit."

It was moments like this when I forgot everything my mother-in-law had ever done or said to annoy me. I told her she was my role model.

"What do you mean?" she asked suspiciously.

"Nothing bad," I said and gave her a hug.

Thomas increased his trips to Indianapolis, sometimes going several times a week in the evenings after work and on weekends. I could see this was taking a toll on him. Although Shirley rarely asked for help, Walter had started calling Thomas with complaints of various forms of discomfort, and Thomas felt a need to check on him.

One evening, Thomas called from the car, saying he was going from work to his parents' house and he'd be home late.

"Is everything okay?" I asked.

He laughed, but I could hear how tired he was. "Oh, probably." Then he laughed again. "Dad wants me to come lower the water level in the toilet because he says it doesn't feel right."

I wasn't sure what that meant, nor if I wanted to know. "So, what are you going to do?"

"Hell, if I know. I guess I'll try to lower the water level in his toilet."

"You're a good man, Charlie Brown," I said.

That night, I thought about who Walter had been to me. I had held a grudge against him for the harsh punishments he meted out in Thomas's childhood. But he was sweet and patient with our children. I had found his love for tinkering with old cars in the garage endearing. I was charmed by his planting of fruit trees: persimmon, apple, pear, peach, and cherry, according to Thomas. By the time I came on the scene, the fruit production had diminished, but not the childhood memories of it.

"We would trick people into eating persimmons freshly

picked," Thomas would say dreamily. "And there was something unique about how sour they were, not like lemons. It was like your mouth was paralyzed in this pucker for several minutes before you could move it again. It was great."

Late that night, Thomas came in after I had gone to bed. I sat up and turned on a light. "Well?"

"He's okay. I fiddled with the toilet and told him I lowered the water level. Then he tried it and said it was fine."

"So, you didn't really lower the water?"

"Nope." He yawned. "But I did hang out with Mom for a while, so that was good. She overheard Dad telling me to watch her spending after he dies. She was pissed and said he's blind and half-dead and doesn't know what he's talking about."

"What about hospice?" I was starting to sound like a parrot that asked the same question over and over.

"They aren't going to lower the water in the toilet either."

"Stop avoiding the question. You know what I mean."

"I don't know." And that was that for another evening.

The holidays came and, for Christmas dinner, our last one in the 20th century, our family went to Shirley and Walter's house and crowded around their dining room table. Walter was brought to the table in his bathrobe, connected to an oxygen tank and an IV stand. He ate a few bites before he needed to go back to sleep.

The new year arrived and Y2K, the threat of modern society shutting down when computers registered the calendar change from 1999 to 2000, didn't happen. I wondered what I'd do with all those gallons of water I'd been collecting in recent months, having figured we would mix it with instant oatmeal if we were desperate. Thomas and I both had the flu, so we ushered in the new millennium with the whole family in bed early. On New Year's Day, Ben went to a friend's house and Alison, who was three, stayed in her pajamas under heavy blankets on the couch, along with Thomas and me. We holed up in our tiny study, darkened by closed blinds, and watched a black and white documentary about Susan B. Anthony and Elizabeth Cady Stanton on PBS while sipping hot tea. Thomas and I coughed and sneezed and cried during the inspiring parts, and Alison occasionally said, "I'm not having any fun."

Thomas's brother, Lee, and his family were unable to celebrate the holidays with us until after the new year. On January 7th, I begged off of going to Indianapolis to see them, since I was still on the mend. Thomas took the kids and called me a couple of hours after they left.

"We're taking Dad to hospice now," he said.

I breathed a sigh of relief. "I'm sorry, honey. He must be feeling pretty bad. Is he aware of what's going on?"

"Seems to be. Anyway, I'll call you after we get there. Lee and Marian and the kids are meeting us."

Thomas called that afternoon to say his father had died a couple of hours after their arrival at the hospice facility. "It was weird," he said. "They got him settled in his room, then Lee and Marian and the kids came, and it was kind of like a party in there. Marian had all these presents wrapped up for everyone, so we started opening them and laughing and talking, then someone looked over and noticed Dad was gone."

I paused to take this in. My first conclusion was not a charitable one. What must it have been like to think, "Hello? I'm slipping away here," as everyone stood around your bed blabbing about school and work and new hairstyles. But then I found myself smiling. Perhaps it was the best way possible to bid the world adieu, surrounded by your family sharing and laughing with each other in the year 2000, hardly imaginable in the early years of a man born in 1914.

27

EVERYONE GRIEVES IN THEIR OWN WAY

I found Shirley's reaction to Walter's passing curious. She had diligently tended to him in the last months of his illness without complaint, but her tone was never generous. In fact, most of the time, she seemed matter-of-fact or even annoyed by the situation. I thought this was a manifestation of the stress of his care and knowing she was losing him, but after he was gone, her impatient tone intensified. In the collection of old photos of Walter, gathered for his visitation, there was a picture of him clowning around as a young man that Thomas's sister, Brenda, commented on.

"I like this picture of Dad. It shows what a great sense of humor he had."

Shirley's response was harsh. "He never had a sense of humor. That wasn't his thing. He wasn't funny."

Shirley wasn't sentimental. She soldiered through the visitation and funeral without shedding a tear and mostly wanted to play with Alison when she could step away from visitors who had come to pay their respects. Occasionally, I would say to her, "Are you okay? Can I get you anything?" and she'd look at me like I had two heads.

"Why wouldn't I be okay?"

I asked Thomas if he thought his mother was glad Walter was gone. He paused before responding.

"Maybe. She never confronted him about anything and either did what he said or found ways to do things for us behind his back," he said. "I don't think it was a good relationship and she had a lot of regrets. He wasn't fun and didn't talk much."

"They were married almost sixty years," I said. "I can't

imagine such a big change."

It seemed like a good change more than a bad one, like she was free to do what she wanted when she wanted. Though still a devout Christian who read her Bible daily, she stopped going to church three times a week. She watched television shows of her choosing and only cooked when she felt like it.

On their first wedding anniversary after Walter's death, I visited Shirley, bringing with me a photograph of Walter standing on a beach, in a frame the kids had made.

"Why are you bringing me this?" she asked, her manner bordering on hostile.

"Because it's your anniversary," I said. "Fifty-nine years."

She rolled her eyes. "I'm not sad, if that's what you're wonderin'." I decided to let sleeping dogs lie.

Years later, as Thomas and I cleaned out Shirley's apartment where she eventually lived after Walter's death, I discovered a wrinkled and worn piece of paper ripped from a tiny notebook on which Shirley had written something. It appeared to be written in 1998, around the time Walter's health started going downhill, because it started with a math problem:

$$
\begin{array}{r}
1998 \\
-1941 \\
\hline
57
\end{array}
$$

Then the following:

We've been married 57 years.

I didn't figure this out all at once. We had been married awhile. We were not interested in church except only at Christmas and Easter. Then we both excepted [sic] Christ at the same time only not together. (That's another story) But at that time I got a different outlook on life.

You both have faults. (Sometimes I think mine were worse.) You know things you don't like about each other but you have to compromise and realize that everything is not going to be perfect or like you want it. You can't throw everything away because you can't agree on something.

Anyhow he was dependable and put his family first.

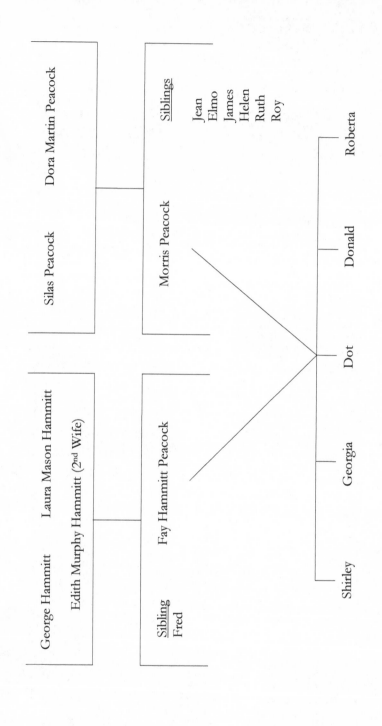

George Hammitt · Laura Mason Hammitt · Edith Murphy Hammitt (2nd Wife)

Silas Peacock · Dora Martin Peacock

Fay Hammitt Peacock

Morris Peacock

<u>Sibling</u>
Fred

<u>Siblings</u>

Jean
Elmo
James
Helen
Ruth
Roy

Shirley · Georgia · Dot · Donald · Roberta

Family tree of Shirley Peacock Kuhn's ancestry

Morris Peacock in WWI uniform

Fay and Morris Peacock

Shirley Peacock held by grandfather George Hammitt
and his second wife, Edith Murphy Hammitt
(Fay's father and stepmother)

Shirley Peacock at orphanage (other children
unidentified), perhaps at Children's Home in Tippecanoe
County, circa 1926

Shirley Peacock and siblings, circa 1928

Shirley and Walter Kuhn's wedding, 1941

Shirley Peacock Kuhn and siblings reunited as adults
with their mother, Fay Peacock

Thomas Kuhn, 1959

Walter, Joe, and Thomas Kuhn visiting Fay Peacock at Central State Hospital

Shirley and Walter at kitchen table

Thomas and Melissa, / Melissa's 30th birthday, "farmer" party theme

Thomas, Melissa, Ben, and Alison Keller-Kuhn, 1997

Shirley Kuhn and Melissa Keller, 2002.
To my knowledge, this is the only photograph of Shirley and me in the same frame.

Part 2

2000-2009

Rules of Commitment

Return to Institutional Life

28

NO LOOKING BACK

"They say you isn't supposed to make any big decisions until it's been six months after your spouse dies," Shirley said. "And it's only been three." Walter had died in January, and this was early spring. But I found myself worrying about this most of the time and looking around for places in Bloomington Shirley might like and be able to afford. She remained in her house with Joe and Dorothy still living above the garage. I kept picturing her in the house by herself, going down to the basement to do laundry with no rail on those stairs. Who would hear her if she fell?

Thomas started taking the kids to visit Shirley most weekends. She must have been in heaven, with Tom, the kids, and no Melissa. At first, having a night or even two nights to myself seemed too good to be true, and I'd catch myself singing "Zip-a-dee-doo-dah" as they pulled out of the driveway. But this grew old quickly, and I didn't like how much they were gone, not to mention the condition the kids were in when Thomas would bring them home on Sundays. Everything was not "satisfactual," and I felt guilty for singing that song in the first place.

"Geez, Tom, did they brush their teeth even once?" I would ask after a brief inspection.

"I'm sure they did," he would say, his furrowed brow and faraway look telling a different story.

"And it's 9:00 at night and they are wide awake. What time did they get up today?"

"Well, they did sleep late –"

"Till afternoon!" Ben would shout, with Alison beside him, popping candy from her pockets and dancing all around to music only she could hear.

I knew what was happening. Thomas was going to his mother's house and lying on her couch for a long weekend nap, as in lasting a whole weekend, and chaos reigned. Knowing I was not invited and not wanting to go anyway, something had to change.

So Thomas started collecting his mother to come to our house on the weekends and my campaign to get her to move began. I had visited four or five senior residences and ruled several out. They were either more than she could afford or in bad shape. One had a distinctly foul odor that prevailed despite the housekeepers' efforts; another served food I couldn't imagine even trying to eat. Cedar Hills was the one I liked best. It was really pretty, the apartments were spacious and affordable, and the managers seemed nice. There were two main drawbacks as far as I could tell. One was the requirement to come to the dining hall for meals, which I knew Shirley would resist, based on the expectation to wear nice clothes and be sociable. The other was the lack of a stove or oven in the apartments. Shirley had always taken pride in the pies she baked. I doubted she'd be happy baking in the community kitchen open to all the residents. Keeping these concerns to myself when Shirley was visiting our house, I called her from my office to see if she'd like to go to lunch at Cedar Hills and get a tour. To my amazement, she agreed, so I dropped what I was doing in order to strike while the iron was hot.

Shirley was rather quiet throughout the tour conducted by James and Maura, the married couple who were the managers, but lit up over the quality of the food. As luck would have it, they were having bean soup, one of her favorites, and she liked the banana pudding for dessert, too. We said we'd think it over and get back to them. On the way home, I decided to just put everything out on the table.

"What did you think of the dining room?"

"Well, the food was good. I wonder how often they have hardy bean soup; I just love hardy bean soup. They said they was havin' chili tomorrow and I like that, too." She paused. "People was dressed nice in there. I guess I wouldn't get to eat in my pajamas."

"Yeah, probably not."

Shirley stared out the window. "But maybe that would be okay. You know, you can get used to anything."

I dared to hope. "What about not having an oven?"

She cackled. "They's afraid us old people is gonna burn the place down!"

"Maybe," I said with a smile. "But what about just having a microwave and not being able to bake pies?"

She answered without hesitation. "I don't care if I never bake a pie again for the rest of my life."

The next day, Shirley, Thomas, and I had lunch with James and Maura, and they did indeed have chili. The tour was repeated for Shirley and me so that Thomas could see the place, too.

"I think Ben and Alison would really like it here," Shirley said. She looked to Maura. "Can my grandchildren come over?"

"Absolutely! We'd love to meet them."

"And can they spend the night?" Another affirmative. Shirley looked to Thomas and me. "I think they'd like them big hallways."

"You know they would," I said, thinking I needed to start talking to them about not tearing around like bats out of hell around other residents.

She decided right then and there. We insisted that she think about it for a few days before signing a contract, an admonition she accepted without enthusiasm. "My mind's made up. What difference is a week gonna make?" This turned out to be true.

Shirley packed up her belongings and left her house and most of the furniture, never showing concern for anything she may have left behind. We found a small kitchen table and loveseat to fit in her downsized space and the move went smoothly.

"I guess Joe and Dorothy will just move into the house now. I don't really care about any of the stuff that's left there. It won't be long before Joe starts selling it all anyway." She laughed and said, "We better get that winter coat I left in the closet!" The stuff that was left there was considerable and would need to be dealt with eventually. She would need to sell the house in order to afford her rent at Cedar Hills in the coming years, but that could wait for a while. We were helping Shirley with this move one step at a time. Thomas had sold her car once Shirley said she didn't want to drive anymore, and the profit helped to get her off to a good start.

Shirley seemed happy and upbeat in her first days in her apartment. Thomas and I took turns eating with her in the dining room, so she wouldn't feel so alone in the beginning. I thought about times when I'd worried over children new to my school not having anyone to eat with in the lunchroom. I was that new kid several times myself and still remembered how it felt. But to walk in as the new person among adults was more daunting than I ever would have imagined. Before she was able to make friends and find her own niche, Shirley was relegated to a table with three men whom nobody else wanted to eat with. I was impressed by her lack of resistance to this. She got to know all three and proclaimed that none of them were too bad, really. She also made it clear there would be no romantic relationships with any of them. Wrinkling her nose, she said, "Why would I want to have to take care of some old man again? I done that. No way."

We started bringing the kids to the dining room in the evenings. At five dollars per person, this was a restaurant we could afford on a regular basis. But soon our old routines took over and Shirley did fine without us at meals. She began to explore the large facility a bit more. After she'd been there awhile, she decided to take the elevator by herself to the second floor and walk around the common area where there was a library, television and couches, and a pool table.

"It's like a ghost town up there after supper," she said. "And something kind of bad happened. When I was taking the elevator back down, I let off some gas. Well, this old guy got on right when I was gettin' off and he yelled, 'SHOOOOO-EEEEEE!' I just kept on walkin' and didn't look back." We laughed and she decided it wasn't that bad after all. Other encounters with residents proved interesting, if not dicey. Shirley often had something to report when I saw her.

"Yesterday, there was a knock on the door and a old man was standing there looking at me. I said, 'Can I help you?' and he said, 'I'm looking for my pants.' I pointed to his trousers and he said, 'Okay, thanks.'"

One day, Shirley and I stood at the window watching an old man walking slowly on the sidewalk outside her apartment. He was carrying a bag of candy and didn't realize the bag had a hole in it. With great effort, he bent over to retrieve a piece that had fallen out, then dropped it back in the bag, only to see it had happened again. This went on for a couple of minutes and I said, "I think I should take him another bag."

"I don't know why you feel like you have to fix everything," she said. "He's fine. This is what I do for entertainment now."

I had forgotten how much Shirley loved to read. The weekly visit of the public library's bookmobile was a gift. Each week, she checked out five or six sizable books, then returned to replace them the next time around. Often, the person who drove the bookmobile made selections to suggest to her. She loved to tell us about the latest novel she was reading.

"It's called *Vengeance*," she said one day. These five girls – one is married to a senator that's mean and powerful. So they kidnap him! You won't believe what they did. After they kidnapped him."

Thomas and I sat on the couch listening. "Cut off his testicles?" I said.

"Worse."

Thomas looked on with consternation.

"They take off all his clothes and take him to SOUTH AMERICA. You see, they kidnapped him. No wait, first he has AIDS – and he give it to the girl – his wife. And she tells him he has and he says he's gonna say she done give it to him."

"Where's the part that's worse than losing your testicles?" Thomas said.

"Well, it isn't like they's any use no more. He has AIDS."

"Yeah, and in South America," I said, getting into the spirit of it all.

"Yeah. So they take him there and make him work in the fields where he won't never see the light of day again."

Now I was confused. "Huh?"

"Well, not in America."

"Is he still naked?" I asked.

Shirley thought for a moment. "They done give him a loin cloth."

Thomas looked at me. "If you and your friends are ever mad at me, I want to keep my testicles."

Shirley jumped back in. "You laugh but they done give him shots—knocked him out. He done woke up in SOUTH AMERICA."

"In a loin cloth," I added.

"Yeah!" she said. "It was great!"

Shirley began to leave us interesting phone messages…

Melissa? This is Shirley. I want to write a letter to the editor of the paper here. Or the Cedar Hills newsletter. About the guy who drives the bookmobile. He's a nice guy. He gave me a book about women talking about, well, I can't say it. You know…well, okay, it's the Vaginal Monologues. That's really what it's called! Anyway, I'm not gonna say that, but I want to write a letter. Are you comin' over tonight?

29

IN THE SPOTLIGHT

Shirley Kuhn has only been at Cedar Hills for six weeks. She brings with her a delightful sense of humor, quick wit and melodic laugh, which leaves you with a joyful feeling about life. Yet Shirley's life was anything but joyful in her younger years.

So began the "Resident Spotlight" about Shirley in the Cedar Hills newsletter soon after she moved in. After describing the circumstances that led to her becoming an orphan and her life once she was in the orphanage, the article reported her thoughts about her lot in life.

Though she first hated living in the orphanage, she soon came to realize that she and her sisters and brother were far better off than most. Shirley read in the newspaper how the Depression had left many without enough food to eat and others without jobs or a place to live. The paper spoke of bread lines for the poor while she was given plenty of good food. "In comparison to them, we were livin' high off the hog," Shirley remembers. "At least we had medical and dental care and a safe, warm bed." The state-run orphanage also provided training in the trade of your choice. Shirley chose to become a beauty operator. Upon graduation, she became a beautician until she met her future husband on a blind date.

Occasionally, Shirley would talk about becoming a beautician after she left the orphanage, but only after I prodded her. "At the Home, I practiced the Marcel style with a curling iron on all these little kids." She laughed. "I guess they couldn't say no! But most of 'em liked it. I had to take some extra training at a school about six months, there in Indianapolis, then I got a job in a beauty parlor on Washington Street. It was called Shirley's, just a coincidence."

"What was that like?" I asked.

"Well, the first time I heard a telephone ring was when I was working there. The phone rang and the owner told me to answer it. I didn't know what to do!" she said.

"So, what did you do?" I asked.

She laughed. "I picked it up and held it. Then someone said, 'is anyone there,' and I said, 'hello!' Believe it or not, I'd never been around a dog either. I was scared to death of dogs when I was 18. There was lots of stuff like that."

A "happily ever after" following her wedding vows was shattered by the beginnings of World War II. Her husband, who had been working at a printing press, was in the Reserves. When the war broke out, he was immediately called to duty and sent to California for three years. Shirley was not able to join him immediately. She took a job at Allison's, a company which made automobile parts. When she finally joined her husband in California, her first child was born the month before her husband was sent overseas.

Shirley rarely spoke of that time, but one story sticks in my mind. "When I was about seven months pregnant with Brenda, we was in Chula Vista – that's by San Diego – because that's where Walter got shipped for training. We took the train to San Francisco for a couple of days. Well, coming back, they wouldn't let any civilians on the train because service men came first. So, Walter got on the train with the rest of the men, and I didn't. Walter was the kind that wouldn't ask for nothin', not even for me, so I got left there."

"Gosh," I said, trying to mask my astonished reaction to Walter leaving her. "How did you get back?"

"Me and this other girl thumbed our way back from San

Francisco to San Diego. 'Course, Walter 'bout had a fit when he found out."

"What did he think you should have done?" I asked.

"I don't remember. But we got picked up by the nicest guy. He wanted one of us to sit up front, but we said we was both sittin' in the back. We had it all planned out what we was gonna do if we needed to get out quick – but he was really nice. He was a lieutenant in the Navy. He took me right to my door."

"Were you and the other woman dropped off together?"

"No, I don't know what happened to her." She shrugged. "He dropped me off first."

My vision of the sisterhood faded to black.

"It was the only time I ever thumbed a ride. Walter got real mad. Maybe it was because he got yelled at by an officer when he saw he left me. Walter said he said, 'Why didn't you speak up? We would have made room for your wife.' I wasn't mad at him though, because I knew he was gonna be gone a long time. Brenda was born ten days before he was shipped out to Guam, then he was gone two years. They never got leaves."

"I can't imagine being apart that long from your husband," I said, "especially with a new baby. But I guess lots of people did it. Did you worry about him?"

"Not really. He repaired ships. All he had to worry about was snipers."

"Well," I said. "If that's all…"

"I did all right, though," she continued. "I wasn't the only one. I got along okay. You just do what you gotta do. It was different back then. We was all in it together." I thought about this sense of a common purpose Shirley referred to during wartime, how different the mood of the country felt back then with everyone pulling together, and pondered whether it helped her to feel like she belonged to something beyond her few familial relationships. I wondered if feelings of patriotism mitigated the void she might have felt without a family of origin she could claim.

After the war, Shirley and her husband returned to Indianapolis and three sons came along following their daughter. She was determined that her children would not suffer the type of childhood she had to endure. Throughout most of their growing up years, Shirley remained at home. To help supplement the family's income, she cut the neighbors' hair and babysat other children. "I made all of my daughter's clothes until she got to the age where she wouldn't wear them anymore. Even then, other people were always asking where I bought the clothes I had made for her," she recalls. She also made curtains and did repair work.

When Thomas read this, he smiled at me. "It's interesting to read this account of her life. She's pretty amazing, really."

"Yes," I said.

"I guess she chose not to talk about the baby she lost. The miscarriage."

"And you were old enough to remember it, right?" I asked.

"Just barely. I remember her being taken away in an ambulance, and I was crying really hard."

"She's never talked to me about it," I said.

"Well, I doubt she talks about it with anyone. I think her reaction was pragmatic. She didn't want another baby."

Later, Shirley worked at the wholesale Kroger bakery, where she iced cakes until she retired. With her infectious laughter, she explained how the cakes would move along a conveyor belt. She and her co-workers iced 6,000 cakes per day. "It was pretty hard sometimes not to look at all those vats of icing and not take a lick before you got around to icing the cakes!" she quipped.

Ben read the newsletter with Shirley when she was over at our house soon after it was printed, and I was listening from the kitchen. He loved the image of Shirley dealing with the conveyor belt carrying all those cakes. "Remember that scene on the *I Love Lucy* show," I called to her, "when Lucy and Ethel were working in a candy factory?" She laughed and said, "Yeah, the one with them stuffin' all the candy in their mouth!" I explained to Ben that it was an old TV show and this was how Lucy and her friend got rid of the candy when the conveyor belt moved increasingly faster and they couldn't keep up. "That's how it felt, sometimes," Shirley said. "And sometimes it was funny. But we sure couldn't do what Lucy and Ethel did. They was cakes."

"Grandma," Ben said, "*Did* you ever taste the icing?"

"Well, maybe once or twice. The worst was when I was chewing gum once, which was strictly forbidden, and it fell in there! I never got it out! I was scared to death someone would find it and fire me, but they didn't. I never did that again."

I guessed there was something worse than that, which I didn't bring up, and that was going out on a limb to get Joe hired at the bakery. He was able to maintain the job for about a year, but then embarrassed Shirley by his abrupt departure before his pending termination. As Thomas told it, Dorothy drove with Joe to work every day and sat in the car throughout his shift, where he would meet her on his breaks and they would have sex. When he paid an undocumented worker he didn't even know to go finish his shift for him, it was the final straw.

Shirley explains that the family's outlook on life changed after they began to attend church at Calvary Baptist church. "I just want to make sure you mention that. I want to give God all the credit for all he did for us," she explains.

Following the paragraphs about where Shirley's children

lived, along with the number of grandchildren and great grandchildren she could claim, there was an acknowledgement of her son, Tom, for taking care of her every need, saying she didn't know what she'd do without his help, that he was the one she counted on. Blah, blah, blah, was what I thought. It was all true about Thomas, and I shouldn't have been surprised to have my efforts go unacknowledged, but I groused inwardly about it anyway. I was quickly becoming the middleman for some strange reason, with Shirley often leaving me messages for Tom, rather than leaving messages for him directly. Thomas handled important matters, such as communicating with Shirley's doctors and managing her medication, as well as picking up fast food when Shirley didn't want what was on the menu at Cedar Hills that day, and Shirley seemed to see me as his assistant in these undertakings.

The spotlight article concluded with this paragraph:

Get acquainted with this lovely lady. She has the knack for making any circumstance appear as though things could always be worse than they are. Shirley knows firsthand how to survive the most difficult things that life can hand you. After all, God is on her side.

Amen.

Phone message that week:

Melissa, people here want to know what you do at IU. This is Shirley. They want to know what you do at IU. I'm gettin' a piece of paper and writin' it down this time. All the old ladies say, "You have such a beautiful daughter-in-law." 'Course they're old and don't see so good. I'm just kiddin'. Okay, this is Shirley.

30

BANG, BANG, BANG ON THE DOOR, BABY

Shirley's apartment became our hub and we were constantly barging in. It was located near Ben's and Alison's schools, as well as the university where I was still a doctoral student working on my dissertation and teaching classes, and the clinics Thomas was directing for Bloomington Hospital. It was easy to stop by and check in, drop the kids off for childcare, or in Thomas's case, take naps on the weekends when I was trying to find him. I learned well after the fact that Shirley was his lookout, sounding the alarm when I pulled up so that he would look alive. Of course, I was partially to blame for this situation, intolerant as I was of Thomas taking a nap whenever I wasn't.

Alison and Ben, who were four and ten years old, often spent time there after school. They loved the long, wide hallways and were encouraged by their grandmother to roam them freely. They engaged in various forms of ripping and roaring around the place, including playing tag, jumping rope and pushing each other in the wheelchair Shirley kept handy for long walks. I worried they would frighten some of the residents and constantly reminded them to slow down when others were about, but Shirley was never going to hold them to this standard when I wasn't around.

"Let 'em bring some life to this place," she'd scold as she threw a ball or even an occasional Frisbee with them in the hall. "It's dead around here all day long. They give old people somethin' to look at," which I had to admit was true.

Occasionally, a resident would express disapproval of the children's rowdy activity. These people landed on Shirley's hate list for the rest of her days, in some cases even after their deaths. It was a favorite topic among Shirley, Ben, and Alison to talk about how much they didn't like that mean Mrs. Arlene Siddons. "She said they shouldn't be playin' on the organ," Shirley would exclaim, as if there were a prayer of my agreement about my children banging on the keys in one of the common areas. "It's out there for anybody to play! I said, 'Well it ain't like anybody else is playin' it!'"

Shirley paused for me to chime in but was undeterred by my silence. "I'd like to see her try to do better! I'll bet she don't even play it. She just thinks everyone should leave it alone!"

Not all the residents were as put out by the children as Mrs. Siddons though. Ben and Alison liked to be around people who were more fun. It wasn't unusual that I'd arrive to hear Ben calling to Shirley, "Hurry, Grandma, ya gotta see this! There's a band here, and Glen's dancing a jig!" Then he and Alison would race down the hallway as if a super hero had come to call.

Although both children liked hanging out at Grandma's, Alison, five-and-a-half years younger than her brother, was the regular fixture over the years. She provided companionship and entertainment for Shirley, and was a friend magnet in the dining room. When Shirley had been new and stuck at the table with three socially undesirable men, Alison helped her settle in, often reporting on each of these new friends in the car on the way home. Raymond took his teeth out before meals. Bert unbuckled his belt and unzipped his pants after them. Jerry put salt on everything, even though everyone knew he wasn't supposed to. All the residents were charmed whenever Alison was served a special peanut butter and jelly sandwich after her grandmother declared she didn't want ham hock and beans, or whatever was featured on the menu that day.

Alison developed a keen awareness of physical concerns most four-year-olds wouldn't consider. After being at Shirley's, she would relay various senior facts of life, based on up close and personal observation. "Grandma always has gas. Last night she took a laxative 'cause it's bad for you to strain when you're on the commode. Sometimes she gets stuck on the commode and needs me to get her up." Shirley would allow Alison to polish her false teeth and try to get them in her own mouth. Once, Shirley laughed and said, "She asked if she could throw them in the dumpster! I don't know why she keeps asking if she can throw things in the dumpster. Can you imagine what all's in the Cedar Hills dumpster? I let her throw a ball in there the other day, but that's all I know about."

Sometimes Shirley would dump out all her pills from the weekly organizer when Alison said she'd like to sort them different ways. It wasn't unusual for me to have to put them back in their proper slots when I'd come to pick her up and find that Alison had lost interest after the pills were in flower shapes of blue, white, and yellow, and Shirley would claim she didn't know how to get them organized again. Looking back, I wonder about my resignation regarding such dangerous activity for a little girl. Indeed, Thomas wasn't much better than his mother when it came to protecting Alison around medication. He wouldn't go so far as to make playing with pills a game, but he did leave them out on his dresser in spite of my concern that some were brightly colored and looked like candy. The day came when I counted them, saw one was missing, and panicked that Alison had swallowed it. When she admitted this might be true, which was as far as we got, we called the poison control hotline and were told she should drink activated charcoal to counter the toxins she may have ingested. It was a thick, black liquid and her resistance was understandable. Thomas prepared a cup for each of them to slurp down and made it a contest, resulting in howls of laughter and a Kodak moment capturing their smiles with blackened teeth and lips, all in spite of my certainty that this should have been a more somber experience. Just another day in the life. If I had freaked out every time something like this happened, ours would have been a scary household.

The power dynamic between Shirley and Alison only intensified as they spent more time together, with Alison calling the shots and Shirley thinking this was simply delightful. Each time Alison entered her grandmother's apartment, she would go through the process of turning down each of her cousins' framed photographs propped haphazardly against the wall, leaving only pictures of Ben and her up. Shirley liked that kind of chutzpah. Sometimes Alison would become intent on beautifying Shirley's apartment, as in when she decorated her door by hanging a monkey Beanie Baby by its neck with a spiral keychain coil on a hook. She festooned her apartment walls with countless coloring book pages of *My Little Pony*. Shirley had a framed cross stitch of the Bible verse, John 3:16, that hung on the wall in the kitchen area, which she and Alison decorated with a bunch of dog stickers, mostly dachshunds.

Alison never cleaned anything up unless I stood there and made her. She was still quite young, but such a force. When I'd come to pick her up, she was often perched on top of Shirley's microwave, like this was normal behavior, and I would tell her to hop down carefully and pick up her toys. The situation was largely about being in Rome and doing as the Romans did. As far as I could tell, Shirley had always had a hard time managing all the stuff one collects over time. The house she left behind was filled with items she couldn't throw out, too. When it was eventually sold years after she moved to Bloomington, Thomas, Joe, and Lee filled a couple of dumpsters with piles of junk without consideration of their value, sentimental or financial. She never seemed to miss any of it – out of sight, out of mind. Thomas was relieved that I wasn't a participant in the purge, knowing how attached I could become to various keepsakes, often at first sight. He was happy to limit the crew to his brothers and him, three men who weren't afflicted with such ambivalence when cleaning the place out.

But Shirley's new apartment was still always a mess, cluttered with Lincoln Logs, Legos, stuffed animals, and *Happy Meal* detritus. This chaos was diametrically opposed to my vision of a proper play area, not that I had been completely successful in this endeavor at home. As a former Montessori teacher, I was all about an orderly environment and sometimes got a little out of control. Like when I tried to set up containers for Alison's numerous little plastic animals, organizing them by their native continents. I'd pick up a kangaroo and say, "I think this belongs in the Australia box," which I had carefully labeled. Alison would let me know in no uncertain terms that its home was now a Groovy Girl bed, which it was sharing with a stegosaurus. Seeing the *Hello Kitty* dolls stuffed in the South America box and *Littlest Pet Shop* puppies residing in Africa, I gave up.

Shirley was there for Alison after school on the days when meetings, classes, or my dissertation research had me working late. By this time, Ben was involved in numerous after-school activities, so he was at the apartment less often. Typically, Thomas or I could stop what we were doing to pick Alison up from school and take her to Shirley's apartment, given the close proximity of both places to the hospital and university where we worked. It comforted me when I was working long hours, knowing they would be having a snack and talking about how her day had gone. After Alison began elementary school, I easily accepted the notion that Shirley's homework help would forever be an oxymoron. Often, they spent their time draped in Shirley's copious costume jewelry and playing endless games of *Candyland*, an activity I was relieved to relinquish. Sometimes, they would work on an elaborate routine Alison had been imagining for a dolphin show, my favorite one being set to the B-52s' song, "Love Shack." Shirley and Alison would describe to me what was happening while playing the song, each part trumpeting the dolphins' leaps through hoops together, or apart, or with Alison riding them, or just dancing on their tails in water. Or the two of them would get into crafts, such as making pretend braces out of tin foil. Once, they made a tool for applying sunscreen, a necessary evil Alison and I fought about each year during swimming season. It was in effect a sunscreen udder made by cutting out the tips of the fingers of a rubber glove. Alison presented it to me saying, "If you put sunscreen on me this way, I won't get mad." When it came to doing a whole lot of developmentally appropriate hanging out without an agenda, Shirley was the best caretaker I knew.

She was there for emergencies, too, like the time we asked Joe to drive Alison to school for us and he vomited on her in the car. When he had realized he was sick, he had turned to his right where his niece sat, rather than to the window on his left – in all fairness, a tough choice to be made without warning. Rather than taking her to school, Joe had the sense to drop Alison off at Grandma's apartment nearby. I've wondered what Shirley must have thought when she opened the door early that morning and found Alison stiffly standing there, her clothes a mess, as Joe pulled out of the parking lot in his truck. By the time I came to take her to school, Shirley had gotten her changed and ready to go. I asked Alison what it was like when it happened. She looked at me in all seriousness and said, "I was quiet on the outside, but screaming on the inside," a line I've revisited in various situations of my own over the years.

Spending so much time in a senior residence center was a new and grand adventure for Ben and Alison. It wasn't the norm, but they had a lot of fun. Sometimes, Alison would bring friends with her to Grandma's and take pride when their eyes would get big as they entered and exclaimed that this place was like a castle. She was envied by her peers, just like Shirley was by hers. Everyone won.

Phone message from that week:

Melissa, someone come into the dining room today in just her underwear. I need some new underwear. I mean, what if you do that and you ain't wearin' your Monday pants on a Monday? This is Shirley.

31

THE CARETAKER

A few months after Shirley's move to Cedar Hills, an opening at one of the dining room tables became available, and Shirley was invited to join a group of three other women. A neighbor down the hall named Patsy had a lot to do with this. They had become friends who tended to see their circumstances similarly and didn't hold back with their opinions. Shirley often asked me if I had known Patsy before Shirley moved in. "She works at IU like you," she said. "In the office." It was fun to watch their rapport developing.

Unfortunately, the managers, James and Maura, left soon after Shirley moved in. They had been professional and impressive, even if Maura had gotten cranky eventually, according to Shirley. Their replacements, especially the wife, Leona, never met with Shirley's approval. Once when Alison and I were there, Shirley and Patsy had a few things to say about her.

"She come over at dinner and tell me how nice I look and it's disgusting," Shirley said. "It's fake. She dances for us and tries to make us laugh and says, 'How are *you* today?' And Patsy and me won't have none of it."

"Truly," Patsy assured me, "it makes Shirley want to throw up. Tell Melissa about the church service."

Shirley nodded her head. "At the church service, the minister always talks about people not sitting in the front row. Y'know, he's joking. Well, Leona dragged a old lady up there and that lady had only been here about a week! I was so mad; well, I went the other way."

Alison pronounced Leona an a-hole. "Alison!" I said.

Shirley shrugged her shoulders. "Well, what's the word for how she's acting?"

"Patronizing."

"Yeah. She's patronizing, and we all hate her."

I had been on guard about Leona soon after she arrived when she asked Shirley to look after a woman named Nelda who was living in the apartment next door. This was in the first months Shirley lived at Cedar Hills, before she had been fortified by her alliance with Patsy. Although she had been uncertain about taking on this responsibility, she wasn't sure how to decline the request. "What does she mean when she says, 'look after her'?" I asked, after Shirley told me this.

"Well, she's depressed, and Leona said I'm her only friend. She has this little dog named Sam."

I laughed. "That's certainly evident -- I mean that yipping dog. But what does Leona want you to do?"

Shirley hesitated. "She said I could get Nelda up and help her get to the dining room for lunch, get her a place to sit. She gets lost."

"That doesn't sound right, Shirley. How do you feel about having to do that?"

"I don't know. I guess Nelda needs me. And I don't know how to tell Leona I don't want to do it no more."

We sat at Shirley's kitchen table and wrote a short, two-sentence script for what she could say to get out of this assignment. She was 80 years old and inexperienced with conflict resolution like this. The passive aggression she had employed over the years with Walter wasn't going to work in this situation. To make her feel better, I told Shirley I'd written things down plenty of times to help me know what to say when I was in a jam. She practiced the couple of sentences I had written, but kept messing them up, which got us laughing. But she tried again.

"Leona," she said with a serious look on her face. "I don't think I should be taking care of Nelda anymore." Then she sat down, defeated. "Melissa, I can't say this."

"Well, do you want me to?" I asked.

"No," she said, "I can do it." She took a deep breath. "Okay. Leona? I wanted to tell you some things about Nelda." I wasn't sure where she was going with this. Noting the puzzled look on my face, she hooted, "And her little dog, too!"

I was laughing again. "Give me that paper. It doesn't say that."

"Okay, well, I'll practice tonight and tell her tomorrow maybe." Over the next couple of days, Shirley lost the script and asked me to write it again, but it turned out she didn't need it after Nelda's dog bit her on the leg. It was traumatizing, even if it wasn't a serious wound, and she was no longer ambivalent.

"I told Nelda, I'll come back if you'll put that dog in the bathroom. She isn't doin' it, so I'm not helpin' anymore," she told me. "Yesterday, Leona asked me to go to her room and knock on the door and get her up and I said no. Nelda never even apologized for Sam biting me! I feel sorry for her; she gets confused. But I'm not gonna do it no more."

Nelda moved out a couple weeks after that. Shirley shook her head. "She's moving in with her son and daughter-in-law and that was what she said she did NOT want to do. Nothin' I can do about it."

It was interesting to see this example of Shirley drawing the line between volunteerism and obligation. She had cared for Walter's parents in their last years, for Walter, for Joe and Dorothy, for her mother in her own way, but Nelda fell outside this circle. I was sad for Nelda but relieved to see Shirley standing up for herself. And Leona remained someone to look out for. What an a-hole, I thought.

Phone message:

Melissa? Hi. This is Shirley. Alison left somethin' here by accident. I don't know if it's a video or a DVD. They's all the same to me. Some is round and some is square. Also, have you been callin' me? The phone's been ringin' all afternoon. I kept sayin' 'hello, hello?' but I didn't know I was holdin' the phone upside down. Okay. This is Shirley.

32

DUBIOUS ENTERTAINMENT

Shirley had been at Cedar Hills for over a year and I was always looking for things to do on the weekends, events Shirley might enjoy, keeping in mind how much she was slowing down. Once she settled into her new home, she seemed more open to various invitations, sometimes even enthusiastic. But there remained an undercurrent of suspicion in her response to me. Maybe this was because the first expeditions weren't to her liking. I had suggested that Thomas take her to the Tibetan Cultural Center in town to watch the Buddhist monks creating their amazing sand mandalas - in hindsight, I don't know why. That night, we ate dinner together, and Shirley's comments about the experience were less than positive. "Well, they was pretty, I guess, but Tom says that after they's done, they take it to the river and dump it in. That don't make any sense."

Thomas sighed. "I tried to explain this, Mom. It's about what is sacred in impermanence."

"That don't make no sense!"

"But it makes sense to them," he continued.

"Maybe that's true, but it's a lot of work for nothin'. I got tired just watching them blow through them straws. It was boring, if you really wanna know the truth."

"Actually, it's like a prayer," I offered.

"Oh," Shirley said. "I get that." She looked at Thomas. "Why didn't you say that?"

I noticed Alison on the phone with Grandma one day in October of 2001 and signaled to let me talk to her. "Grandma, do you want to talk to Mom?" she asked. Then, "Well, here she is anyway."

I took the phone. "Hi, Shirley. Jeff and Carol's daughter, Sophie, is clogging at a festival near town this Friday. I think it will be fun to watch. Do you want to go?" Shirley had known Jeff since he and Thomas were in middle school.

"Well," and she paused. "Who else is going?"

I rolled my eyes. "It will be me and the kids. I think Thomas has other plans."

"And *what* is it?"

"It's a fall festival in Ellettsville, just a short drive from here. Sophie is a clogger, remember? Her group is going to perform."

"Oh, yeah, she's cute! Y'know Alison says she's a clogger, too, but she don't need no lessons." Alison was nodding her head to music she heard through a pair of earphones. I laughed with Shirley. "I know. She just shuffles her feet back and forth and says she's got it. So, anyway, would you like to go?"

"Oh. Well. I guess that would be okay." She paused again. "If that's what you want."

"Shirley, I just wanted to know if you'd like to go. I'd love for you to join us if you want to come."

"I said, okay," was her answer, her voice becoming shrill.

It was a date.

Ben, Alison, and I went over to pick Shirley up. As usual, she was ready to go and waiting for us. Her hair had been freshly coifed in the in-house beauty parlor and she wore nice slacks and rubber-sole shoes. "I got a coat and a sweater. Do you think I need both?"

"It wouldn't hurt. I'm not sure how cool it's going to get."

At this, we began the long walk from Shirley's apartment to my car, approximately 20 feet, once we were positioned with her holding my arm, never the other way around. Shirley was moving more slowly now and her osteoporosis was becoming more noticeable. After she was in the car and seat-belted, I returned to the porch to fold up and load her wheelchair. With no room to spare inside her apartment, Shirley kept it there, out in the elements. It was an old, manual chair with a heavy, rusted stand and squeaky wheels. Its vinyl, olive green seat sagged like an old lawn chair. Mostly, it was used for the kids' entertainment down the hallways of Cedar Hills, but sometimes it came in handy when we were going somewhere that would require walking. It was a pain to fold up and haul into the car, but the back of our station wagon held it easily.

I had never been to the Ellettsville Fall Festival and wasn't prepared for the crowd. I began to tense up when I saw how hard it was going to be to find a parking place nearby. Shirley kept saying, "Just drop me off on some corner somewheres," but that seemed unwise. The sun was still bright and hot before sunset, and I worried about how long it would take to get back to her as she waited. Maybe this wasn't a good idea after all. I thought about Thomas hanging out at home and his confusion about why I'd want to take this on. I kind of hated him in that moment of my second guessing.

Finally, I saw an unoccupied bench on a side street near the festival and pulled over to deposit Shirley until I could park the car. "Ben," I said, "you can stay with Grandma. Alison and I will park the car and come get you." Sensing she was about to miss out on something wonderful, Alison began to protest.

Shirley waved me off. "She can come, too. Stop worrying all the time."

After pulling over and settling Shirley on the bench with the kids, I whispered a bit of terror into eleven-year-old Ben's ear. "Do NOT let Alison run off and make sure you stay right here with Grandma. I mean it." He nodded. A driver showed his impatience with me blocking a lane by honking, and I wanted to give him the finger as a way of showing mine, but resisted. I always found the taboo of mothers giving anyone the finger ironic, so often stuck between a rock and a hard place as they are, even when it's self-imposed.

Once the car was parked, I rushed to retrieve Shirley and the kids. They were smiling and laughing on the bench, enjoying themselves as Grandma provided commentary about people walking by.

"Look at that bald guy and all them tattoos. They's ugly."

"That colored boy's pretty fat, ain't he?"

"What is that old lady doing wearing them short shorts? Ugh."

"Look, there's a Chinaman."

I reconsidered the wisdom of leaving the children with her. Ever.

Pushing the wheelchair through the crowd while keeping tabs on Ben and Alison proved challenging. They ran ahead, then circled back to point out something to Grandma, and though this made me anxious, she seemed to be having fun. She insisted on stopping and directing me to buy them cotton candy as we made our way to the stage. Alison climbed onto her lap, adding to the weight of the chair I struggled to push forward. She brandished the cotton candy all around while I formed a shield with my hand over Shirley's hair. Shirley was oblivious to this, singing her version of "Stars and Stripes Forever," the lyrics replaced by "da-da, da-da-da, da-da-da."

We finally got to the stands minutes before the performance was scheduled to take place. Shirley and I settled on the bottom bench. Alison and Ben ran up and down the bleachers with friends after handing over the sticky remains of their cotton candy for Grandma to hold when I refused to provide this service.

Following their introduction, Sophie's clogging group appeared on stage with sequined outfits and winsome smiles. They kept their upper bodies remarkably straight while tapping their feet in complex patterns that added perfect percussion to the routine. They were enchanting to watch, especially Sophie, of whom we were particularly fond. Alison shuffled her feet forward and back on the sidelines while Shirley cheered her on. The performance lasted fifteen minutes.

Then it was time to go home.

Sophie's mother, Carol, offered to take everyone to get ice cream, but Shirley was getting tired and cold in the night air. Noting the disappointment on the kids' faces, Carol suggested that she take Ben and Alison and that I could pick them up at her house after taking Shirley home. It sounded like a good idea.

It wasn't until after they left that I realized my error. I would have to leave Shirley somewhere by herself to wait while I retrieved the car. And now it was getting dark and cold outside. Even she seemed doubtful about this prospect, so we decided to soldier forth together with her in the wheelchair.

If I thought it was difficult pushing the wheelchair on a smoothly paved road earlier, I hadn't realized how much harder it would be on seriously cracked sidewalks. At first, we took it slowly over a few uncomfortable bumps. But we soon encountered a crack much harder to navigate. Having pushed strollers over rough terrain, I thought I could do this, remembering when to lift up or bear down on the handle as I pushed forward. It turns out this is much easier to do when pushing a baby versus an adult. No longer masking the effort I was expending, I groaned as I tried with all my might to move my mother-in-law over this chasm. After pushing her up, the wheelchair slammed back down on the cement and she yelped.

"Oh, gosh, Shirley, I'm so sorry. We'll just take it slowly, okay?"

She nodded with uncertainty and began to peer ahead for bad patches.

"Here comes another one, Melissa. Now hold on. What are

we gonna do?"

I stopped and looked around, grateful for a chance to catch my breath. "Well, we could move on to the street, but with all this traffic, that doesn't seem like a good idea." Shirley looked at the cars passing by and laughed nervously. "I don't wanna do that!"

"Okay, well, I could help you out of the chair whenever we come to a big bump, then you could sit back down."

Seeing the upcoming terrain, she frowned and said, "They's way too many cracks coming up. I can't get up and down that much. I'll just walk."

"Oh," I tried to be polite here as I envisioned us still walking late into the night after the festival was over and everyone had gone home. "It's a really long walk, Shirley. Let's just try to keep going with the wheelchair." She hesitated and looked around, like she was searching for someone else to go with before she said okay.

We continued miserably, jerking along until one of us – I don't remember who – began to laugh following another bang onto the sidewalk. Suddenly, we were immobilized by our hysteria, me doubled over and her wiping her eyes.

"You said this would be fun!"

"I really thought it would!"

"Well, it ain't so fun right now!"

At this point we were spotted by a knight in shining pickup truck, who pulled over and said, "Ladies, you look like you could use some help." I paused to size him up, but really, almost any alternative was better than what we'd been doing. His kindness seemed genuine as he showed us how he could help Shirley into the front seat, then load the wheelchair into the back. There was an awkward pause and I realized he was hesitant to say I'd need to ride in the truck-bed with the wheelchair. "Melissa don't mind riding in the back," Shirley said. "She got us into this mess in the first place!" Like they were the best of friends.

All I could do was laugh and thank the guy as I piled in after the wheelchair, grateful for his charity. I held on to the side rail, tipped my head back, and looked up at the stars, letting the cool breeze dry the sweat I'd worked up.

It was a quiet ride back to Shirley's apartment. We were both worn out. As I drove to pick up the kids, I practiced various ways to respond to Thomas when he asked how the evening went. I settled on the nonchalant version, the one that would get me to bed soonest without having to eat crow.

Shirley began to increase the number of phone messages she left, now most nights:

Melissa, that Chinese cook of ours? That you said opened a restaurant somewheres else? You said they's Asian, but he ain't Asian. He's Chinese. From China. This is Shirley.

33

THE STOCKINGS WERE HUNG
BY THE CHIMNEY WITH CARE

Once Shirley moved to Bloomington, she always spent the night on Christmas Eve. We attended the service at our church, starting at 7:00 P.M., so dinner was a bit rushed, but it was worth it to me to sing "Silent Night" by candlelight each year. Of course, this came with its own hazards. Young children were supposed to use battery-operated electric candles for safety purposes, but Shirley couldn't bear to disappoint Alison, so she traded with her for a real candle with its cardboard skirt to catch the dripping wax. This always happened after I had done battle with my daughter, explaining why she couldn't hold an open flame until she was older, so I often sang "Silent Night" with gritted teeth. Shirley's permanent was always heavily lacquered with hair spray, and while she held Alison, who merrily waved her lit candle in all directions, I focused my Christmas prayer on Grandma's hair not catching fire. Each year, I willed myself to stop picturing my difficult mother-in-law as a giant human torch lighting up the sanctuary and found my fascination with that image disturbing whenever it came to me.

After we extinguished our candles and returned them to their baskets to be sorted and used for next time, we would load into the car and head home, some years on clear roads and others with me eyeing Shirley's pumps and wondering what we'd do if we slid off an icy road going home and had to get out. When we'd get home, we'd go through a succession of typical traditions with me watching the time and thinking about tasks to do after the children went to bed, with or without visions of sugar plums. We would read the Christmas story from the books of Matthew and Luke, unless everyone pointed out that this had already happened at church, then Alison and Ben would be allowed to open one small gift. For many years, we read The Polar Express, ending it with all of us shaking small jingle bells to show that we still believed in Santa. Sometimes, we remembered to take a picture of the children. There's one with Ben in pajamas he was still willing to wear and Alison in some faded chenille, zip-up robe she had discovered in the free clothes basket at Cedar Hills, with a faint smell of something I couldn't quite place.

Lastly, we would put out milk and cookies for Santa. Ben believed in Santa Claus with his whole heart and often wrote him a sweet note. I saved them over the years, my favorite being the one where he wrote:

Dear Santa,

We hope you like the cookies. When you're finished, please bring your dishes to the sink and rinse them off.

Love, Ben

Thomas read this to Shirley and me, adding in a needling voice, "Please, Santa, we want to have a merry Christmas. Everyone needs to clean up after themselves." I was all about such training at the time. Shirley, who never picked up after herself, leaving a trail of tissues and gum wrappers throughout the house, acted as if she had gotten an early Christmas present, just like the kids. I had found the note funny, too, but less so after she read it aloud repeatedly, laughing non-stop.

When it came to believing in Santa Claus, Alison had a different view than her brother's. As early as four years of age, she looked up the chimney and said, "A big fat man is coming down that hole? I don't think so." As Unitarian Universalists, we welcomed all perspectives on this matter.

Finally with the children in bed asleep, Thomas and I, like other bleary-eyed parents who had overspent for the big day, would get to work putting together toys to be discovered in the morning. Shirley would have gone to bed by that time, too. In her first years in Bloomington, we hadn't added on a guest bedroom, so she stayed in a makeshift bedroom in our study next to the family room. One Christmas Eve when she was with us overnight, we had gotten a Baby Alive doll for Alison that talked when you pressed its tummy. When we put the batteries in, the doll barked out, "I love you, Mommy!" loud enough to wake the dead in the silence of that holy night. Shirley came tearing out in her curlers and kerchief, shouting, "She's awake! Alison's awake! I heard her!" We told her it was just the doll, but she didn't seem to believe us at first. Finally convinced, she headed back to her room, only to dash back out in alarm when the doll blurted, "I want my ba-ba," from across the room unbidden.

"She's awake! She's awake!"

"Shhh!" I said. "She's not awake, and you're going to wake her up. It's that blasted doll. I don't know what's wrong with it. I guess we need to take out the batteries until tomorrow morning." Before we got to the battery removal, there were two more outbursts, one from the doll and one from Shirley, and Thomas threw his hands up in the air, saying, "Jesus, Mom, will you cut it out? We're trying to fix this damn thing and we're tired."

This struck the three of us as very funny, and we began to laugh uncontrollably, despite our attempts to muffle the sound. Finally, we heard a tiny voice from upstairs.

"It's too loud down there," Alison called irritably, her good behavior act for Santa having worn thin.

"Your mom's watchin' a TV show about baby dolls!" Shirley called.

Alison seemed to tune this out as she stomped back to bed without looking down the stairs. Noting her lack of interest in our careful display of Christmas bounty, I looked at Thomas and said, "Either we're doing something very right or very wrong; I have no idea which it is." After all, the only one who needed several escorts back to bed on Christmas Eve was Grandma.

34

TOO CLOSE FOR COMFORT

I came home one evening and discovered Shirley was there.
I knew this even before I saw or heard her, because her wads of
tissue were everywhere, like tumbleweeds on the prairie. Thomas
and his mother were engaged in a standoff in the family room.
"You have to stop ordering things," he told her.

"I ain't gonna order stuff no more!" Shirley exclaimed.
"But this was a honest mistake. I didn't know my feet was gonna
swell and these socks is too tight. I got an envelope to send 'em
back in."

"What about the envelope the company sent? And the
receipt?" he asked.

"Well, I didn't know they was gonna be tight! I threw it
away."

"You have to stop ordering things," he said.

"I know."

Thomas groaned, then walked into the kitchen where I was
unloading bags of groceries and getting out what we needed for
dinner. "You're good at returning stuff like this," he said.

"Hey, don't look at me," I said, out of Shirley's earshot.
"I'm staying out of that crazy-town with your mom. She really
does have a problem with ordering stuff, and it's all little stuff like
those socks."

"Maybe if she lived here, we could keep her from doing it."

I froze in the middle of transferring the quart of milk to the
refrigerator. "Lived here," I said.

"Yeah, it's probably not a good idea."

I counted to five as I continued putting things away.

"Who brought it up?" I said, more menacingly than I
intended, which is what happens when you have a skillet in hand.

"Well, she did, of course. *I'm* not gonna do that."

"Why'd she bring it up?"

"She was just saying how expensive her rent is every month and that she wished she could give it to us instead."

"Do you think that was all there was to it?" I said. "Or that she really wants to live with us? Because I'm thinking that isn't such a great idea."

"Oh, don't worry, I know, and we wouldn't take her money, anyway." As he walked out of the kitchen, I heard him say, "Well, not much." I wondered if this was going to be a regular topic. And if Shirley read in Thomas's reaction that I didn't want her moving in.

As we ate dinner, Shirley regaled us with stories about her life in general, including one about the new, young doctor she was seeing. After two years as a resident of Cedar Hills, she was aware of everyone else's business in all her stomping grounds, from her residence to her doctors' offices. "Did you know his parents live at Cedar Hills?" she said. "He says he wants 'em in a nursing home, but they like where they are. He wants 'em on the first floor. I told him I been on the first floor all along, and I love it. He wants them on the first floor if they's a fire. The firemen says they's responsible for getting you out – well, I don't know if I like that – would you like that?" She didn't pause for a reply. "He's Edna's doctor, too. I told him we all may need him because of Edna and that new scooter she's always on. We all hit the deck when we see her coming. And Bernice keeps passin' out and fallin' on her head. I think it's something in her mind. She was in that Wee Willie's restaurant – you know, I probably told you about this." "You did," I confirmed, knowing it would make no difference in the retelling. "And she went to the restroom and did it and had to yell, 'Help! Help!' With her clothes down. I mean her drawers were around her ankles and don'tcha know the manager that come in to help her was a young, good-lookin' guy!

He says to her, 'don't worry, ma'am, I've seen it all.' Well, he has now!"

By now, Ben and Alison had finished and excused themselves, but Shirley kept on talking. "Okay, so today, it was supposed to be bean soup. All there was was flour and it was *white*. The menu said it was hardy bean soup. So I was expectin' hardy bean soup. And I said, 'this ain't no hardy bean soup.' And the assistant manager – that new, old guy – says it's Albino Bean Soup. I said I never heard of that and he just turned and left. Just like that. Well, it wasn't no hardy bean soup, and that's what I had my heart set on."

I got up to clear the dishes and load the dishwasher. Thomas looked like he was falling asleep. I tuned out for a moment, then realized Shirley had moved on to another topic. "Well, she's a mess. I mean, I've had her food in my lap. And if I see her do this one thing one more time. Here's what she does. She takes her napkin and cleans out her nose. Then she spreads it out on the table. Then she looks at it. Then she folds it up and sticks it under her watch. Every night. I told Patsy just to look the other way. We's supposed to be friends with Adele, but the moral of the story is don't ever shake Adele's hand, so help me God! She gives me candy, but it's always wrapped."

I poked Thomas to wake up as I brought coffee to the table, mostly for Shirley, something wholly unneeded that evening. "Is Adele the one that's been at your table for a while?"

"Yes. That seat opened up when Blanche found another table. We was all relieved to see her go."

"I remember Blanche," I said. I had suspected she wasn't going to last long when I joined the women at Shirley's table one day for lunch and heard Blanche say, "Every night I dream about Boy George and I don't know why."

When Thomas returned from driving his mother home, the kids were asleep and I was in bed reading the paper. "How was the drive back?" I asked, as innocently as I could.

"Oh my God, when she is wound up, I just can't listen to her after a while."

"Mm-hmm."

"I know what you're thinking," Thomas said.

"Yeah, you probably do." I yawned and turned out the light.

Phone message:

Melissa, is you tapin' "Three Wives" for me? I mean "Sick Love." I mean "Big Love." This is Shirley, by the way.

And there's something else. Another woman come to the dining room in her drawers. Just plain old ugly cotton pants and nothin' else. And she was late so everyone saw. I've seen her at your church. She's got thick glasses. Anyway, I need to get some good underwear in case I lose it and go to the dining room like that. I want something pretty. I'm thinkin' red or purple. This is Shirley.

35

SHIRLEY'S LAST BALL GAME

Shirley could be reflective when looking back on her parenting. "I tried to be loving and put them first. If it was about scrubbin' the kitchen floor or goin' on a picnic, we went on a picnic. But there are things that I wished I'da done – like go to things they done at school or the sports they was in."

It did astound me when Thomas shared that his parents never attended any of his track meets or wrestling matches. They didn't even come to his high school graduation. He had shrugged his shoulders. "They never saw things like that as important." Even knowing Shirley didn't experience good parenting as a child, I couldn't quite grasp such a lack of attention paid to one's children.

Grand-parenting Ben and Alison proved to be Shirley's redemption. Once she moved to Bloomington, she attended all school and sports events. There were school plays, science fairs, piano recitals, poetry cafes, 4H exhibits, and lots of ball games. Uncharacteristically demure, she would smile and nod and say nice things about her grandchildren to anyone who greeted her. She seemed to have fun and, although she was worn out by the time we took her home, was ready for whatever activity the next day would bring.

The last time Shirley saw Ben play baseball, he was about 12 and still in Little League. The games were fun to watch in the evenings under the lights and spectators could provide as much entertainment as the players. Ben's teammate, Oscar, had an ever present grandmother who called him Oscar Meyer, loudly and often, in a gravelly voice that smacked of a lifetime pack-a-day habit.

"Okay, Oscar Meyer, you gotta get this one," she'd say

when Oscar was up to bat. "First, pull your pants up." As Oscar did as he was told, his teammates, feeling his humiliation, looked the other way. "Well, now you've got a wedgie." she'd shout. "Pay attention, boy, this one's yours. Good swing, Oscar Meyer, you got it." And then, "What happened, boy? Should've practiced more!" Then to the crowd, "He ain't payin' attention."

Then she'd swat her knee with her visor, scratch and spit. Poor Oscar, Thomas and I always thought. Poor Oscar. Part of me loved Oscar's grandmother, of course, but Shirley, shocked and outside her comfort zone, didn't know what to think. Mostly, she looked to Thomas and me to know what to say and do.

We were of no help, however, during a rousing celebration after a close game that ended in victory. The boys, proud and elated, were gathered in a tight bunch with their families. After the coach praised them and there were hip-hip-hoorays all around, one child forgot himself completely and threw his cleat high into the air above the crowd. No one reacted quickly enough to prevent it from hitting Shirley on her back when it came down. I can still hear what happened in that instant. She shrieked.

"SHIT! DAMMIT! SHIT!"

It's hard to adequately describe the crowd's response to a nicely dressed grandmother screeching such invectives. Everyone stopped talking. Alison, six years old and unable to handle the discomfort of the scene, kicked Thomas hard in the shin. All eyes fell upon our fucked-up little mess of a family and triage proved challenging. Shirley needed comfort and a muzzle. Alison needed a reprimand. Ben needed to be saved from this painful disgrace in front of his teammates. The little reprobate who had caused the ruckus was weeping, his face buried in his mother's side. Everyone gathered around him to offer consolation while giving our small group a wide berth.

The only thing that was missing was my inappropriate laughter, so I grabbed Shirley and took off for the parking lot before adding this finishing touch. We sat in the back seat of the car and waited for the rest of the family.

"Well, it hurt!" Shirley shouted when an awkward silence followed the initial injury check.

"I know. Are you okay?"

"What was that kid doin' throwin' his shoe up in the air like that?"

"Something he'll never do again, I imagine." And the first giggle came up.

"Why are you laughing?" she demanded.

I fell apart and said, "Oh, I don't know…"

"You'da said some things, too, if it was you!"

"I probably would have said much worse."

"This is gonna hurt tomorrow, y'know."

"I do know, and I'm sorry for laughing."

Shirley sighed. "Those benches is getting too hard for me to sit on anyway."

It was a sobering moment. "Now wait, you can still come to games," I said. "Think about Oscar's grandma. Think about when I don't understand the umpire's calls and cheer at the wrong times. Nobody's perfect. And we can bring a cushion to sit on." But seeing the look on her face, I knew it was the end of an era.

36

NOBODY PUTS BABY IN A CORNER

Joe and Dorothy arrived for an overnight visit on a Friday evening in the summer of 2002, along with their latest little dog, Baby #4 or so. This one was ancient and decrepit. He was blind, snaggle-toothed, sickly, filthy, and very, very cranky. I never touched him, which is just as well, since he was unpredictable and might have bitten me with the few teeth he had left.

We hadn't seen Joe and Dorothy for some time, mostly due to the busy pace we had set for our lives at that time. I was finally finishing my dissertation, preparing to graduate and considering my options for what would follow. I knew that universities like Indiana University didn't hire their own graduate students in tenure-track positions since this was seen as research incest. Newly minted Ph.D.'s were expected to find jobs elsewhere, only to return if there was a job for them after they had earned tenure in a different academic setting. We didn't want to move again and I didn't want to commute while the children were still so young. There was a lot to figure out.

At dinnertime, Baby sat in Dorothy's lap, eating meatloaf from her plate and drinking from her glass. Alison kept looking to me to send them both to the time-out bench, her response in direct contrast to Ben's matter-of-fact acceptance of the scene. He asked Dorothy if Baby would like some ketchup on his meatloaf. I was reminded that Ben had spent more time with Joe and Dorothy than Alison when we lived only a mile away from them in Indianapolis. He was harder to shock.

Early Saturday morning, Thomas returned to our bedroom after going downstairs to put the dogs out. He had a look of disbelief on his face. "I don't know whether it was Baby or Dorothy, but someone has shit all over the first floor."

I sat up in bed. "Oh, God. I feel so badly for you about that."

"You're not going to help me?"

"Well, no. But when my family defecates all over the house someday, you can remind me of the position I'm taking." Feeling guilty, I asked, "How bad is it really?"

"Very bad."

"Yikes. And Joe didn't clean it up?"

"No," Thomas said, his anger rising. "I guess he thought the poop fairies would do it." Then he stomped back down the stairs.

I buried my head under my pillow as I heard Thomas retching and thought about Baby not being the first to experience gastrointestinal distress from my meatloaf. Who lets their dog take a dump in someone's home and doesn't clean it up? I thought. Thomas lasted about five minutes on his own before heading back upstairs for inhalations of odor-free oxygen. "I can't take it."

"I thought you were a nurse," I said. "Shouldn't bodily fluids be your thing?"

"I thought you were a principal," he shot back. "I remember how often the question of the day was, 'what's that smell'?"

"Yeah, but the custodians took care of that stuff," I whined. "I can't do it. I'll throw up. Why aren't Joe and Dorothy – okay, Joe anyway – cleaning it up?"

"I haven't wanted to deal with them, but I guess I better go wake up Joe. Dammit, I can't believe they had to bring that stupid dog."

"Lemme know what he says," I said with a big yawn. In my defense, it was really early for a Saturday, like 6 AM.

A few minutes later, Thomas returned with even more alarming news. It turned out that Baby wasn't to blame for the fecal explosions downstairs. "Oh, my God," he said. "It was Dorothy."

"Whoa," I said. "How did that happen?"

"Joe just said she's sick. When I asked why she had to be sick in three different rooms, he didn't answer."

"Where is she now?" I asked.

"He's got her in the shower. He says she's finished."

"Well, that's good. Do you have any medicine for her?"

"Probably, but I doubt she needs it anymore."

Thomas wrapped a towel around his mouth and nose and headed downstairs again, this time with Joe there to help. I was relieved that Ben was spending the night at a neighbor's house, but of all days for Alison to wake up early, it had to be this one. She tiptoed into our bedroom in her footie pajamas, her blonde bed-hair sticking out in all directions, a sly smile on her face as she realized it was still early in the morning. I concluded that the situation downstairs was not something I wanted her six-year-old brain to have to process and came up with an idea to keep her upstairs.

"Hey, Lambchop. What are you doing up so early? Come get in bed with me, and we'll sleep some more." Nothing doing. She was bright-eyed and bushy-tailed, so another strategy was needed. I said, "I've got an idea for something fun this morning. Would you like to get in the bathtub and play for a while?"

It worked like a charm. Alison was accustomed to bathing at night, so the novelty was irresistible. She splashed around until her little fingers and toes were wrinkled, a good 45 minutes. Before she got out, I went downstairs to see if the coast was clear. Thomas had opened all the windows and set the ceiling fans at full speed. Dorothy was sitting out on the deck with her hair drying in the sun, drinking a cup of coffee. Her tiny body was wrapped in a towel. I whispered to Thomas, "Why isn't she dressed?"

"She didn't bring a change of clothes. We washed what she was wearing and now they're in the dryer," he said.

"I guess I'll keep Alison upstairs a while longer." Seeing her aunt on the deck almost nude would bring up difficult questions. Before I went back upstairs, I checked in with Dorothy. Stepping outside, I took a seat beside her and patted her hand. "Hi," was all I said.

"I made a mess," she said, her voice so plaintive that I had to remind myself to take a deep breath.

"It's okay, Dorothy. It's okay. Are you feeling better now?"

"I guess."

"Do you want more coffee? Or some toast?"

"No." She stared in another direction and I decided to give her some privacy, because she seemed to need it and because I was at a loss for what to say next.

Much to Joe's credit, he ended up cleaning up the mess mostly by himself. I was surprised and touched by this act of responsibility and apparent devotion to his elderly wife. They left soon after Dorothy's clothes came out of the dryer, before Alison came downstairs to say goodbye. After they left, Thomas and I wondered aloud about how things were going with them in the house by themselves in Indianapolis, how isolated they were. We realized that we needed to check on them regularly, make sure they were okay.

The next day, I picked up Alison after she had spent some time at Shirley's place. As soon as she got in the car, she demanded to know, "Where did Aunt Dorothy poop in the house?"

I closed my eyes and mentally cursed at Thomas for telling Shirley. "What? Did Grandma tell you that?"

"She said she crapped all over." Thank you, Shirley. Thank you so much.

Joe and Dorothy didn't return to our house until the

holidays that year. As Thanksgiving approached, my sister and I compared notes about Thanksgiving plans. She asked me how many I was expecting and I replied without irony, "Twelve. Thirteen if Baby comes." I realized my resignation in that moment, and I just didn't have it in me to care anymore.

I set the tables for twelve, knowing that Baby wouldn't want his own chair, and entertained the futile hope that Joe and Dorothy would leave him at home. In a way, they did. When they arrived empty-handed, I blurted out, "Where's Baby?"

"Dead," said Joe. "Died yesterday, and we buried him last night."

Dorothy was shaken and inconsolable, and ate by herself in the kitchen. I wondered if this would be the last little dog named Baby. Much to my surprise, I was heartbroken, too.

Phone message:

Melissa? Hi. I want you to tell Tom that I was watchin' Ofrah today and they said you could eat bacon even if you got the gout. I'm pretty sure that's what they said. But Tom says no more of that since I got the gout. Barbeque, too. They said on Ofrah the only things you can't eat are things I don't like anyways. Like liver and kidneys and brains and herrings — is them fish? Hey. Will you pick up some barbeque at Kroger? This is Shirley, in case you're wonderin'.

37

PARENTAL JUDGMENT

Every once in a while when I was particularly annoyed with Shirley's overindulgence of the children, I realized it could be worse. I was pretty sure I wouldn't tolerate lectures about what I was doing wrong as a parent. My suspicions were confirmed one evening when Ben attended his first middle school party. He had changed schools in seventh grade and was making new friends. The invitation – from a girl named Jolie, whose email address started with "babygrrrl" – evoked simultaneous thrills and anxiety. He really wanted to go. Rather than going to Grandma's for our typical Friday night routine, he chose this foray into the world of middle school social life.

"Gosh, Ben," I said a few days later while navigating Jolie's father's directions, "I don't know this neighborhood at all." We ended up in a remote area in the early evening darkness of late autumn. After driving past the driveway several times, we determined it must be the place by process of elimination. There was no address or sign or balloon floating above the mailbox to help us out. We were accustomed to houses like ours that couldn't be seen from the road, but puzzled when all we found was a barn at the end of the driveway. There was a lighted path just beyond the barn, but we didn't see anyone around. We looked at each other as we sat in the car.

"Maybe this isn't it," I said. Ben looked out the window and said he didn't know. At that moment, a group of about seven or eight girls poured out of the barn, saying, "Ben is here! Hi, Ben! Ben, Ben, Ben!" As he stepped out of the car, they surrounded him with this chant, jumping up and down. One girl held her elbows akimbo and performed a cheerleader high kick.

"Come on, Ben!" they shouted as they pulled him into the

barn. Ben laughed uneasily, and I followed behind thinking this was odd. When we stepped into the barn, we could see different colors of light bulbs had been strung and there was a boom box plugged in. One of the girls hit the button on the CD player and suddenly they all began to dance in a circle around him singing to shocking lyrics that included, "Lick it, baby, oh yeah." My head began to swim. Ben stepped out of the circle when the song ended, smiling tightly and still gripping the brightly wrapped present for Jolie in front of him. He looked at me for help.

"So, hey girls," I said, trying to sound smooth. "Which one of you is celebrating a birthday?"

Jolie waved her hands and said, "Me!"

"Well, happy birthday, Jolie! What a great barn. Where's your house? And your parents?" Returning to her gyrations, Jolie managed to point toward the path. "By the campfire up there," she shouted above the music.

"Oh! Well, that sounds fun," I shouted back. "Are other parents there, too?"

"Just Skylar's."

"Okay. Well, I think I'll go say hello," I said as I gave Ben a questioning look. He stepped out of the barn into the safe quiet and looked up at me wide-eyed.

"Do you think any more boys are coming?" I asked, no longer trying to be cool.

"I heard them say this other guy is coming in a while," he whispered back.

"What do you want to do, honey? Seems pretty weird in there." Now we both were laughing from the jolt of the scene.

"I don't know!" he said. "If I leave, I'll look dumb."

"What if I stayed nearby at the campfire?" This was a shaky offer from me, not knowing what I was going to find there.

"That looks dumb, too!"

I looked at him and suggested that we both take a breath.

We inhaled and exhaled and still felt uncertain. "Tell you what," I said. "I'll go say hi to Jolie's parents and come back down in just a couple of minutes. That will give you some time to think about what you want to do."

The tiny group of parents around the campfire wasn't very welcoming, not that I expected them to dance around me or anything like that. I had to ask which of them were Jolie's parents. After complimenting their barn and campfire, there was an awkward pause.

"Okay!" I said, a little too enthusiastically. "What time should I be back for Ben?"

The mom and dad looked at each other. "Whenever is fine," one said. "Most of the girls are spending the night."

"Are there any more boys coming?"

They laughed and shrugged their shoulders. I left hoping Ben hadn't settled on my offer to hang out at the campfire in the few minutes I was gone. But I wasn't going to leave him there without a plan. He was standing just inside the door of the barn by himself now. We kept our distance from the group and murmured a few ideas to each other. He was still fretting about what it would look like to leave as soon as he arrived.

"The only place I know around here is Wal-Mart," I said. "I'll go there for a while and come back in 45 minutes. How does that sound?" Ben didn't have a cell phone yet, so we weren't dependent on the stream-of-consciousness communication that would later become common between parents and children. My idea sounded good to him.

I walked around Wal-Mart absentmindedly, relishing my ability to think about nothing. Having completed my Ph.D. in recent months, I was enjoying the luxury of time frivolously spent after years of scheduling every minute of every day to complete this task. I had been offered a visiting professor position in the special education program in the IU School of Education, later to be funded as a clinical professor position, a job I was eligible for as a recent graduate because it wasn't tenure-track. This felt like a burden lifted and my relief over the question of what I'd be doing next was considerable.

When I returned to the party shortly after I left, several more boys had joined the group and the girls' attention wasn't focused on Ben alone. Things had settled down considerably. Ben seemed at ease playing a game of tag in the yard and quite willing to throw me under the bus. "Mom. What are you doing here already?" I felt my right eyebrow rise involuntarily and beckoned to him to speak to me privately.

"Everything's okay now," he said, dropping the fake attitude when it was just the two of us. "Why don't you come back in an hour?"

"Okay, will you be ready to go then?"

"Yeah."

"Will you pretend you didn't ask me to, like you did just now?"

He laughed. "Sorry."

It didn't make sense to drive all the way home, so I went to Shirley's apartment because I didn't want to go back to Wal-Mart. I knew I'd need to leave her place soon after I got there, but hadn't made plans for anything else anyway. Thomas and Alison were there, too, hanging out and watching television. I came in laughing and shaking my head. "You won't believe what I just saw," I said. "I don't think we're ready for this." Shirley's reaction to what I relayed about the party was surprising.

She glared at me and spoke in an accusatory tone. "You shouldn't have left him there. What was you thinking?"

My temper flared instantaneously. Following a pregnant pause, I said, a little too quietly, "What do you mean?" Thomas picked up on the vibe and was on point right away.

"I mean anything could happen! You don't know! That

wasn't good judgment."

"Not good judgment?" I enunciated, louder this time. "You're telling me I don't have good judgment? Let's talk about that."

I found myself being escorted by my husband into the corridor outside Shirley's apartment before I could continue. "Whoa," he said. "Let's stop and take a breath."

"Do not tell me to take a breath! I can't believe her acting superior about good judgment," I spat. "She signed a permission slip for you to hand over at the border when you went to Mexico by yourself! When you were 17! For a month! I'd like to talk about that!"

He dropped the soothing tone when he saw it was having the opposite effect of what he intended. "I know, but she sees things differently now. And she's just scared."

I ignored this. "She never knew where you were or what you were doing at Ben's age, night or day! And from what you've told me, she should have! You and Joe used to hop train cars when you were in third grade! And tried to explode shotgun shells when you were in kindergarten!"

Thomas nodded his head. "It was different then."

"I will not listen to this from her. She helped Joe grow pot in the backyard!"

"Okay, she just knew about it. She didn't help out that much." He paused. "Do you want me to go get him?"

"And leave me here with your mother?"

"Right. Do you want me to go with you? We can swing by afterward to get Alison, and Mom will feel better knowing he's okay."

"Or I could go and you could tell her not to worry about it because your wife knows what she's doing." Like I knew what I was doing. We didn't alter our plans.

I could tell Ben was ready to go when I got there. I saw

him sneak an eyeball-rolling look at his friends when he said goodbye, something about which I chose not to comment once we were in the car. When I asked him how it went, he seemed happy to have gone and happier to be leaving. Details were not forthcoming, and I thought about whether this was how it would be henceforward. He turned on the radio and looked out the window – probably talked out, I figured. He did look over after a couple of minutes. "Thanks, Mom," he said.

Our affable silence got me thinking about my irritation with Shirley. I had been dangerously close to starting a sentence with, "Listen here, old woman…" and I wasn't proud of it. Grudgingly, I thought about how hard it must have been to know how to parent when she'd grown up unparented. And that when Thomas was an adolescent, she was working full time in the Kroger wholesale bakery, taking care of Walter's parents, and bringing her mother home from the hospital every week on her day off, as well as visiting her on Sundays. I was pretty sure I would never do anything as crazy as allowing my teenage son to drive to Mexico by himself without plans or a single acquaintance to look out for him. But it was a shaky moment as I realized that good judgment wasn't guaranteed, even if you'd been raised by great parents like mine.

I stopped by Shirley's place again as a peace offering. Thomas and Alison had left, so she was there alone. "Was it fun?" she asked.

"It was okay," Ben said with a shrug.

"Did everybody dance?"

"Sort of."

The party had been different from parties I attended as a 12-year-old, not to mention ones of Shirley's youth at the orphanage. Admitting to myself I had no idea what I was doing half the time, I accepted Shirley's parting squeeze of my shoulder as an apology, the best she could offer. I patted her hand as Ben and I picked up our coats to leave.

38

TELL ABOUT THAT TIME

Hanging out in Shirley's apartment could be fascinating; you never knew what direction the conversation might go, even when it had a predictable start. From the time Shirley moved to Bloomington, her entire social life had centered on her conversations in the dining room of Cedar Hills. One major topic was what various adult children and grandchildren were accomplishing in the world. The first time she was interested in what I did for a living was when she needed a response to people asking this question.

Shirley, Alison, and I were hanging out at her apartment, sitting on the couch with our feet propped up on the coffee table. "I told them you work at IU. Patsy's gonna retire at IU. Have you ever seen her? She works in the office. Tell me again what you do, 'cause people keep asking." Sometimes I wondered if she forgot what I did on purpose, this not being the first time she'd asked me since she'd moved to Bloomington.

I waited a beat for the back-handed compliment that would follow what she was asking. "They say you's so pretty and sweet. I tell them you's just okay."

"Oh, Shirley. You're too good to me. So what I do is teach people how to be teachers." If I said any more than that, it would be too much.

"I told 'em you was workin' on your disposition, too. They want to know how that's comin'." Regarding my doctoral dissertation, I smiled and said, "It's actually done." Then regarding my disposition, I added, "But it's probably not going to get any better than it is right now."

"Okay, I'll tell 'em that."

Shirley gazed at her bare feet. Each of the toes curled down severely and the nails were yellowed and thick. "Them are called hammer toes and they's ugly," she said. She held them up for us to examine, which we had done many times before.

"Can you wear those sandals that have the thing between your toes?" she asked Alison and me.

We reminded her again that, yes, we could.

"Well, I can't. It just bothers me; I can't explain it. But my feet have always been trouble. When I was 16, I had surgery on them at the Home. That was the thing about living there. If anything was wrong with you, they'd fix it, just like that," and she snapped her fingers. "And it was on the government's dime."

She looked her feet over some more. "They cut the liters in my toes to stretch them out, but it didn't work." I knew better than to ask again what liters were. Shirley didn't know the last time I asked, and I was willing to bet this was still the case.

Shirley sighed. "Sometimes things happen, and they never get better. But not always. When Tom was a little boy, he almost lost his arm in the neighbor's washer wringer. But he was lucky there weren't no permanent damage. I 'member hearin' him screaming from down the street." Thomas walked in right on cue and clutched his arm involuntarily when he overheard what Shirley was saying. She did not stop to greet him.

"Remember our neighbor, Gertie? Gertie Gill. I 'member her lyin' on the couch with all them flat curlers on her head. They was brown and flat. And she had a monkey, a spider monkey, climbin' all over her. She was dirty. This bird was always flyin' around her house, too."

Thomas shook his head. "Say what you want about Gertie Gill, but she saved my arm." He paused. "I remember I just wanted to touch it, the wringer, and see what it felt like. It grabbed my arm so fast, and I couldn't pull it out. Gertie came running and hit this big red button to stop it. If it had gotten to my elbow, well..." he shivered at the thought. Then he laughed.

"Hey, remember her son?"

Thomas looked at me. "Her son would ride his motorcycle through the house, full speed, in the front door and out the back. One time he hit his dad." The story continued as I tried to process this. Alison had a neutral expression on her face. I hoped she wasn't paying attention.

Shirley said, "Oh, yeah, his dad was a drunk. He was always movin' slow." Thomas was laughing harder now. "Right, and Gertie Gill's son hit him with his motorcycle and he flew straight up in the air. I was so scared when I saw it; I just ran away as fast as I could. I don't even know what happened." Hardly another Pleasant Valley Sunday, I thought, when the old Monkees song came to mind.

Shirley nodded her head. "She was seein' somebody."

I asked, "Cheating on her husband that was a drunk?"

"Yeah, and she would send Brenda across the tracks with notes for him, pay her fifty cents each time. I was so mad when I found out."

I tried to steer us back. "What do you remember about the operation on your feet, Shirley?"

"Well, it was supposed to correct the tendons, but it didn't work. I had to stay in the infirmary for a year!" She paused and laughed. "At the same time of my surgery, a group of boys was in there for circumstision." I kept my eyes trained on Shirley, knowing Alison was looking to see if I would correct her grandmother's pronunciation of this procedure. "They weren't babies neither. And you should have seen them cryin' and runnin' all over the place with band-aids on their you-know." Alison was familiar with the term, circumcision, but still found it endlessly fascinating. She began to chant, "Penis, penis, penis!"

Shirley looked at her granddaughter, all of 7 years old. "Children know so much these days. She knew words like vagina when she was only a baby. When I was a girl, I didn't even know

234

I had a vagina! And I sure didn't know about penises! We called them weenies back then."

There was nothing like Grandma's version of an old time story.

From the 1937 annual report of the orphanage Board of Trustees to the Governor:

Physician's Report

General Surgery

In this branch of our department we had the removal of tonsils for sixty-two patients; circumcisions for fifty-one patients; nine appendicitis operations, all acute cases; one operation for removal of diseased thyroid bone; the removal of the distal phalanx of a finger, necessitated by infection.

Orthopedic and Bone Surgery

In this division we treated four cases of fracture and fore-arm with good recovery in all cases.....One patient was operated for deformity of toes and one for a deformed elbow, both had improvement.

Phone message:

Melissa, tell Tom not to transfer all that money from savings to checking. I'm havin' a hard time tellin' 3s and 8s apart and they's a big difference between them two. This is Shirley.

39

DRAWING THE LINE

Throughout her preschool years and now in second grade, Alison continued to spend a lot of time after school at Shirley's apartment. I would prevail upon her to pick up toys before we went home, though I knew this was a losing battle. Shirley would say it was her place, so why didn't I leave well enough alone. Often I only had Alison put away a couple of items before we called it a day, accepting the mounds of clutter as the norm.

I had to admit that problems like these were minor when I would see how much fun they were having. Shirley received positive attention for having a family around, this being coveted more than any possession or privilege in a senior residence home. She was the belle of the ball when we set up a table for Alison to sell Girl Scout cookies as a Brownie, with Shirley bossing the other residents around like she owned the place. "What do ya mean, you can't buy cookies 'cause of your diabetes?" she'd say. "How 'bout that cake you ate at Lou Elle's birthday party?" When 98-year-old Harold approached the table at a snail's pace with his aid supporting him by the elbow, Shirley said too loudly, "He's got no business ordering something that's gonna take six weeks to get here."

"Shh," I said, and looked at Alison to remind her of her manners, despite Grandma's. My expectation to be kind was challenged when he leaned over to sign his name on the order form and a long string of drool slowly made its way to the paper. Shirley showed her disgust by sputtering something unintelligible, then used the napkin under her coffee cup to wipe it up.

As it turned out, the six-week delivery time indeed had been ambitious for Harold. Shirley was not charitable about his passing. "Everybody's sayin', it was such a shock, and I say,

'Why? He was almost a hundred! We's all gonna go the same way.' He was 98 years old and I don't feel like goin' on about it or sheddin' a bunch of tears. He had no business makin' that order."

"Well, I just wanna know who's gonna pay for all these cookies," was what Alison had to say, focused on her chances of earning her troop's top cookie-seller badge.

There were times when I talked to Shirley about giving Alison too much free rein of the building. The hallways and common areas were always deserted after 6:00 p.m., and my daughter, who was never afraid of the dark, would happily wander around the big building to her heart's content while Shirley, having changed into her gown for the night, watched television in her apartment. Alison would inspect the latest collection of donated clothes to be given away, kept in a box in the laundry room, picking out stained and ratty nightgowns to bring home and wear in place of cute sets of pajamas I bought for her. Or she'd move around chess pieces on a board in the library area, likely left out to continue an all-important match between two of the residents the next day.

Once I came to pick Alison up around 7:00 and got nervous when I didn't find her right away. The place was so quiet, and all the lights were out. Finally, I saw a small light down the hall in the community gathering room. There, I found her, all by herself in front of the computer that was there for the residents' use. She was so fixated on what she had found, which was a video of childbirth up close, that she was taken by surprise when she saw me. I couldn't help laughing. "What in the world, sweetheart? What have you found?"

When I saw her distress at being caught in this clandestine act, I suggested that I join her and we could watch it together. Upon our return to Shirley, I stressed, again, that Alison shouldn't be allowed to prowl around by herself at any time, but especially at night. Shirley would promise to comply, but the trouble was less about her agreement and more about her willingness to stand up to her tyrannical granddaughter.

This problem came to a head a year or two later when Alison was about eight. She had befriended a child named Macy, the granddaughter of one of the Cedar Hills maids, who regularly accompanied her grandmother to work and was allowed to run amok like Alison. There had been an incident, which neither Alison nor Shirley wanted to talk about. A couple of days later, I had picked up Shirley to take her to an appointment. I knew she was stalling when she acted like nothing had happened and asked me for the umpteenth time if I knew that her friend, Patsy, was retiring from "the office" at Indiana University. Then she told me about their dinner the night before.

"Last night, Patsy and I was in the dining room and they brought out this cheesy ball all puffed up, a cheese puff, and it was BURNT. I mean black on top. Poor Patsy tried to cut the top off, but it was burnt inside, too! I was lucky. I was eating a taco that Tom brought me. I guess I could've gave Patsy some of my taco, but I only had one and that was for me. I told Patsy to complain. And Missy, that new manager, had the nerve to come by our table and say, 'This meal was awesome.' Well, it wasn't *awesome*, it was burnt. You see, it was a puffed up piece of cheese, a cheese puff. And it was black on top and that was what we was supposed to eat."

After an awkward pause, she said, "Alison said you wasn't gonna let her come over so much no more." Her chin was raised, a clear sign that she was challenging me.

"We didn't say that, Shirley. Well, maybe Tom said it when he was so mad at her Sunday night, but he didn't mean it, and Alison knows that."

"Well, I been worryin' you think I done lost it."

"We don't think that," I said.

"Or got the old timer's."

"We don't think that either."

"Well, maybe I do 'cause I just don't know why I let her get on that bus, and I knew right away that I shouldn't've."

When Thomas had come to pick Alison up the previous Sunday evening, he found his mother desperate and distraught after letting her young granddaughter get on a bus, without any adult supervision, heading out to "some Pentecostal church," the name and location of which she had not thought to determine. It took some doing to find out where Alison had gone with Macy. After a long trip, driving too fast on winding country roads, Thomas arrived and threw open the door of the church, only to realize that it had no foyer and he was walking directly into the service.

Alison had turned crimson upon her early retrieval and departure. She stomped out, wearing her Old Navy Halloween-themed tee shirt with a picture of a Dalmatian dressed like the devil. Having just missed the baptisms, she was furious, not contrite, and Thomas told me the ride home had been unpleasant. That night, after processing with Alison what had happened, why it was wrong, why it should never happen again, and determining a consequence for her misbehavior, she had described the superiority of this church. It was apparent to Thomas and me that we could lose her to fundamentalism based on fascination alone, ripped from the steady and inclusive arms of our Unitarian Universalist church. She was enthralled by the waving of arms in the air, the laying on of hands, the public declarations of faith, and the tears and hugs, as long as she remained an observer and no one hugged her. Macy had told her about speaking in tongues and nothing – nothing – in Alison's church could ever compare to this weekly drama. I had sighed after Alison's emphatic statements, having gone through something similar when Ben's friend, Conner, had gone to church with us one day and pronounced that it wasn't a real church because they didn't talk about being saved. It seemed that when it came to religion, our children, not unlike other children, were highly suggestible.

Alison's misbehavior at Cedar Hills, too often sanctioned by her grandmother, albeit reluctantly, brought out my declaration as the alpha authority. I had gone through this with Ben, too, although it hadn't been called for as much since he spent less time at Cedar Hills than Alison. "Listen to me," I said in my most serious tone. "When Grandma looks unsure about whether you should do something you want to do, that means no. It doesn't matter that she can't say it. I'm saying it. You're taking advantage of how hard it is for her to say no to you and you have to cut it out." It wasn't a conversation; it was a decree. Regardless of how short my tenure as a school principal had been, I could draw on the experience of laying down the law when I needed it most and, for the most part, it worked. In situations like this it worked for Thomas, too, since he was never going to be that kind of parent. He was cookies and I was vegetables, and when we worked as a team, we were happy to remain in our comfort zones. The unfortunate flip side of that dynamic was when we weren't working together, we each became more extreme with our tendencies. I became the sergeant-at-arms, and Thomas decided ice cream for dinner was perfectly acceptable. Most of the time, however, we were a great combination. Although I sometimes wished I could be as playful as Thomas, I had to admit that I was more content coming up with new chore lists, point systems for earning a trampoline, and things like that.

Back in the car with Shirley, I turned to her. "I know you won't let her talk you into something like that again. And Alison knows she was wrong to push so hard to go."

"Everybody makes mistakes!" she exclaimed.

I nodded my head. "Yes."

"Even you!"

"Yes."

There was a pause and Shirley asked, "Well, when?"

"What?"

"When did you make a mistake?"

"This morning when I got up and yelled at everybody." I didn't add that this had followed twenty minutes of early morning meditation, including two recitations of the Prayer of St. Francis.

"Oh," she laughed. "Hey, did you know that Patsy retired?"

Despite putting the fear of my wrath in Alison regarding her behavior, I remained ambivalent about her safety in Shirley's care. I knew Shirley would do anything to protect her, anything except deny her granddaughter's demands. We're lucky nothing tragic ever happened when she allowed Alison to run around the complex alone or play by the decorative fountain and pond in front of the building and so close to a busy street. And I have reason to believe there was a dumpster diving incident, although this was never confirmed. Now that the stage of my life when I needed childcare is over, I think about the risks that were taken and balance them against the benefits of structuring our family time this way. I'm grateful Alison was able to spend so much of her childhood with a grandmother who adored her, and that she never suffered anything calamitous as a result of that adoration.

Upheaval

40

IN TRANSIT

In the years after Shirley moved to Bloomington, Joe and Dorothy slipped into a kind of dark hole. They moved from above the garage into what Thomas fondly called "the big house," but they were lonely and isolated from the outside world without Shirley and Walter. After the last dog named Baby died in 2004, it was clear that Dorothy could no longer care for a pet and there would be no more animals rescued. This source of joy in her life was over. Now it was 2005 and, in his fifties now, Joe watched Dorothy, who was in her eighties, sink into dementia. He was constantly afraid that she was endangering their lives by forgetting to turn the gas stove off, among other things.

Shirley, now 85, stayed connected to them by paying their bills, which I worried about, knowing she was burning through the savings she needed to live on. She paid their utility bills, gasoline bills, medical bills, grocery bills, and more, in addition to her own rent and expenses. "Her savings are dwindling," I said to Thomas, and he nodded his head in that way that meant he knew something needed to be done, but probably not today, and tomorrow wasn't looking so good either.

Certain we should be checking on Joe and Dorothy since no one had heard from them in weeks, I asked Shirley for status reports. "Phone's probably cut off," was Shirley's theory. "He hasn't sent me a bill in a while. Probably don't got any stamps neither. I bet he's sellin' off them street lamps Walter put up in the yard, remember them? You was with us when he bought 'em." I cringed at the memory of Walter, Shirley, 4-year-old Ben, and me, detouring away from the highway for hours to buy these massive street lamps from some dealer when we were on our way to the Covered Bridge Festival in Parke County.

"He's probably sellin' the pots and pans I left behind, too, and anything else he can get his hands on." She laughed. "I think some of Walter's pills was still in the medicine cabinet when I left!"

"And there's no way he's going to get a job?" I asked, in spite of knowing full well the answer. Joe thought part-time jobs at places like McDonald's were beneath him, when the irony was that they were likely too challenging for his limited skills and mental health.

There was one time, many years before, when Joe and Dorothy surprised us all by trying to act like self-sufficient adults. They moved to northern Indiana where Lee had gotten Joe a job in one of his factories. Joe and Dorothy lived in an apartment and even paid their own bills. But it only lasted a few months. Joe showed up at the factory one day to announce he'd found another job that would pay him twenty cents more per hour. He quit without considering the likelihood that his new boss would not be as interested in his success as his former boss. It wasn't long before the grand experiment had been declared a failure and Joe and Dorothy moved back to Shirley and Walter's garage in Indianapolis.

I began to push Thomas to go check on them, having conjured in my mind terrible things, like Joe snapping over Dorothy's care, maybe a suicide pact between them, or a murder-suicide combination, with blood and stench still undetected by the neighbors. One day I threw a fit to get through to him. "Okay, I'm going and you're going to look like a scumbag if I find them dead," I said.

Thomas was unfazed by any danger to his image, but knew

it was time to pay them a visit, unannounced since the phone actually had been shut off. Although they were alive, he found them in crisis. Joe had not known what to do when Dorothy fell and broke her hip. Thinking she had sprained her ankle, he put her on the sofa, where she had sat in excruciating pain for days. Thomas never went into full detail about what he had found there. He mentioned that the bathroom was too disgusting to even step into. He had carried Dorothy to his car as she screamed in anger that she didn't want to go and had taken her to the emergency room, sure he'd be suspected of elder abuse when it came out how long ago she'd incurred the injury.

There were no abuse accusations, but in the emergency room it became clear that Dorothy would not be living at home any more. Everyone thought she wouldn't make it through the surgery to repair her hip, but she did. We placed her in a nursing home near Shirley and Walter's house so Joe could visit her each day. It was euphemistically named the Cozy Manor. Thomas felt awful about all of it and agreed that we should see it as a stop-gap measure.

"We need to move Joe to Bloomington," I said.

"I know, but he won't want to leave Dorothy."

"Yeah, but he can't be in the house alone," I said. "He told me he gets scared. Since we can only handle one thing at a time, let's move him here, then see what to do about Dorothy after that."

We began to make plans with Joe to move him to Bloomington, which was a complicated process, including getting him evaluated and diagnosed for the first time since he was a child and applying for disability funds. Thomas and his brothers cleaned out the house so that it could be sold and Thomas found Joe a small apartment in town. He moved him in and set him up for weekly appointments at a center for behavioral health care. We did not try to get him a job. Shirley acknowledged the wisdom of this decision, saying, "If Joe works, he'll bring people home with him, and they'll all end up with crabs."

Joe was available to take his mother to appointments and to pick up items like Lucky Charms and Cocoa Puffs cereal at the grocery store for her, along with a regular KFC carryout order, which was a welcome relief to Thomas and me. After a while, he stopped making regular trips to visit Dorothy in Indianapolis, saying he couldn't afford the gas.

Dorothy's Medicare began to run out, and it was clear we'd need to do some research to understand what to do next. She sank into a deep depression at the Cozy Manor. I was alarmed by her despondency and started visiting whenever I could get away, once a week when I was working with my students in their field experiences in Indianapolis. I would find her under the covers of her bed, grey, toothless, and in a fetal position. She had become so small, like a sick and helpless baby who longed to return to the womb. The nurses said it was hard to get her to the dining room for meals and once she was there, she wouldn't eat more than a couple of bites of food. It was a terrible situation.

Remembering that she loved Native American artifacts, I once brought her feathers instead of flowers, but couldn't tell if she noticed them. I would look for things to say after long pauses as we gazed at each other, me smiling, Dorothy waiting for me to speak. I asked her the same questions every time I visited, about her meals, whether she could eat and how she was sleeping. I asked if she watched the television that was always on, if she had favorite shows, if she knew she had just had a birthday and what she thought about that. Sometimes I'd ask several questions at once, even when I was telling myself to stop, or I'd ask a question and explain what I meant before she had time to comprehend it. I was so out of my league. I'd talk about the new year and how amazing it was that it was 2005. Sometimes she would look like she had something to say and I'd stop to hear it. Usually, nothing was forthcoming or she'd mumble something and even repeat it when I moved in closer to try to understand. Each time this happened, the disconnection felt profound and I'd move on to the next trivial topic, sure that I was Nurse Ratchet from *One Flew Over the Cuckoo's Nest* or anyone else who patronized the infirm and talked too loudly. I tried reading to her. Remembering her expressed desire to be a monkey swinging through the trees, I thought *The Jungle Book*, by Rudyard Kipling seemed like a good choice, although I couldn't tell if Dorothy was listening. Mostly, I was keenly aware of my life force in this hushed and sour crypt where sadness and confusion permeated the space between us. Sometimes I imagined my energy was blinding in contrast to the lack of it all around.

Dorothy's roommate usually spent her time answering an imaginary telephone. My friend, Maura, who once met me there to offer support, quietly dubbed her Flaky Florence and I laughed in spite of myself. I was grateful that Maura was upbeat and intent on lightening my mood. She watched me kiss Dorothy on the forehead to say goodbye, telling her I hoped she slept well and that I'd be back soon. As we left, I complained that I didn't know what to say to Dorothy, at which point Maura smiled, companionably put her arm around me, and offered more authentic examples of topics and questions. "How about, 'Looks like some bad karma playing out here, Dorothy, what do you think?'"

There was one day that Dorothy exhibited a rare burst of energy, surely chemically induced. She talked and talked, laughing at her own jokes, none of which I understood. Almost everything she said was unintelligible except the sentence that rang out loud and clear in the commons area as she confided to me, "He don't do me in bed no more." Later, she spat and yelled "pussy" at people who walked by, also painfully understandable. I took deep breaths and tried to make sense of this sordid mess. Each time I left, I wondered if I'd ever see her again and silently wished her a safe journey.

I talked to Thomas about moving Dorothy to Bloomington. After all that had gone into moving his mother and brother and selling the house, he was not enthusiastic. Additionally, the challenges of day to day care of his mother were increasing. He had come from Shirley's place, where he had posted signs everywhere, saying, CALL THOMAS BEFORE YOU TAKE A PILL. He had tried putting out pills for one day at a time, since no organizational system prevented her from taking her Friday pills on Thursday, etc. That day, he had set up her pills in two different cereal bowls, one green and one yellow, to help with instructions when she called. But later in the afternoon, she left a message, saying, "Well, Joe come over, and we was hungry. So we made popcorn and we used them bowls on the counter. And when we was washin' his bowl, well, up floated one of them pills. That's when I remembered why them bowls was sittin' out there. I don't know how else to say it. I think Joe done ate the other pills with the popcorn. Does he need to go to the emergency room? Also, you gotta come over and give me some more pills."

Maybe he was tired of being the family member who did the lion's share of all this work. Maybe he was just tired. But we'd finally found a place near us that would accept Dorothy on Medicaid and in her advanced state of dementia. I could have given him some time to get with the program, but kept thinking about Dorothy stuck in the Cozy Manor all alone and couldn't help but push the matter. All the time. "So, what would you want your family to do with you?" I asked Thomas.

"Shoot me."

"No, really."

"Shoot me."

"We can't leave her there anymore. If she's here, we'll have to pay better attention to what she needs."

"Exactly."

"I'm serious."

"Me, too."

I chose to ignore him and proceed as if we were on the same page. "The nursing home said they'd pay to transfer her in an ambulance."

Thomas shook his head. "Well, they lied. Or they're morons who probably believed it when they said it, but it isn't true. We'd have to pay for it, and it's a lot of money."

"I'm not sure if that's true, but if it is, I guess that's what we have to do. She's a limp noodle, but unpredictable. She's going to be disoriented. You don't want to be responsible for her while driving."

"Not a problem," Thomas said. "You're the only one she recognizes these days, so you should sit in the back seat with her and hold her up. Joe would be worthless, so it's gotta be you. It's only an hour."

"I'm not doing it." I don't know what had come over me, given the significant progress we had just made. "She needs an ambulance and if you try to drive her, I'm not helping."

Two days later, I was at a conference out of town and called home to check in. Thomas told me that Dorothy was safely ensconced at the Sunrise Care Center, her new home in Bloomington. I couldn't believe it. He had gone by himself to the nursing home, put Dorothy in the car, and completed the uneventful trip all for the cost of a half tank of gas. I went to see her when I was back in town and asked her how the trip went. Her eyes sparkled when she uttered one word: "Fun."

I acknowledged being wrong about the ambulance and was relieved to have saved a thousand dollars or whatever Thomas had threatened it would be. Thomas was similarly apologetic about moving Dorothy. "I get it," he said. "I just haven't wanted to face it. She's going to be better off here – this is the right thing to do. Maybe she can learn to walk again." My eyes widened. "Okay, well, we should at least buy her a new set of dentures."

Alison was on the periphery of this discussion and interjected here. "No, remember when Grandma spent a lot of money on that set of new teeth and she didn't even take care of 'em?" Thomas and I exchanged a look that acknowledged too many adult conversations around our 9-year-old. For good measure, she added, "And I'm not visiting her if she's going to lick me."

Dorothy was happy in her new home, really happy. Not sad or agitated like before. She still reminded me of a baby, but now she smiled beatifically with a toothless and otherworldly grin. The Sunrise Care Center was a dramatic improvement over the Cozy Manor. At the case conference, her caretakers asked what Dorothy's favorite art medium was, and if she'd like to plant tomatoes with assistance in the raised beds of their courtyard. It was clear that she was the nurses' favorite, probably because she was happy. She didn't say much to them, but she smiled all the time, and they babied her in the sweetest ways, braiding her hair and feeding her ice cream throughout the day. At one point, I asked, "How many times is she eating ice cream in a day?" Angie, the head nurse, looked a bit defensive. "Eight or nine times," she said. "She's so tiny. She needs the calories, and ice cream makes her happy." I loved this 'why not' attitude and felt better about Dorothy's care than I had in a long time.

One day, I brought in a photograph of Dorothy as a young woman to show the nurses. It had been a tiny black and white picture of Joe's that had remained sharp when I had it blown up to a 5X7 size. Dorothy is a stunner in it. She is wearing stiletto heel shoes and a stylish dress that shows off what looks like a 20-inch waist. Her hair is long and dark with straight bangs cut high on her forehead – very Betty Page. Although it wasn't easy to identify in this picture, she was standing in front of the Alamo in San Antonio, the year unknown. Everyone's reactions were beyond satisfying. They gasped and took it from me, walking from station to station to share and gush over. I couldn't tell if Dorothy understood that it was her in the picture, but she wore a shy smile that told me maybe she did.

Gone were the days when I struggled with what to say or do when I visited. Dorothy talked to me now, albeit in language that was mostly indecipherable, and she hung on to my every word, agreeing with whatever I said. I jabbered away, saying things like, "I don't understand women who dread their birthdays when they're just in their 40's." She narrowed her eyes as she processed this idea, then spit out the word, "God!" with surprising conviction. I wasn't sure whether she comprehended what I was saying and was putting in her two cents, or just read my facial expressions and reflected them back. It was never going to be sparkling repartee, but she vigorously participated in the conversation, this give and take. It was good for both of us.

"Hey, Dorothy," I'd say. "Remember when we used to dye our hair? Now we're both older and grayer – and smarter, too, don't you think?" Dorothy's jaw would hang slack for a moment before she she'd say, "Yeah," emphatically. I would continue. "Shirley still dyes her hair, y'know. She's the only one in the place where she lives with brown hair. Everybody else has let it go, but she's hanging in there." A moment would pass. "Yeah," she'd say. Then we'd share a chuckle about our mother-in-law.

My favorite moment happened each time I arrived for a visit. I would hug Dorothy, and she would beam at me. After settling into a chair, I'd ask, "Dorothy, do you know who I am?" Studying my face and smiling broadly, she'd say, "No." "I'm Melissa," I'd say, and she'd throw her hands into the air, yelling, "Melissa! Oh, God!" Then we'd laugh and eat ice cream while looking at picture books.

Joe came every day to visit, actually twice a day to share lunch and dinner with Dorothy in the dining room. This was a relief when I didn't always make it for my weekly visit, especially considering that I avoided mealtime for visits anyway. It was hard for me to avoid gagging over the smell and look of pureed beef, which Dorothy ate even after her new set of teeth was made. She wasn't going to wear them, no matter how much they were adjusted to fit.

I began to relax a bit, enjoying the liberation of not caring about how the situation looked. "No, that younger man that visits her every day is not her grandson; it's her husband," I told the nurses. It was fun to watch them reframing how they saw Dorothy after hearing this information. They looked at her and said, "Well, you go, girl." Dorothy smiled and said, "Yeah."

"Yes, we are sisters-in-law." I continued. "No, that's what I meant. We have the same mother-in-law."

I tried to get Shirley to visit Dorothy a couple of times, but she refused. "I think you'll drop me off there and not come back," she said. I was flabbergasted. "What? For Pete's sake, Shirley, that's crazy. You know that isn't going to happen. And seriously, you should see this place. There's a cool sensory room for people with dementia like Dorothy. It's a great facility with all kinds of state-of-the-art stuff. You'd like it." I knew I had misspoken the moment those last words left my mouth. She eyed me warily. "I'm not goin'."

Shirley's refusal to visit felt like a relief on days that seemed particularly strange in the nursing home. I didn't want to deal with her reaction to various patients and the ironic background music playing on the stereo like "I'd Really Love to See You Tonight" by England Dan and John Ford Coley, or Tommy James and the Shondells singing "My Baby Does the Hanky Panky." Dorothy often sat near a woman named Ida who would interject in a sing-song voice that sounded like a parrot when

Dorothy and I were talking. "Oh, my goodness, I didn't know that." "Oh, yes." "Well, maybe." "Don't know about that." She was our little Greek chorus.

"Dorothy?" I'd say. "Did you ever have chickens when you were growing up?" Dorothy had shown some interest in the chickens Alison was raising since joining the Monroe County 4H Poultry Club. And Ida would chirp, "Don't know about that," as Dorothy nodded her head tentatively. I'd try again. "Were they all hens or did you have any roosters?" Ida responded with, "No, well, no. I didn't, no, well, maybe."

Once when I got there, Dorothy had gone temporarily missing, having scooted on her behind all the way down the hall and into another wing when no one was paying attention. However, for the most part, she was carefully attended, with her mattress moved to the floor to keep her from falling out of bed at night.

Although Dorothy remained in good care at the Sunrise Care Center, her happy times didn't last forever. After about six months, we reached a point of diminishing returns. Bringing in new clothes or trinkets didn't seem to interest her. Once she responded enthusiastically to an old Elmo doll of Alison's and played with it for a few hours, but mostly she wasn't attracted to such things any more. At some point, I got it in my head that she could still read and tried to make a communication board for her. But I gave up before getting very invested when I saw she wasn't willing to try it out.

She remained the caretakers' favorite even after she became less responsive. They treated her like a doll, painting her nails a soft, sweet red, like a spot of Technicolor on a black and white picture. Sometimes, they pulled her hair back into a bun and exclaimed how cute she looked. She'd smile and say, "Good!" then pull it out as they walked away. Dorothy had never liked having her hair pulled back. As late as her mid-80s, she had worn it long, straight, and dyed jet black.

I studied Dorothy's relationship with the nurses closely, not because I distrusted it, but rather because I was curious. How was it that some people invited such affection? I wondered if, when I'm in a nursing home someday, I'd be given ice cream all day long, just to see me smile. I guessed not, knowing I wasn't like Dorothy, sweet and beatific. It wasn't that serene was an unnatural state for me, but a kind of crankiness or cynicism had set in in recent years. I could work on it, but was overwhelmed at the thought. Looking around at the other patients in the ward, I decided I'd be more like Fredene, who usually looked stern and unapproachable, but sometimes smiled and talked to me when I talked to her. No one painted her nails or played with her hair. Fredene was no one's doll or baby. Fredene was no one's fool, likely perusing all her mental files, out of sequence, but no less rich – memory and imagination and desire and regret. This was a sweetness I could aspire to in the advanced dementia ward, a private, dignified, and quiet place of repose. Looking around at the antics of other patients and listening to the Bee Gees' "Night Fever" on the stereo, I decided not to get my hopes up.

41

DISASTER RELIEF

Over the years, I could tell when Cedar Hills was abuzz with political discourse. Shirley would present the controversy of the week a little too forcefully in a voice that wasn't quite hers, betraying the influence of other seniors pontificating in the dining room. Like an ideological pinball, she recklessly careened from side to side. Sometimes it felt like a sneak attack. She'd shout accusingly, "Melissa! I'm talkin' to you! Do you think they's such a thing as hate crimes?"

Following the aftermath of Hurricane Katrina, she was trying out a new idea about fiscal responsibility that didn't quite fit the context of her life, the one that included growing up in a state-funded orphanage, and having Joe, a son who was financially dependent on both his mother and government disability checks. Like wearing an ill-fitting coat that wouldn't button down the center, the person beneath was still visible.

"They ought to make all them people around the hurricanes move out of there!" she bellowed at me.

I had just walked in the door for a quick minute to get Shirley's signature on a birthday card for one of her great-grandchildren and reacted to her pronouncement with confusion. "What?"

"Well the government can't keep bailin' them out every year. That's OUR MONEY!"

Okay. Hurricane Katrina. Now I was up to speed. "Shirley. You can't empty an area that large; you can't make all those people leave their homes."

"Well, why not? Every year, we have to spend all our money on 'em and they don't even care!"

"You and I don't know how they feel."

"Well, who cares how they feel when they just want the government to build them a new house every year." Her voice rose even louder. "Do you think the government should have to build those people a new house every year?"

I started to respond, then paused to take another approach. "Y'know, there are children down there. They can't help being homeless. Kids like Ben and Alison."

"Hey, Ben's got a job. He's learning how to take care of hisself. He's workin' hard baggin' them groceries."

I checked my watch. "Ben has been working a total of four hours at his first real job. It's a little soon to count him in. What about you? The government paid for the orphanage where you lived, right?"

There was a pause, just long enough for me to ask myself, again, what I got out of winning arguments with her. In that moment, I recognized Shirley's return to what she actually knew, her own life back in view. "Well, yeah," she sighed. "And it's good the government's payin' for Joe, 'cause I couldn't keep it up. I guess I oughtta just shut up."

I shook my head and sighed. "I'm glad the fate of the Gulf coast isn't up to either one of us."

I glanced at my watch again and realized I needed to get back to work. Shirley caught me before I got out the door. "Did you hear about what they done at breakfast yesterday?"

"Who?"

"Dana. She and Claude is the new managers. Well. After breakfast, Dana, that's her, asked everyone to go upstairs to the chapel and pray for Cedar Hills."

I stopped and looked at her. "What do you mean?"

"That's right, they's worried cuz the place is half empty, so we's supposed to pray more people'll come."

"Wow, are you kidding?"

"I know. Ain't that the limit? I told Dana that I don't have to go to the chapel; I pray in my apartment. I wish I could say I don't care, but I don't want to have to go someplace different. I know I complain about the dining room, but who knows about somewheres else? It could be really bad."

I pledged to pray for Cedar Hills, too. Walking more slowly to my car, I wondered about this dingbat Dana and how long she'd been in charge. The quality of managers had gone downhill over the years of Shirley's residence and I tried to see how many of them I could recall.

Perhaps the nadir of the rapid managerial turnover in recent years was Harley and Missy. Shirley had had a lot to say about them both. "Harley was so tacky; he did not look like a manager. I mean put on a shirt and tie, and some teeth. He had the dumbest laugh. And he wore them thin undershirts, y'know, eggbeaters, and he had these big tattoos and his armpits showin' when he reached over you to serve coffee. Ugh. Did I tell you he spilled coffee on my hand one time?"

"Yes," I said, resigned to her telling it again.

"I said, 'Hey,' and he said, 'well, you moved your hand.' Honest to God, that's what he said. Patsy was sitting right there and she heard him. Missy had some tattoos, too. She said, 'I can show you two of them, but I can't show you three of them.' Besides, I think they should have been married." She had paused for a moment to think. "All the other managers have been married. Patsy and I thought it was funky. About Harley and Missy. One time, she come to our table and squatted on her hands and knees between Patsy and me. Said she'd heard a rumor that I preferred the other couple. Can you believe that? And remember what they found in their apartment when they left?"

"How could I forget?" I said. There were boxes of earthworms, which they were growing and selling, to whom, I never heard.

From here, Shirley moved on to others in the Cedar Hills

management parade. "'Member that woman with the wild hair – her name was Lela, but we called her La-La. She had this spiky red hair. She did not know how to approach old people. And she had a girlfriend."

"Mm, hmm."

"A girlfriend."

"I know; I got it the first time."

"Now Howard's wife was pretty nice; you could talk to her. Not like LaLa. I wouldn't bother with her; she wasn't worth it. There was this other lady and I didn't care for her neither. Patsy and I decided we wasn't even gonna learn her name. She intimidated you. She made you feel like a five-year-old; you can ask Patsy." Shirley laughed. "I don't know why I'm bankin' everything on Patsy. Anyway, she would get up to make the announcements, and she says, 'Todaaaayyy…we're going to have this and this.' Like we was five years old. That made me mad. And she's got umpteen hundred degrees, but that don't mean you do your job good. Right before she was gone, she was sayin' at dinner announcements to flush three times every time we go; before, during, and after. Ask Patsy if you don't believe me."

"I believe you," I had said.

Similar to when I was visiting Dorothy, sometimes an image of myself as a resident under such circumstances would flash before my eyes. Over time, it was getting easier to imagine. And I wasn't envisioning such a profound change in my demeanor that I wouldn't be the old lady responding to Dana's instructions to pray in the chapel by saying, "Are you kidding me?" Truly, it seemed that the older you get, the more people try to pull this stuff. The reminder to flush three times came to mind. Regarding urgent prayer directives, I hoped I didn't become someone who shrugged her shoulders and moved with the crowd down the hall to the chapel, figuring it would be easier than making waves, maybe even safer that way, given that people like

Dana could be in charge of my welfare.

My sister used to say she hoped her mind went before her body, which sounded dubious to me. She loved to talk about a woman she knew who believed she was the manager of the senior residence where she lived. Lynne said she walked around the place snapping her fingers at employees and threatening them with termination. The best part was that she appeared to be loved by all the people she reprimanded and they played along that she was the boss. I suspected that a charming kind of dementia was rare however. With my luck, I'd be the one smearing feces on the walls. At Cedar Hills, this person existed in the form of Agnes Belfont, who according to Shirley, couldn't get anyone to clean it up. Shirley knew this because Agnes had asked her to help with a little mess on her wall. Having to learn this lesson the hard way, Shirley bore witness to something so gross she couldn't even describe it without hysterical fits of laughter, more from disbelief than a lack of charity. Even Agnes's family had declined support in this matter, and how awful was that? Shirley said they picked her up every Sunday for church and dinner, but never came in anymore. "How bad can it be?" I asked naively. And Shirley cackled, gleeful at the shock value potential, "Go see for yourself!" to which I declined. Alison, who by now had seen it all, put in her two cents. "Agnes's room smells like crap."

At this, I stared at Shirley. "Please tell me Alison hasn't visited Agnes's room."

"I told her to stay in the hall!" Shirley said. "She just peeked in. She didn't come in."

I left a message for the manager, inquiring about the situation, and decided that would have to be enough, but not without pangs of guilt. I was grateful Shirley didn't have advanced dementia and that she had a lot to say, even if much of the time it drove me crazy. And I was even more grateful that she had a sense of humor, which was encouraged by her son who adored her and thought she was hilarious. I hoped I would be surrounded someday by people who thought I was funny, even if my befuddlement became a primary topic of their conversation. I hoped that if I became incontinent, someone would have the good sense to set me up with a proper level of care. I hoped that Cedar Hills would indeed go out of business if people like Agnes were left to fend for themselves in squalor. And I hoped I didn't lose all the little scraps of paper on which I had been recording quotes from Shirley for a good ten years before I had a chance to compile them for posterity.

Phone message the next day:

Melissa, can you get me some chili from Wendy's? With cheese and onions and anything else comes with it. Tonight, they served this watery soup and called it cream of celery soup. Like they dragged a piece of celery through some water. It sure wasn't no cream! Oh. This is Shirley, by the way.

42

MEDITATION HELPS

I rose early the morning of Thanksgiving 2005 and wandered down to the basement, picking up clutter in preparation for my in-laws' arrival. At the bottom of the stairs was a small pink object that made me hesitate. I bent over and touched it gingerly. It was squishy and reddish-pink, like an animal's organ. Since we'd moved to the country, our cats and dogs regularly presented spoils of a daily hunt, so I had become less squeamish about such things. But this was strangely clean and separate from the body from which it must have come. Carefully, I placed it in my palm, keeping my hand open, and carried it to Thomas in the kitchen.

"What do you suppose this is?" I asked.

His reply was matter of fact. "That's a kidney from the turkey. The kids were throwing the giblets around yesterday."

And so the day began.

As soon as Alison awoke, she got into the spirit of preparation by hauling in from outside the life-size, light-up reindeer lawn decorations purchased the day before, plugging them in and moving them from one strategic spot to another, including in front of the refrigerator and then the stove. Now that she was in third grade, she was taking a more active role in hosting our guests. Her plan for the table setting involved squeezing the reindeer in places around the already crowded table. The scene reminded me of my mother getting me out of her hair when I was a kid by sending me out every Thanksgiving to find beautiful leaves to include in her table centerpiece. I hated the job, mostly because there were no good leaves to be found in late November, just ones that were torn, brown, and muddy. When I protested, my mother insisted, sometimes adding that edge to her voice that still struck terror. The leaves looked gross on the table each year, but this remained my job at Thanksgiving for many years of my childhood.

Back in the present, when I saw Alison walking around the dining room table and pouring Raisin Bran on each plate, I found the words flowing so easily from my mouth. "Go find some beautiful leaves." I met her resistance not with steely resolve but negotiations more typical of our relationship: the reindeer could stay for the moment, but there would be no more pouring of breakfast cereal.

Thomas picked up Shirley and brought her to the house before everyone else to cook these flat noodles that were not homemade like the ones from his childhood, but nostalgic for him nonetheless. I liked seeing him excited about a particular dish he loved, and the over-the-top hubbub involved in Shirley boiling frozen noodles for a side dish didn't send me over the edge as much as when she had cooked them in the past. At this point, my priorities were less about food or even surviving the whole ordeal, and more to do with taking it all in moment to moment. I'd restarted a regular meditation practice.

Shirley stood in the kitchen with the newly transplanted reindeer and shared her dose of daily wisdom from her trusted companions, the hosts of the Today Show. "If you want to have a nice Thanksgiving, there's three words you should never say. One of 'em is 'shut up.' SHUT UP. What was the other ones? All I can remember was 'shut up.' SHUT UP." As various family members arrived, she repeated this helpful information such that "shut up" appeared to be our traditional greeting.

Our meal was uneventful. I timed my bites to avoid the moving head of a reindeer colliding with my fork. Unlike my family of origin for whom political debate was a competitive sport, the Kuhns stayed on the polite surface of social exchange. There were minimal entanglements in the family's relationships, as far as I could tell over the years. Sometimes when we spent a holiday in Cincinnati with my family, someone would be on the outs with someone else, but this was a tension I was used to. In Thomas's family, everyone was careful with each other, with the exception of Shirley, who operated without a filter most of the time. And Joe had decided for Dorothy that the two of them would eat Thanksgiving dinner at Sunrise Care Center that year, from what I could tell, because they were serving Salisbury steak along with turkey. He had planned to join us after dinner. As the rest of us ate, topics of conversation tended to be safe. Several family members talked about their annual tradition of hitting the stores in the wee hours of Black Friday, a practice I may never experience. We hadn't gathered as a group in a while and I was struck by how little we knew each other, which affected the depth of conversation available to us. Thomas's nephew was asked about the world of banking, Lee about the world of engineering, and I was asked, once again, where I work and what I do. Most answers were short and to the point. We were not a group that elaborated.

Shirley, however, could be counted on to make interesting contributions to the conversation. She talked about the custodian who had gotten fired at Cedar Hills. "He got fired because he was impertinent. Not impotent. They's a difference between them two. There's a new guy. He's G-A-Y, but he sure cleans good."

I had the radio on for background music. When a classical piece began, Shirley said, "Well, I wonder if Cookie is listening to this and will go on and on about it tomorrow." We asked what she meant.

"I mean she thinks she's better than the rest of us, and we're ready for her to find another table."

I had wondered about Cookie, too, who had recently moved in. She had a conspiratorial way of leaning in at the table and talking about the "hoi polloi" across the room, indicating whom she meant with a slight nod of her head in their direction. She also used words like "egads" and "gobsmacked" whenever something unexpected happened, as in, "Well, I am *gobsmacked* that they have the temerity to serve this casserole again in the same week."

Cookie and Shirley were like oil and water. Shirley may have been unhappy about the casserole, too, but likely defended it if Cookie said it was bad. Shirley described their latest altercation as we ate dessert.

"Yesterday, she kept talking about that guy again." She looked to me for help. "Y'know that guy she's always going on about – koff, koff…"

"Tchaikovsky," I prompted.

"Yeah, and I just had enough. She was all shocked that we didn't know all he done and I said, 'Hey, not all of us is into opera, okay?' You should have seen her face."

As we finished eating, Ben's friends, all teenage boys, stopped by to see if he could hang out with them. I could see our dinner ending quickly, as in the past. Before the boys left, Shirley crossed the group to get to the couch, saying, "That was a good meal," farting all the way and oblivious to the boys holding their waists and falling to the ground with silent laughter in her wake.

Later that evening, when only six of us were left, we played a game. It was a form of charades with a machine that made a ticking noise, which increased in volume and speed as the time to guess the answer came to an end. We divided into three teams of two. Thomas was paired with Alison, who acted out "Jurassic Park" by baring her teeth in a menacing way for a full minute. Uncle Lee teamed with Shirley, who was equally challenged by the rules. Joe and I were the third team. Joe is functionally illiterate, so when it was our turn, I read the word for him by whispering it in his ear, then encouraged him to act it out so that I could guess it. Making up the rules as we went along, I dare say it was fun, complete with laughter, encouragement, and even good-natured teasing.

That evening as I climbed into bed exhausted, it occurred to me that this had been a good Thanksgiving. No arguments, good food, shared work, lots of laughter. And as I drifted off to sleep, I remembered something too often forgotten in the chaos of hosting Thanksgiving dinner, which was gratitude. Life is good, I thought, as I drifted off to sleep.

Phone message:

Hi, Melissa. I just saw they're gonna have that series again. I can't think of the name of it. It's where the guy has three wives. Now he's gonna have four. That sounds interesting. This is Shirley.

43

WOMEN AND MADNESS

Often when Shirley spent the night at our house, she would rise early and put on a pot of coffee. Next, she would walk around the house, inspecting the bookshelves for anything that caught her eye. This always made me nervous for a reason I never shared with her. On our honeymoon in the Philippines in the mid-eighties, taken 7 months after our wedding when we could both take time off from work, Thomas had snapped a naked picture of me in our bungalow on Mamburao Island – full frontal, ah, youth. At some point, I had stuck the picture in a book and promptly, uncharacteristically, forgot which book it was. Friends promised that if I died before finding the picture, they would gather at the house immediately after my last breath, systematically going through every book on every shelf until the picture was discovered. I would be spared posthumous humiliation of its discovery at the annual Red Cross book sale. (I have since found the photograph tucked into an old copy of *Women Who Do Too Much*, and deemed it unidentifiable compared to my physical self today, therefore no longer a concern.)

Shirley never discovered this photograph, but sometimes as I descended the stairs in the morning, she would greet me with a hostile denouncement of a book she had pulled off the shelf, acting as if I were the offending author. The day I came downstairs and found her reading Phyllis Chesler's seminal *Women and Madness*, clearly agitated, I held my breath and prepared for the diatribe. But it didn't happen. "Melissa. Where'd you get this book?"

"Morning, Shirley. I don't know; it's old. I probably got that in the 70s or early 80s."

She stood up. "Well, I been reading it and it's true. And it's what happened to my mother."

I refreshed her cup of coffee and poured a cup for me, too. "What do you mean?"

"I mean the way they done stuck her in Central State. Like she was nobody. And this book says it happened to lots of women. If your husband didn't like the way you made coffee, he could just leave you there."

I nodded my head. "What do you remember about your mom going to Central State?"

"Well, not much, really. I just don't think it shoulda happened. And by the time I got her out, her life was over. She had to go to a nursing home."

"How old was she?"

"I don't know; I'd have to figure that out. Whatever she was, she looked much older. She was a smoker. She started some fires, but not on purpose."

The story of Fay's commitment is a sketchy one, full of questions, vague impressions, and contradictory anecdotes, all of which would break your heart. To this day, I find myself wondering who her friends were, or her keepers, and whether anyone ever really knew her.

I've stitched together patches of information about what happened to Fay by gathering material from various perspectives. After Shirley's death in 2009, Thomas, Alison, and I visited what is left of Central State Hospital, which was shut down in 1994. The only building open to the public has become the Indiana Medical History Museum, formerly the Pathology Building of the institution. Thomas had spent a nursing rotation at Central State during his training, after his grandmother had been moved, so he had an inside perspective of the place. We also visited the Indiana State Archives and were allowed to make copies of hand-written records from Central State Hospital of Fay's diagnosis – schizophrenia, hebephrenic type, which was described as a type of schizophrenia characterized by disorganized speech and behavior. There were a few interviews of family members regarding Fay's condition. Her maternal aunt described her in 1937 in this way:

Patient has been very peculiar or "silly like" all her life. She would laugh at things that would make other people cry. Her relatives always expected her to lose her mind when she got older. She said her life was a book and it will be some day on the screen. She arranged her hair and tried to look like a movie actress.

Many of the descriptions of Fay referred to her as different, childlike, and silly. When I first read this, the image that came to mind was actually Dorothy. But Fay's aunt also said she was fearful that Fay might hurt her and her young daughter. It was unclear whether this was the aunt's child or Fay's. Her aunt said that Fay had tried to smother her child when sleeping with her, that the child had "hollered" and got out of the bed, and Fay pretended to be sleeping. This is where any comparison to Dorothy ended.

Additionally, there were interviews of Fay about her family and life prior to her commitment, what happened to her, various treatments she was given, and the failed attempt in the late 40s to move her into the custody of her youngest daughter, Roberta. I also gleaned stories from Dot and Roberta's daughters, told to me years after Roberta's death. If my mission in this research had been to get all the facts straight, I would have been a frustrated woman. Not until I arrived at a different kind of understanding about Fay's life was I able to accept the incomplete story as inevitable. What I uncovered will never fit into an accurate timeline, but rather it's a subjective truth that assigns various people's interpretations to Fay's circumstances, based in part on the established mores of the times and all that was and wasn't known about mental illness.

Fay was committed to Central State in 1928, a particularly unfortunate time to be mentally ill in America. However it was still better than it had been in the recent past. By the time Fay arrived, the men and women had been separated into different quarters, which resulted in decreased violence against the women in particular. Fay lived in a massive building called Seven Steeples, which housed the Women's Department. When I visited the library in the old Pathology Building, I was fascinated by the profound name change of a series of volumes organized by years. *The American Journal of Insanity* became the *American Journal of Psychiatry* by the mid '20s, indicating the promise of a different perspective on mental illness. Thanks to the leadership and advocacy of heroes like Dorothea Dix, mental health patients had not been housed in jails and poorhouses since the turn of the century, but in mental institutions where various forms of medical practice were always developing. Unfortunately, the practices during the decades in which Fay was a patient included lobotomies, "prolonged narcosis" or long periods of being kept comatose, ice water baths, "cerebral stimulation" with injections of sodium cyanide, removal of body parts believed to be sending toxins to the brain, and the treatment of syphilis with strains of malaria, all without patient understanding or consent. It was generally accepted that doctors knew what was best for their patients. Regardless of the mission to provide more humane care for the destitute and mentally ill, by all accounts, conditions in mental hospitals in the early and mid-20th century were deplorable.

Combing through the records of Fay's time at Central State, none of the infamous treatments known to have been inflicted on others were indicated for her. I found this curious. She was described as a meek person, so perhaps her behavior wasn't considered aberrant or something to suppress. But so many years and no records of rough treatment whatsoever? There are reports of medications, earaches, cataract surgery, but nothing stands out that could be considered questionable. It's possible that Fay escaped such terrible "remedies" at the hospital. It isn't possible that she escaped witnessing their implementation on other patients. She lived in a frightening world where dangers lurked in unexpected places.

Many years later, when we drove to downtown Indianapolis, locating the old Pathology Building on Washington Street, Thomas recalled from his childhood the Sunday afternoon visits there each week after church was out. There's a picture we have of him with his grandmother during one of the visits, standing outside on what appears to be a sunny spring day. He looks about seven years old. "There was a bridge on the way that we liked," he said. "We called it the Singing Bridge because of the sound it made when you drove over it. We always raised up our feet when we were on it." He didn't remember much about his grandmother at that time, just that she was very quiet and smiled a lot. He remembered the iron fence that surrounded the property and patients standing at the fence watching the outside world. "I think our visits must have been really important to her. But we hated them," he said with a sigh.

Shirley was the most reliable of Fay's children when it came to visiting and caring for her in the decades of her commitment to Central State and later when she lived in a nursing home. Although Georgie eventually lived nearby, she refused to spend time with this person she never really knew. Don's disconnection extended to the entire family, except when he needed money, according to Shirley. Dot and her husband helped with a couple of crises, like when they retained an attorney to respond to a government bill that said the children of Fay Peacock owed a considerable sum of money to Central State. Dot visited her mother, but was the first to admit that she didn't do this as often as she would have liked, and was grateful that Shirley was there for her every week.

Roberta appears to have been the sibling with fervent but unrealistic ideas about saving their mother from her fate, given Roberta's limited resources to support such plans. In February of 1948, Fay was discharged from Central State to live with Roberta, who would have been twenty-two at the time and only a few years out of an institution herself. But Fay had to be watched all the time. The records report she was careless with her cigarettes, exposed herself to Roberta's neighbors, and constantly made strange noises, saying she needed to do this to adjust her eyes. Roberta had a husband and small children to care for. Fay was returned to Central State a couple of months after she had left, her experience living in the world outside declared a failure.

"I felt bad about it for her," Shirley said about that time, "but I didn't want to take on the responsibility, so I didn't say anything."

In the notes from the Central State archives, there is a statement saying all Mrs. Peacock's records between 1948 and 1954 are missing, and indeed, there are none to be found. In 1954, Roberta tried again to take her mother out for a thirty-day leave of absence, but returned her after 22 days when she said Fay had screamed and become mildly combative with her. This was Fay's last overnight experience away from the hospital or subsequent nursing homes in the 32 years that remained of her life.

Throughout the decades of Fay's commitment, the one constant in her life was her oldest daughter, Shirley. It had to be a depressing affair each week to visit her on Sundays and take her home on Fridays for the day, but Shirley never faltered, and to my knowledge, Walter never complained. "It was bad there," Shirley once told me. "Big hunks of plaster would fall on your head, and all the sinks was this color," she said holding up a walnut. "Just awful. They had these group showers they would hose down. One thing my mother wanted to do every week when she came home with me was to sit in the bathtub full of scalding hot water. And she'd always talk about making her bed every day. The matrons were always inspecting her bed and the area around it, I guess, and she was afraid of getting in trouble if it wasn't picked up. The place was so smoky you could hardly breathe in there. Everyone could smoke wherever back then, and they set Central State on fire all the time. People was sittin' on the floor and leanin' on the walls, banging their heads over and over."

Although Shirley was sketchy on the details of when this happened, she had a vivid memory of going to visit her mother one week, only to find the doors locked and a sign posted saying there had been a fire and the inmates had been moved, no indication of where. She was stunned that she hadn't been contacted and frantically did what she could to finally find her mother in a big hotel where many had been relocated. "I drove out there in the pouring rain and found my mom worried sick that I wouldn't find her. She cried and said, 'I thought I'd never see you again.'"

In 1970, Fay was discharged from Central State to the custody of Barton House Nursing Home. There was a short description of her health status at that time in her Central State records.

Mrs. Peacock continues to have little insight into her illness, but she has been no management problem on the ward for some time, and it is expected that she will have few problems adjusting to the nursing home. She is quite eager to make the move.

Eventually, Shirley was able to move her mother to a better place, where she remained until her death in 1986. "This place was much nicer and new," Shirley had said. "She was on

Medicare, and Medicaid, and Social Security. They sent me a check every month and I had to account for every penny spent with all this paper work. Some people was takin' it and usin' it for their self, I guess."

Eventually, Shirley took on the care of Walter's parents in her home, all the while maintaining her steady routine in Fay's life. Whenever she talked about her mother, her tone was both fond and matter-of-fact about her lot in life. She focused on the little things that could make a difference in her mother's life, which must have added up considerably over time. She once laughed about her mother's simple wishes. "She was real skinny, and she ate candy like you wouldn't believe. She loved them chocolate turtles. And she was always beggin' me to smoke with her. One time I did just for fun, and I said I don't know how anyone stands this. I never minded her doin' it though, as long as she was outside."

Shirley had seen more than her share of women and madness, regardless of the Central State patients' health status when they were committed. She knew more about the dangers of losing control of one's destiny than most people would ever be able to imagine. However, rather than talk about what she couldn't change, she chose to do what she could and did it unfailingly.

44

ROUTINE MAINTENANCE

Typical enough for her age, Shirley's weekly schedule was anchored by doctor appointments. Thomas or Joe drove her most of the time, but sometimes I filled in. In the fall of 2006, I was doing more than usual with Thomas in Biloxi, Mississippi as part of a volunteer team aiding victims still suffering the effects of Hurricane Katrina. He had been deputized by Homeland Security and was living in a tent set up in a K-Mart parking lot. He spent his days working in makeshift clinics in churches and going door to door with soldiers, asking elderly and indigent residents about their health and trying to figure out what medicines he should prescribe after their pills had floated away in the flood.

Compared to these virtuous deeds, one could argue that I had it easy back home holding down the fort. But in the few weeks Thomas was gone, I struggled with maintaining all that needed to be handled each day, never having considered how much I depended on him to make our lives work. Shirley's demands seemed more numerous and involved. I was feeling buried under a big project at work. The kids had a lot going on and the typical random crises seemed to pop up more frequently. As determined as I was to be positive and encouraging when Thomas would call to check in every few days, my frustration sometimes got the better of me and I didn't behave admirably. I was so proud of him, but the whinier side of me took the lead too often. One evening, I was particularly annoyed because Alison, who had become an avid fan of fishing along with her brother and dad, had gotten into Thomas's stink bait, something he had left sitting out in the garage, where the odor had intensified in the sweltering heat of early autumn. She had discovered how much our dogs loved this delectable treat and fed it to them on dog biscuits. This resulted in everything she and the dogs encountered smelling like an unwashed behind, and I was beside myself. On top of that, our hamster, Spunky Junior, had escaped from his cage again and the children and I feared for his safety from our two cats. I had strategically placed his cage with a hamster wheel in the hallway between our three bedrooms, knowing he liked to work out at night, the squeaky rotations often waking us up or showing up in our dreams. I thought one of us would wake up to the familiar sound and close the cage door before he scurried away. Sure enough, he had been true to his fitness routine and I would jump out of bed when I heard the wheel turning, but by the time I'd get there to catch him, he was always gone. This was the kind of problem Thomas excelled at solving, me not so much.

When Thomas called that night, I was exhausted. I did my best to listen carefully to his modest tales of self-sacrifice for people with real problems before I blurted out, "Do you know you left the stink bait out? And now the whole house smells like it. And Spunky's on the loose again, and I can't catch him, and the cats are going to kill him while we're sleeping; I just know it."

Thomas sighed. I pictured him rubbing his temples as he spoke. "Melissa. You know what to do. Just put some tin foil by our bed and some hamster food on it. And a big bowl to put over him. Then when he comes to eat it, you'll hear his little feet on the foil and catch him."

I tried to count to five before speaking, but didn't quite get there. "Well, maybe *you* should come home and set up the tin foil. And you should listen for his little feet. It's not as easy as all that."

There was a pause before Thomas responded. "Okay, well, that's what you should do. And this isn't the best timing, but I forgot to tell you about one of Mom's appointments tomorrow, at least I think it's tomorrow. You should call Dr. Titche's office in the morning to check on the time. Maybe Joe can take her, but you'll need to set that up." I pictured Thomas hanging up and returning to his cot on the hot asphalt of the parking lot, wondering if he might extend his stay and continue his magnanimous work for people who knew how to show some appreciation.

The next morning, I called the doctor from my office to determine Shirley's appointment time, then tried to get in touch with Joe to ask him to take her. When he didn't pick up, I assumed he'd forgotten again to charge the phone we'd gotten him. I moved a few things in my schedule around and called Shirley to say when I'd be by to take her to see Dr. Titche.

In the past, Thomas had often reported on exchanges between Shirley and her doctors that made me laugh. She had a feisty way of questioning authority that was fun to watch, especially if you weren't the one being questioned. Or feeling sorry for yourself. There were occasional misunderstandings, like when Shirley checked "yes" to all the questions on a form she was given, including, "are you being abused." I kept this in mind when I took her for a routine check-up, determined to catch problems before they arose.

As soon as we arrived, the receptionist handed Shirley a form to fill out in the waiting room. Sitting next to her, I tried to be nonchalant as I checked out what she was writing. After a moment, Shirley said loudly, "Are you trying to copy off my paper?"

I noticed a few curious glances and laughed. "No," I said, determined to keep things light.

"Then why are you sittin' so close and watchin' what I'm writing?"

"I thought you might need some help," was my feeble reply, delivered in a quiet voice.

"Some help," she said, again at full volume, as she caught the eye of another elderly patient who was shaking his head in solidarity.

"I mean, I didn't know if you could see it okay," I continued, whispering and wishing we could move into an examination room for the rest of this exchange. Shirley paid no mind to me signaling that we should keep our conversation between us.

"I can see it FINE. See? This question says, 'do you need religion'."

"What? Let me see that." I reached for the clipboard in spite of others looking at us.

"Well, it says somethin' about religion and that's good enough for me," she said. "Everybody needs religion."

I gave up. "Okay, I'll leave you alone. I didn't mean to pry." Finally, Shirley's name was called and we moved down the hall to an exam room. Without an audience, she was less interested in sparring with me and I was thinking about what a pain in the butt she was, certain that I must have been Bloody Mary in my last life. We sat in silence.

After a few minutes, she looked my way. "What are all them papers in your bag?"

"Oh, just papers I need to grade. I'm carrying them around so that I'll do a few here and there when I get a chance."

"What's wrong with now?"

"Nothing, I guess, but I'm thinking the doctor will be here any second."

More silence followed, without eye contact. She spoke up. "You coulda got some done by now."

"I know. Stop bugging me." This broke the tension. We both were laughing when the doctor came in, which made a nice impression and might have been helpful had she checked the box about elder abuse again.

Dr. Titche was young, not just by Shirley's standards. His tone was warm and professional. "Good afternoon, Mrs. Kuhn," he said. "How are you feeling today?"

"Like I need a new body." Taking in his uncertainty, she let him off the hook. "I'm just kiddin'. I'm okay."

Now he laughed, too. "Okay, Mrs. Kuhn, I'm going to say three words and I want you to see if you can remember them when I ask you at the end of our time together. Okay?"

Shirley knitted her brow. "Okay."

"The words are ball, tree, and chair."

"Ball, tree, chair. Those is easy. Who couldn't remember that?"

He smiled. "Great, but I'm going to ask you to say them again later."

Ball, tree, chair, I thought. I wondered if she'd remember and how significant it was if she didn't.

"Mrs. Kuhn, do you know what the date is?"

Shirley didn't hesitate. "It's the 15th of March and the year is 2-0-0-6." This impressed me. I would have had to think for a moment.

"Great," he said and checked a box on his clipboard.

"And it's Tuesday," she added.

The doctor nodded. "That's right."

"Well, I know that."

He asked about the medicines she was taking.

"What do you wanna know? Is my words slurred? A-E-I-O-U!"

"You sound great to me," he said. Shirley knew all the answers to the doctor's questions. He appeared to cut the interrogation short when she started to get huffy. I decided I liked him. He did have a couple more questions about her diet and exercise, however, and Shirley became even more impatient.

"My daughter-in-law has some papers to grade." I looked over and smiled.

"Okay, we're finished, Mrs. Kuhn," Dr. Titche said. He

wrote some instructions on a piece of paper and said, "I'll see you next time."

"So, you think I'll still be here?" she said with a crafty smile.

"I do. Okay, do you remember the three words I wanted you to keep in mind?"

She practically shouted, "Ball, tree, chair!" He laughed, shook her hand, and wished her well. I decided to keep to myself the fact that all I could remember in that moment was ball.

When Thomas returned, we were all relieved to see him. He resumed his care of the family, returned to work, caught a wild-eyed Spunky Junior and relocated him in his cage, and never asked about the stink bait that had gone missing from his tackle box. I acknowledged the need for two people to be in charge of our two-kid, one-grandmother, one-brother, one-elderly-sister-in-law, three-dog, two-cat, ten-chicken, and one-hamster life, musing about the order in which the dependents would have to be abandoned if Thomas decided to stay with Homeland Security.

Phone message:

Melissa, this is Shirley. It's Patsy's birthday and we want to have some of them you-can't-blow-me-out candles like you have. Do you have some left over from Tom's birthday cake? Okay.

45

DOROTHY'S LAST THANKSGIVING

Shirley had her hands on her hips. "If Dorothy comes for dinner, I ain't comin'."

"That's not very nice," I said.

"Well, I ain't nice. Joe don't want her over here with us neither. Nobody wants her with us 'cept you. Besides, are you prepared to pulverize her food?"

"What if we brought her over to the house after she ate dinner? It's embarrassing, but pureed meat makes me retch sometimes."

"Well, if you wants to retch, you should see the mugaloney soup they done served at Cedar Hills last night. It was supposed to be hardy bean soup, and I had my heart set on hardy bean soup." I'd been with Shirley long enough to know that she was talking about mulligatawny soup. "Maybe we could bring her over for coffee and dessert," I said.

"Well, that might be okay, but it won't be easy gettin' her here."

Thomas walked in. "Mom, what is that you're eating?"

"Nothing!"

"It smells like barbeque." He looked at me. "Melissa, did you bring her that?"

"I'd rather not say." It had been a weak moment, and I didn't think I'd get caught.

He rolled his eyes and looked back at Shirley. "You have to stop eating that stuff."

"Well, what if I like it? Havin' the gout ain't the end of the world. That's what I heard on Ooprah. Maybe tomorrow, you'll be pulverizing my food, like Dorothy."

Thomas looked at me. "Is she coming for dinner? Because

y'know she doesn't know it's Thanksgiving." I thought about how the apple doesn't fall far from the tree.

"But we do," I pronounced. "What if we eat early and then bring her over, see how it goes?"

Thomas's nod indicated his resignation, but Shirley went down fighting. "I'm still sayin' it's a bad idea."

The family gathering for dinner in 2007 was small. Just Shirley, Joe, Thomas, the kids, and me. Shirley was telling us about Lee's new wife, Colita. "What country is she from?" I asked.

"Hong Kong. No, wait, she speaks Taiwanese, so she's from Thailand. She used to be Buddha, but not anymore."

Ben made an attempt here. "Grandma, that's like saying she used to be Jesus. You mean Buddhist."

"Well, with her, she used to be Buddha, but not no more."

Alison got up to throw away the gum she had been chewing, which inspired our next holiday topic of conversation. "Children do not appreciate their chewing gum," Shirley said. "They go through a whole pack in a day! I used to make mine last for three whole days. And I'd stick it on the bedpost at night." This led to other chewing gum stories. Someone recalled the time when Alison was a little girl playing under the table at a restaurant and how she had come up chewing gum none of us had given to her. Shirley put in her two cents here. "You know you don't find so much gum under the tables like you used to."

There was a pause as we took this in. Ben broke the silence. "You still feel for it, Grandma?"

Thomas laughed, saying, "Old habits die hard."

After dinner, Shirley and I stayed behind while the others took a car and truck to pick Dorothy up. The truck was needed to transport her wheelchair. My anxiety increased as Shirley kept up her trash talking about my poor judgment. "Did you pulverize her pie? Is you going to take her to the bathroom? I'm just sayin'." I drank an extra glass of wine.

Our barking dogs heralded the group's arrival and I hurried outside to welcome Dorothy. Everyone looked vaguely upset, except my tiny sister-in-law. True to form, she was beaming at us all. I looked from one person to another. "What?" I said.

No one spoke as Joe pulled down a bent and scratched wheelchair. When Ben lifted his aunt and settled her into the chair, she was listing to one side, so he immediately picked her up again and carried her into the house where we settled her on the couch between two big pillows. Ben turned to me. "I was driving, but it wasn't my fault. That truck of yours is a wreck." I'd never heard Ben refer to our truck, which he considered his own most of the time, as our truck.

Alison took it from there. "Ben hit a big pothole and the back of his truck came down and Aunt Dorothy's wheelchair flew out, right in front of us!"

"On the highway?"

"Yeah! And Dad and I were in the car!"

"What did you do?"

"We yelled!"

"Did it scare Dorothy?"

Alison rolled her eyes. "She didn't even see it. When we yelled, she jumped. Then she asked if it's raining." I poured another glass of wine.

Thomas filled in the story of Ben's touch-and-go retrieval of the wheelchair from Route 37, dodging cars whizzing by, and Joe paced, muttering to himself and wringing his hands. "They's gonna put me in jail," he kept saying. "In jail, man. I gotta fix it."

Trying not to sound too woozy, I couldn't resist that old familiar call to take charge of this group. "Joe, nobody's going to put you in jail. It was an accident."

Thomas shook his head. "I've already told him to leave it alone and we'll work it out." But Joe sat on the floor and took the wheelchair apart until he had it broken down to twenty parts, each looking worse than when they were assembled.

"I told you," Shirley crowed, and I kept drinking. Nobody felt like having dessert. We tried playing the game, *Taboo*, not as a competition exactly, but a way of being together without the television, which I was secretly dying to watch, anything to escape what I knew I'd hear about from Shirley for the rest of her days.

I took out the video recorder and showed Dorothy how she could watch herself on the little monitor as I taped her, which she loved. She smiled and nodded and took her teeth out and put them back in repeatedly, all with complete fascination. She wasn't accustomed to having them in her mouth.

When it was time to take Dorothy home, I took stock of my sobriety and Thomas's expression of I-told-you-so, then said to Ben, all of 17 at the time, "You're just going to have to handle this, honey." So, Ben, who had outgrown his uncle as a playmate when he was five, accompanied Joe and Dorothy back to the nursing home, wheelchair parts in hand, and insisted on telling the truth, despite Joe's fervent pleas to say that's what it looked like when they picked it up. Ben reported that the night staff said it was the best laugh they had had in months, we were never sent a bill, amazing to this day, and Dorothy was provided a better wheelchair. Everyone was happy.

It was Dorothy's last Thanksgiving and, in spite of the fact that she didn't know it was Thanksgiving, and it was a bigger inconvenience than any of us could have imagined, I was glad she was there. In two years, it would be Shirley's last Thanksgiving, complete with pulverized food and memorable moments, and their departures would be felt for many years to come.

Phone message:

Melissa, Tom showed me a picture of Ben with two girlfriends on the football field. It was after the game. Did he have to buy them both something to eat? This is Shirley.

46

DOROTHY BLASTS OFF

"Well, she's a tough old bird," was Shirley's response to Dorothy lingering through two hospitalizations in recent months. I asked myself how many women referred to their daughters-in-law this way. Dorothy was slipping away from us. Sometimes when I visited her, I couldn't wake her up. She had lost her appetite altogether and no one could get her to eat. The nurses said that with Alzheimer's, the muscles that allowed her to swallow atrophied. I shook my head, thinking about this horrible disease and wondering whether Dorothy knew we were there or could hear us talking. I actually hoped she couldn't hear everything, like what Joe said at one point when the nurse was placing an IV in her arm. He announced in a conversational way that, after she died, he was going to join a singles club. Good lord, I thought, does it ever stop? He had been upbeat, telling us that the cleaning lady at Cedar Hills had requested his sperm donation. "Huh," Thomas said. "I think of women looking for somebody like a brain surgeon."

At one point, Joe whispered in Dorothy's ear that she was about to go to another planet now. I wondered if Dorothy was wishing someone would go ahead and launch her.

Thomas was frustrated with Dorothy's hospitalizations during which she'd been pumped with fluids then returned to Sunrise. "This is bullshit," he said. "Nursing home administrators don't like to have patients die there, so they ship them off to the hospital. She's DNR and it's wrong to keep putting her through this. I'm calling to see where the hell hospice is."

A decision was made to let Dorothy die in peace, safe in her warm bed. I hoped for Joe's sake that this wouldn't happen when we were on our family vacation, but it did. We were in

Washington, D.C. when Joe called to say Dorothy was dying. We called Shirley to see if she could provide support until we returned. "Well, I told him to get over to your house and feed Alison's chickens. I think he forgot about it," Shirley said.

Thomas rubbed his forehead and closed his eyes. "Mom. We'll find someone else to feed the chickens. Listen, I've written out several pages of notes about what to do if this happens."

"Well, let's hope he's wearing his glasses 'cause he can't hardly see no more. Remember when he thought those dog biscuits you left out were cookies for him? And he can't read what you wrote anyway. I give him a list, but you never know what he's gonna bring when he goes to the store to trade for me. But I'm not complainin'. Last week, I told him not to get me them white hairnets and he did it again. I told him they're for old people. Well, and Melissa, I guess." Shirley could never get over the fact that I had let my hair go grey.

"I'm right here, Shirley," I said. "You're on speaker phone."

"I don't know about all these special kinds of phones no more. Don't try to explain it."

That night, Joe called my cell phone and said, "She's gone. Dorothy's gone." It was hard to know what to say over that distance. When we ran out of words and Joe didn't want to hang up, we just listened to each other breathing until I said we'd call back in a few minutes. A series of phone calls began between Thomas, Joe, Shirley, a social worker, the funeral home director, and Thomas's assistant at work who was checking on Joe until we could get back in town. All the phone calls with Joe were confusing. He declared, "I'm a free man!" then talked about being afraid to send her to the creamery where they kill people.

It seemed there was no time or place that was conducive to all that needed to be worked out over the phone. And sadly, there was a general lack of reverence by the time Dorothy died. Her passing had been imminent for a long time, and everyone had said their goodbyes. Even Shirley, who had to face her fear of me leaving her at the Sunrise Care Center, made one trip after all. Ben and Alison, now 18 and 12, had been appropriately sad with the news, but couldn't be expected to remain in this state indefinitely. Shirley called as the kids were going to bed in our hotel room. They were doing their adaptation of the phrase, "Goodnight, John-Boy," from "The Waltons," a television show they had never seen.

"Goodnight, stinky breath that makes me want to vomit."

"Goodnight, bung hole."

"Goodnight, stinky breath that smells like my bung hole."

"Quiet!" Thomas said, having lost his patience as he finished the call with his mother. He hung up the phone. "So Joe was over at Mom's place today saying he's afraid he's going to hell if he has Dorothy cremated. Mom says she's reassuring him because she doesn't want him coming over every day worrying about it. It's all about her. Anyway, the funeral director is calling back now that everything's gotten confused."

Thomas called Joe and told him we'd be home soon. He did some fast talking about Dorothy's interest in Native American customs, claiming to be part Cherokee, and indeed she could well have been. "Cremation is a Native way," he told Joe. "And no one's going to hell." I wasn't sure where the conversation was going when I heard him say, "Yeah, I'm sure they cremated white people, too," then, "Well, when I said Native, I meant Indian," then, "No, I never saw that TV show."

The funeral director called and Thomas stepped into the hotel hallway to talk with him. He put the speaker on so that I could listen, too. "Yes," Thomas said, "Joe is the one that has to sign the death certificate."

"Well," the funeral director started to respond, but paused. "Is he... competent? He kept talking about people getting killed at a creamery when I think he meant crematorium." This is when the equivocating began. Joe had never been competent in matters of such significance, but always had Thomas there to help him out. Thomas explained to the director that Joe had the power of attorney, but he really didn't make any sense if you talked to him, so he should use Thomas as the go-between.

Thomas's assistant, Bonnie, had her usual sideways take on the situation, which she shared with me on the phone that evening. Thomas had called her with a request to help Joe sort things out. "Yeah," she said, "Joe's gonna have another woman soon. He isn't bad looking, now that Thomas got that cyst removed from his face, and he sure doesn't look 56. He's got a truck, and he's on disability. Someone's gonna grab him up fast." I remembered Ben telling me that Joe had said when Aunt Dorothy died, he was going to find him another woman, a young one this time. But I knew it was best to cross that bridge when we came to it, and I hoped we wouldn't come to it for a long time.

We probably should have left immediately, but Thomas and I had decided to stay one more day. We tried to get the kids to go to Mt. Vernon with us, but they were tired and wanted to hang out at the hotel. I told them I thought they might be sorry if they missed it, prompting Ben to mention every few months, and eventually every few years, "Hey, Mom, still not sorry," my warning having liberated them from potential regret. When we finally left for home, we were weary and on edge from all that had transpired, and the quarrel in the car between Ben and Alison was predictable. It started with name calling, where they completed each other's slurs. If one said, "butt," the other said, "munch," etc. Thomas and I eyed each other. At least it wasn't the "that didn't hurt" game from when they were littler, consisting of Ben punching Alison increasingly hard, while she laughed and said, "That didn't hurt," until it did and all hell broke loose. This looked like an amiable kind of squabbling and Ben had Alison in stitches with his noisy flatulence, which Thomas and I tried to ignore.

Eventually, the name calling escalated and a couple of shoves were delivered. I snapped and said if anyone farted or fought from then on, I was going to throw out the window the only thing of value I could think of, which were cookies we had packed for the car trip. It wasn't one of my better consequences. Ben didn't care about the cookies and tortured Alison, who vehemently protested when he passed gas relentlessly until I said forget it and he knew he'd won the match between Alison, him, and now me.

Shirley called Thomas's cell phone and I talked to her for a bit. She said we needed to get home quick. "Now Joe's sayin' we shouldn't have had her cremated. I told him that Dorothy said she wanted to be cremated and throwed in the woods, but he won't listen to me and he's hangin' around here too much. He's got this box that she's in and he doesn't know what to do with it. I don't want him leavin' it here." Little did we know how long Dorothy's remains would sit in Thomas's closet before he could get Joe to distribute his wife's ashes.

I tried to hand Thomas the phone, but he declined it, leaving me to say, "Shirley, we can't talk right now. We'll see you tonight. Okay, I'm hanging up now."

Thomas picked a fight with me right in front of the kids. "Geez, that sounded rude, Melissa. Would it have killed you to talk to her some more?" I couldn't believe it. "Are you kidding? I can't believe you would say that to me. You're the one who refused the phone."

"Right. I'm driving."

"Oh, please. And let's do a quick check on how much time

you've spent on the phone with *my* family lately." Ben and Alison exchanged a look. Alison laughed as Ben shouted, "They're fighting! Throw Mom's book out the window!" They were comrades again, and Thomas and I weren't speaking, our family dynamic in balance once more.

Joe's response to the planning of Dorothy's memorial service and placing of an obituary in the newspaper swung wildly between a variety of emotions, including grief, relief, and sadly, embarrassment about her advanced age. Thomas tried to enlist Shirley's help when supplying information for the death certificate and obituary. "I know all her records are missing, but when do you think she was born?" he asked. Shirley thought she'd been born around 1916, but she wasn't a reliable source. "Say she's 89. That makes Joe feel better."

Thomas sighed. "Mom. This is a legal document."

"Well, I know that. Let's see. When was she born? I know it was in Texas somewheres. She done had a tough life, that's for sure." Coming from Shirley, this was saying something. "She worked in the tobacco fields when she was a kid. And her mother died when she was little; I think she said she was just 30 years old. She told me once that her middle name was Carmen. Dorothy Carmen Linville Kuhn."

"So her maiden name was Linville?" I asked. "Not Fox? I remember when you said it might be Fox. Do you think that was her first married name?"

"How should I know? And you might as well give up on asking Joe 'cause he sure doesn't know. What's important to him is that none of this goes in the paper."

Thomas said, "I'm putting an obituary in the paper, Mom."

Shirley berated him. "Why do you have to go and do that? Joe don't want it in the paper. He don't want people to know she was so old. He says people's gonna make fun of him. Besides, all these nosy ladies I eat with every day are gonna ask questions. And what am I supposed to say?"

"Ah," Thomas replied. "But it's Joe we're worried about here? Joe's embarrassment?"

"Well, me too, I guess."

"Mom. She was a person. It doesn't matter what you and Joe think."

I was proud of Thomas standing up for what he believed when it would have been easier to comply with Shirley's wishes. Dorothy was a person. We didn't know many details about her long life, but she had been here, she had had an impact, and it deserved to be acknowledged.

We had a small memorial service for Dorothy in our home, led by our church minister who had all the right words of comfort and kindness for her passing. It was attended by our family, including Thomas's sister and her husband, and Thomas's first wife, Jaime, who had known Dorothy long before I came on the scene. We played Carrie Newcomer's song, "Bare to the Bone." The lyrics couldn't have been more fitting.

Here I am without a message
Here I stand with empty hands
Just a spirit tired of wandering
Like a stranger in this land
Walking wide-eyed through this world
Is the only way I've known
Wrapped in hope and good intentions
And bare to the bone.

47

A LOT TO PROCESS

Shirley sent Joe to our house whenever she could. "He's hangin' around here too much 'cause he's got nothin' to do now that Dorothy's gone." I understood her complaint. It wasn't easy having Joe at our house either. It could be a lot of effort since he didn't want you doing anything but sitting around and listening to him. Grading papers was out of the question, along with doing laundry, paying bills, or making a grocery list. My heart sank each time I saw him pulling up the driveway, especially if Thomas wasn't home. "Mom said Tom needs me," he'd say. "She said I needed to leave her place and come over here."

Thomas tried to get him to help with chores around the yard. "He's worthless," he said. "It's worse than having a teenager. He'll rake about twenty leaves then sit down and smoke." But we knew he was lonely. We gave it our best shot, which unfortunately looked a lot like saying, "mm-hmm" and "uh-huh" while trying to slip in a glance at the newspaper and hoping he didn't notice. It wasn't that he'd get mad if he noticed us straying, but rather, diverted, such that the new topic of his monologue would be whether we could take time to talk with him. Surrender seemed like the best option.

Ben leaving for school was one of Joe's favorite topics. "Yeah, Ben's goin' to college. Has he already left? He's gonna meet lots of girls, man. He'll have a TV and a stereo and he'll meet them girls. Thanks for the reception." I thought he meant the macaroni and cheese we'd just eaten. "Do you mean supper?" I asked.

"No, the reception for Dorothy."

"The service at our house?" I asked.

"Yeah." Joe looked around before continuing. "I admit it, I

have to admit I done met two girls. I felt guilty, but I met 'em. They's in my apartments. Like down the way. It was before Dorothy died. I don't have to feel guilty no more, but I still do. We watched a forno, too." I looked to Thomas for a response, given that a discussion about pornography was way beyond my purview as a sister-in-law. But Joe saved us both the trouble.

He pointed to a vase. "I guess Indians made it."

"Actually, it came from China."

"The Chinese. They done tried to be the U.S. of A. and now they's scared of lead paint. They don't want no American factories because they's lead in the paint. Yeah, that's the Japs. Jap-a-nese. I got Japanese beetles on my tomato plants, but they didn't come from Japan. They don't got nothin' to do with the Japs."

Knowing how much Joe's slurs bothered Thomas, I cringed, but then noticed he was no longer with us. Looking around, I found he had escaped to the porch. As was typical in these situations, I went outside and whispered to him to get his butt back in there, and he laughed, knowing he'd been busted. Joe could then be counted on to come find us on the porch without skipping a beat and his droning would continue. "Yeah, Ben's off to college. I'm gonna be the big 6-0 – yech – better get a woman. If you don't have a steady woman by then, I don't know. I'm gonna get me a woman, but this time I'm gonna be careful. I'm gonna do some DNA testing to make sure they don't have the all-timers."

There was a pause, then Thomas asked, "How are you going to do that?"

"Well, maybe not the DNA, but I'm testin' 'em, man, for diseases. Bunch of college girls movin' into my place. They kicked the bad people from my place. They's keepin' out the blacks and the Mexicans."

Again, this was what Thomas hated dealing with the most.

"Don't say that."

Joe was unfazed. "Some of them guys, you could lose your money. Remember that guy in school that jewed me?"

Thomas sat up straighter. "Joe, don't say that. It's offensive."

"Well, that's what he did."

"When you say that, you're putting down people who are Jewish and it's offensive."

Joe looked confused. "I ain't talkin' 'bout the Jewish. I said he *jewed* me. He *jewed* me. He ain't the Jewish." After hearing this helpful explanation repeated, Thomas snapped at him. "When you come to Melissa's birthday party, I do not want you talking to anybody about blacks, Mexicans, Japanese people, or Jews. I mean it."

Following an awkward silence, Thomas took a deep breath and told Joe that their mom had just called and needed him to run some errands for her.

During this time, I reflected on how much I had feared the day when Joe would be left without Dorothy. Early in our marriage, I had talked to Thomas about what was planned for Joe after Walter, Shirley, and Dorothy died. I never got anywhere with him about this and let it go after hearing a similar story from a friend, whose in-law had ended up in need of considerable assistance when she landed in a predictable situation, and that my friend's incessant worrying hadn't made any difference. Shirley was still alive, but I could see the day I had dreaded coming, and still didn't know what we should do to mitigate the inevitable. "What if something happens to us?" I asked Thomas. "What will happen to Joe?" This was not a conversation Thomas grew up around, the "what-ifs" and "what should we do now to prevent problems in the future." Although Thomas's siblings never discussed this with him directly, it was clear early on that he was the only one who was going to take care of Joe. We chose to assume responsibility for various family members, first Shirley, then Joe, then Dorothy, when we moved them to Bloomington.

Throughout the week, Joe left long, rambling voice mail messages. "Hey. The guy across from, uh, the paper recycle place by the railroad? He welded, I went over there and he welded my charcoal grill and he got his guitar out and playin' and he gave me a air compressor and I painted it red. This is Joe. Call me."

"Yeah, Tom, put me in that PH, PCH, Publisher's Clearing House contest. This is Joe."

"I got somethin' in the mail. The Catholic Church's tryin' to get me. I don't know about that. I ain't no Catholic. They's sendin' me letters – says they gonna buy me a house and a shirt. I have to see that to believe it. They sent me some beads, rose beads. It's a good luck charm. I put it by Dorothy's picher. This is Joe."

Similar to the conclusion I had drawn in the 80s, I realized, when it came to Joe, we would cross each bridge when we came to it, having no idea how daunting each bridge would be, not to mention how many.

48

VARIABILITY OF THE HEART

Sometimes meditation just didn't do the trick when it came to getting ready for the holidays. And it was unpredictable. I really thought I'd be okay preparing Thanksgiving dinner that year for our small group – only Thomas, the kids, Shirley, Joe, and me – but I was tense. I swore a lot and went through the motions of food preparation in a complete state of exhaustion. It had been a tough semester and sleep had been brutally sacrificed. Thomas, on the other hand, was in fine spirits, and the more I cursed and even called him names like moron and nincompoop, the more he laughed, which made me laugh, too. He was clearer about holiday priorities than I. I could say this was a blessing, only because that's the kind of thing people say around the holidays, not because it ever came naturally to a glass-half-empty, cranky kind of gal like myself. In fact, I had noticed that it annoyed me when people talked about their special blessings, and I wondered if it always had.

Our meal began with me asking everyone to talk about a blessing in their lives. I was trying to be a good role model and had a lot of work to do to balance out all the swearing. Shirley rolled her eyes. "Ain't it enough that we're alive? That's all I got to say."

I couldn't argue with that, so everyone got off the hook. But I tried another tack. After Thomas read a blessing from a book, I suggested that we toast to those people whom we love that couldn't be with us. Ben said, "So, like Mariah?" Mariah was Ben's current girlfriend. "Or do you mean somebody that's dead?"

I sighed. "Passed away, with us in spirit; okay, dead. I'm thinking about Poppy and also her cousin, Martha, who died this summer. She was such an incredible person, and I know a lot of people are missing her. I'm so glad I got to see her last year."

I looked to Joe sitting next to me and asked if he had anyone he wanted us to remember in our toast. I had purposefully omitted Dorothy, who had been gone less than a year, so that he could be the one to honor her. He responded by asking Thomas whether, when he became a nurse, he had to read a book. Thomas said, yes, and then we moved on to everyone else who was more adept at following the directions. Shirley was last. "Oh, well, I guess Walter."

I nodded my head. "I think about Walter at Thanksgiving, too."

"Well, I wasn't really thinkin' about him, but you made us do this and now the food is gettin' cold!" Food served piping hot was always Shirley's priority. Also, she was still getting over the year before when I tried to make everyone sing "Come Ye Thankful People, Come."

Unlike many holiday meals of the past, Joe fully participated in the dinner conversation, or at least had a lot of things to say. He talked about his new haircut and his concern that it didn't make him look younger than his 56 years. "I says to her, 'don't cut my cowlip off.'" Alison rolled her eyes. He then proceeded to talk about Walmart's name brands for less and somehow segued into pollution and that living in the country was best. "How 'bout all that carbonoxide, man. You can't even breathe in the city, no matter how many dorphins you got."

"Yeah, but you smoke, Uncle Joe," Ben said as he quietly removed Joe's hands from his upper arm. Joe had been feeling up his biceps, gingerly squeezing them and giggling, a lot. It was bizarre, but Ben stayed polite, enduring Joe squeezing his arm throughout the entire meal. Ben remained composed unless we made eye contact and started laughing, so we tried not to look at each other.

Joe continued. "I guess Dorothy's in Lake Lemon now." Thomas nodded his head. "That was a good place for her remains. I think she'd appreciate that." Joe shrugged his shoulders. "I guess so. I wanted to take her somewhere else, but you made us stop at the lake. That's okay."

Thomas started to respond, then thought better of the matter. He had finally gotten Joe to agree to distribute Dorothy's ashes, which had been sitting in a box in our bedroom closet. They had agreed on a place in Brown County, the scenic county adjacent to ours, thinking it would be perfect because Dorothy loved being in natural settings. Thomas told me that Joe said he was bored during the 40 minute drive and complained that it was taking too long to get there. When Thomas asked if he had some other place in mind, they were passing a nearby lake, Lake Lemon. They stopped and Joe said, "Let's do it here. I'm hungry." And so it became Dorothy's final resting place.

Changing the subject completely, Thomas began to tell us about his favorite new biofeedback toy from a company called HeartMath®, which he had brought home for all of us to try. He described the way you hook up a sensor to your earlobe or index finger, then breathe deeply and try to eliminate stress in your body while you watch the results on a computer screen. There were charts that showed the green, blue, and red zones indicated by your heartbeat variability, green being the best and red the worst. There were also accompanying games he wanted to show us after dinner, which I knew would be soon, never being ones to linger over coffee and erudite conversation.

"One game," Thomas said, "begins with a black and white woodland scene on the computer screen. As you approach the green zone, color comes in around the edges of the picture and there's a sound of little bells. I've gotten it to change to color all the way and even got it to the point where little animals come in."

"Little animals?" I asked.

"Yeah, like deer or a rabbit goes hopping by. Once I saw a naked woman behind the waterfall." I knew he was full of it on that last part.

Shirley guffawed. "Ha! I don't get it. Everybody's saying we have to not have stress. Well, there was this laughing group you could sign up for at Cedar Hills." She practically spit out her words. "Stupidest thing I ever saw. There they was, HAHAHA, HOHOHO. I stood outside in the hallway and laughed so hard at them." In response to our laughter, she added, "Well, it's funny, they's so stupid. See, you's laughin', too! Okay, let's go see what this is about. It sounds real dumb. Alison's got a full plate of food still. That would feed ten Chinamen! Did your mother ever say that, Melissa?"

"No."

As we headed to the computer for Thomas's demonstration, Joe said he was afraid that we were all going to be meditators now, like zombies. He closed his eyes and put his arms out straight, a la "Night of the Living Dead," bumping into longsuffering Ben whom he was following.

After Thomas showed us how the game worked, Alison hopped into the driver's seat. Still mad that I made her change her clothes for dinner, she stayed in the red zone, but didn't seem upset about the picture staying black and white. She shrugged her shoulders and said it was just her first try.

Ben was up next. He sat down, stuck his finger into the sensor, and, presto!, there was color, there was sparkling blue water, a doe and her fawns, even the bunny, all appearing with a sound of little tinkling bells. Everyone cheered, mostly in amazement over his immediate and sustained residence in the green zone. Shirley shouted, "You trained him up good. Let everyone do your worryin' for ya."

Thomas looked at me, my mouth agape, for I was the one who had done his worrying for him. Nights of lost sleep over his ability to accept whatever consequence we doled out for various transgressions, with him deciding he could just live without the items we took away after all. This was the boy who wouldn't read a book to save his life, the one who, sitting on the toilet upstairs before dinner, had called Alison on his cell phone to request that she bring him toilet paper. And she had. Spellbound by the screen, I stood behind Ben and grumbled, "Unbelievable." He laughed and breathed deeply in the land of living color.

Is he Buddha? Thomas and I wondered later that evening. *Or just a bum? Or both?* Thomas muttered, "Yes, we have a lot to learn from Ben. He's going to live a long time – in our basement."

After an impressive amount of time in meditative bliss, I kicked Ben off the machine and tried it myself. Thomas encouraged me to go to my happy place, and I sneered. I imagined everyone elbowing each other behind me, then tried not to think about such things as I inhaled and exhaled slowly and deeply. Standing behind me, a little too close, Shirley tried to be helpful. "Think about a new car you don't have to pay for. And it's your favorite color. What's your favorite color? It gets good mileage. You need that nowadays. Gas has done gone out of control. Did you see the prices at Marathon yesterday? Shooo-eee, they are through the roof! So you need good mileage. I'm just sayin'."

"Mom." Tom said with exasperation. He escorted her out of the room as she shouted, "Well, have you seen them prices?" "It doesn't matter," he told her. "That isn't Melissa's happy place. It remains undiscovered."

Alison jumped up, rubbed my shoulders, and kissed me on the cheek. This was the nicest she had been to me all day. She took a sip from my glass of water and I involuntarily blurted out, "We shouldn't be sharing, I have a sore throat." Too late. All her good will vanished and she scowled at me. Needless to say, I stayed in the red zone. I never saw the bunny.

While cleaning the kitchen, I paused to run upstairs to the bathroom and, to my mortification, stopped up the commode. This made me reconsider a recent claim made by my friend, Suzette, about going through a period of massive bowel movements that stopped up the toilet, like it was a developmental stage all middle-aged women experienced. I tried to fix it myself, but needed help. And there I was without a cell phone… I stood at the top of the stairs and told Thomas I needed help with something. The look we exchanged was the kind of communication we had taken 23 years to develop. His expression indicated his understanding that I was dealing with something embarrassing and mine said, watch it, I'm on the edge here. Trying to avoid his mother's attention, he said, "Does it require…tools?" I nodded my head and laughed. It occurred to me that this is how we do it. I throw down a challenge, he makes a joke, and I laugh, thereby releasing the stress that, as Shirley said, we couldn't seem to stop talking about. I realized that if I ever lost my sense of humor or, worse, if Thomas ever lost his, there would be no point in watching scenes of the forest as we breathed in and out, for humor is what we ran on. Elegant we would never be, but laughter remained in good supply. As it turned out, this was the best Thanksgiving blessing I could imagine.

Phone message:

Melissa? This woman showed up naked in the dining room. Another time she wore her diaper over her dress. Turns out she's been takin' all the dessert dishes of an evening. She got twelve, one at a time. She wanted a set. I just thought you'd find that interesting. This is Shirley.

In Need of Assistance

49

RELIGIOUS TRAINING

We started 2009 warily. Having seen Dorothy's death firsthand, I was more aware of what decline looked like, even if it was happening in ways that weren't always obvious or that I tried to ignore. I knew that it could strike quickly and without warning. Thomas and I were busier than ever. In addition to teaching full time at Indiana University, I was now directing the undergraduate special education program, and Thomas's responsibilities continued to grow as he added a wellness clinic to the occupational health and urgent care clinics he had been directing for some time. Alison had started middle school, and Ben, having decided he didn't want to be in school at that time, was living in an apartment in town and working in the IU Psychology Department, making materials in a wood and metal shop to be used in various forms of research. Our lives were full, but we could easily see to Shirley's needs almost every day, given the convenient location of her apartment close to our places of work. Sometimes I felt stressed when I was in her messy apartment and unable to clear off a spot to sit down. But other times, the setting had an opposite effect on me, and I would sit down on a pile of papers on the couch without even attempting to find another place for them. I'd put my feet on the coffee table, eat whatever fast food I had picked up for us for dinner, and watch a montage of old people falling down on *America's Funniest Home Videos* with Shirley, who saw this as the height of hilarity. Every once in a while, I tried to organize Shirley's papers and memorabilia from her childhood, but never got very far.

One afternoon at Cedar Hills, Shirley and I were looking at a picture of children kneeling and praying in their pajamas in a Soldiers' and Sailors' Children's Home centennial celebration book called *The Home, 1865-1965*. I asked her, "Did you do this?"

Shirley rolled her eyes. "Yes."

"Every night?"

"They made you."

"Did it mean anything to you?"

"No. After we said, 'now I lay me down to sleep,' we'd say, 'God bless so-and-so,' y'know, and we always had to say the governess's name first." I was reminded of the children in the musical, "Annie," chanting in unison, "We love you, Miss Hannigan."

It was interesting to think about Shirley's resistance to prayer, given her devout faith as an adult. She and Dot shared their memories of requisite praise and supplication once, starting with a description of their dining hall experiences. Shirley had been talking about seeing Georgie get in trouble for not eating her peas. "Old Schumacher, that's what we called the matron in there, was watchin' to see if she ate her peas, so Georgie counted out ten peas on her plate and made everyone laugh. Old Schumacher walked up and dumped a whole big spoon of them on top. And when Georgie wouldn't eat 'em, she had to go to the superintendent's office. I don't know what happened after that because that never happened to me. I stayed out of trouble. But I hated cooked turnips and carrots that was cooked and fatty meat. Have you ever had roast beef with a lot of fat on it? Some like it but it made me sick. So, I stuffed it all up my britches, y'know them bloomers kids used to wear, and the elastic kept it long enough to dump it in the bushes when I was done."

After reciting the blessing used in the dining room, Dot giggled. "Remember that prayer you used to say, Shirley?" Dot said. "'Praise the Lord and the Holy Ghost. Whoever eats the fastest gets the most.'" They both laughed.

"You had to say it quiet or you'd get in trouble! There was a special blessing for the dining room." Shirley said.

"We never sat at the same table, but I remember hearing you say it!" Dot replied. "Y'know, it's kind of hard to explain, because we had to go to church, but we couldn't talk to anyone about Jesus because it was a state institution."

"Right," Shirley said. "They was the state so they wasn't allowed to."

"So, what were the sermons about?" I asked.

"God and doing good deeds. I learned all the stories like Joseph and his coat," Shirley said.

"Was there Sunday School?"

"No."

"So, no baptisms?"

"Not there. They couldn't," Shirley said. "Some kids went to other churches outside the Home, like if you were a Catholic or a Jew. But I guess they wouldn't get baptized either." She laughed. "I guess none of those little kids got saved!"

"Did you wish you could talk to someone about God?" I asked.

"No."

"Well, I wished I could," Dot shared, "but I never did. I began to talk to God when I was a little girl. When they would take us kids into town, I'd see children walking with their dads holding their hands, and I wished I had that. So, I pretended I had a dad to hold my hand, too, and I called him Father God. And no one knew." Her eyes welled with tears. "It was like he was holding my hand the whole time."

I wondered about all those children going to church, listening to sermons, reading Bible stories – but lacking permission to talk about what any of it meant. The orphanage appeared to embrace the culture of Christianity, but for children for whom this message resonated, they were on their own.

50

SUSPICION OF SHOPLIFTING

It was evening and Shirley was calling with questions which I let our voicemail pick up. "Melissa? Was you strip searched? By the woman? Patsy wants to know. I thought you said they done checked your underwear. This is Shirley, by the way."

"Melissa, this is Shirley again. The girls want to know if you was arrested. I couldn't remember what you said about that."

It had been a long day.

When Ben decided to take a break from school and moved to his first apartment in Bloomington, he needed various housewares to get set up. For the most part, I had enough surplus of everything to supply him what he needed, but decided to check out the Monroe County History Center Annual Sale to see what I might find. He still needed a set of dishes, which was the kind of thing one could expect to see there for about five dollars. Ben had agreed to meet me, despite his insistence that he could get by for quite a while on a large supply of disposable dishes and cutlery Shirley had bought for him.

After waiting around for a few minutes, I gave up on Ben and went in. I wasn't shocked that he'd not shown; in fact, he had been distancing himself from me in noticeable ways. Just the night before, I couldn't remember the celebrity Snoop Dogg's name and said on the phone with him, rather randomly, "Who says f-shizzle?" His rapid response was, "Not you, not ever."

I had forgotten that no carts or baskets were provided at this sale and hadn't brought any bags in with me. As I gathered odds and ends, I put them in my purse, leaving it wide open so everyone could see I wasn't trying to steal them. After I'd been shopping about twenty minutes, still no Ben, a couple of men approached me and asked that I go with them to another room.

They seemed really nice. "Sure!" I said, thinking they might be interviewing customers about the sale. We went to a back room and they asked to go through my purse.

I was confused. "Excuse me?"

"Ma'am, someone told us that you were taking things without paying for them." My heart began to pound. "Well, not *yet*. I haven't paid for them *yet*," I stammered. "But I certainly plan to before leaving."

"Do you mind if we examine what you have?"

"Of course not," I lied. "I'll show you everything myself. I think it totals less than eight dollars."

"That's all right, ma'am; we don't need your help."

I was too dumbfounded to express my indignation. There was a female officer who went through my purse, pulling out the objects in question, plus things that were not. The men asked what I was intending to do with the sale merchandise. "Pay for it," I said. I was seething, but this was secondary to my humiliation.

"Okay, then. We're sorry to have bothered you, ma'am."

Looking around to see who my accuser might have been as I reentered the sale room, and wondering if this person even existed, I thought about leaving my selections there. I resolved to buy them instead, if anything, to show that I could. As I went through the line, a kindly older woman wearing a green volunteer apron was the cashier. I hesitated, then decided to share what had happened to me. It was satisfying to see how appalled she was. "I'm so sorry," she said. "This is the first year we've hired security. We certainly never imagined them accosting people before they had a chance to pay." She asked me to come back next year and I said I would, with a basket next time.

It's hard to describe how affected I was by this experience -- preoccupied, to say the least. I went through a McDonald's drive-through to buy a Diet Coke, paid at the first window, then drove away without picking up the drink. I thought about friends who had described such accusations, and realized I'd never known how awful it could feel.

I called Ben. "Where were you?" I demanded.

"Sorry, Mom, I meant to come, but I guess I forgot. And I have a surprise."

"Oh, yeah? What's that?"

"I went to the pound and got a dog!"

Shirley responded to this story like it was her birthday. I recognized too late the strange thrill she exhibited and the fodder I had provided for dining room conversation among her friends. The need for excitement among this little assemblage was like a fifth food group, utterly necessary and missed in times of scarcity. "Tell me again," Shirley said. "Why did they tap you on the shoulder? Is that when they done took you to another room?"

"Well, I told you, they thought I was stealing."

"Was the room in the basement? Was anyone else around?"

"Not in the basement. I don't even know if they have a basement in that building. There was a female officer who looked through my purse."

She looked at me expectantly. "That's it," I said.

Thomas and I listened to the voicemail messages Shirley left before we went to bed. "She has you leading a prison revolt by now," he said.

I laughed. "Well, I'm glad something good's coming from this."

It took a couple of weeks for the story to die down in the Cedar Hills dining room, a period during which Shirley's popularity spiked impressively. While others bragged about their children's achievements, Shirley trumped them all, still saying she didn't really know what I did for a living, but that I had recently been patted down for contraband and might even have a record now.

51

COMRADE DORIS ROLLS AWAY THE STONE

Easter dinner had been thrown together this year. Coming in from out of town the day before, I hadn't the time or the energy for anything special. I assessed the contents of the refrigerator and pantry. There were eggs Alison and I had dyed earlier that week that could be devilled, a few potatoes, and some asparagus, a bit past its prime. That evening, I went to the store and picked up a roasted chicken and a couple of pies, thinking this would be enough for our group of six with Shirley and Joe joining us.

When we sat down to eat, Shirley announced that she didn't like asparagus, that it was her least favorite vegetable. This was typical, as much a staple of our dinner conversations as "Pass the salt." I challenged her. "Shirley. Name two vegetables that you like."

"Broccoli."

"Nope. You said at Christmas broccoli was your least favorite vegetable."

"Was you servin' broccoli then? Oh."

"Try again," I said. "Just two vegetables." She continued to think, clearly at a loss. Ben shot me a look of reproach, and Alison jumped in to save her grandmother. "You like green beans," she said.

"Yes!" Shirley practically shouted. "I like green beans." I counted to three. She continued, "But not barely cooked. They should be cooked for several hours so's the bean can't stand up. Once when we was in California, this woman barely cooked them. It was unbelievable. I mean they was practically raw. I could barely eat 'em." She paused. "But that's how Melissa cooks green beans, I guess."

"Any others?" I cooed.

"What?"

"Vegetables you'll eat."

She thought for a moment. "Well, I'm sure they's somethin'. They put something in the cushie at dinner last night. But I don't know what it was." Since I had already been unkind, I didn't pursue the obvious – what is a cushie? It was Thomas who asked. I had assumed this meant they were serving couscous at Cedar Hills, but it turned out it was quiche. This was a reasonable mistake on my part, since Shirley usually called quiche "quickie," "quishy," or "squishy."

After we said the blessing and loaded our plates, I asked the kids if one of them could tell the Easter story. Never having sent Ben and Alison to Vacation Bible School, I was aware of all the Bible stories they hadn't learned and tried to fill in whenever I could, including various mnemonics I'd been taught. I could still remember the Old Testament story of Shadrach, Meshach, and Abednego, thrown into the fiery furnace by King Nebuchadnezzar, because my teachers had taught me the phrase, "Shake the bed, make the bed, and into the bed we go!" Ben's telling of Jesus's crucifixion and resurrection was good, better than I expected, and it was nice that he didn't seem to be holding a grudge toward me for picking a fight about the vegetables a few minutes before. After he got to the part about the rolling away of the stone and Jesus appearing to the disciples, Ben stopped, and said, "And there's something about the disciple named Thomas." This had been Alison's favorite part in the past, since it was her dad's name. When I tried to fill in the story of Doubting Thomas, Shirley piped up.

"Don't forget he was chasing a pig."

I knitted my brow. "Wow," I said. "Really? I don't remember that."

"Oh, yeah, you know. 'Tom, Tom, the piper's son. Stole a

pig and away he run.'"

"Okay." I gave a meaningful look to the kids that said, we'll work this out later. But the comment left me wondering. Had Shirley genuinely confused Doubting Thomas with a nursery rhyme? Was she just messing with me? I scrutinized her facial expression. Busily cutting her meat, she was the picture of indifference.

After a while, Shirley said, "Melissa, you probably don't even teach about the Bible in your Sunday School class. Your church don't use it, do they?"

"They do, but I think we should use it more in the curriculum for the kids," I said.

"Well, what is you teachin' them kids that's more important than the Bible?"

"Last week, we talked about Dorothea Dix, because of all the great things she did and because she was a Unitarian."

"Dorothy Dix? Well, she's still alive!"

"No," I said slowly.

"Yeah, Dorothy Day's alive."

"Well, that's someone different. Dorothy Day was a famous communist, but she's dead, too."

"A communist! You are wrong!" she cried. "She was wholesome and she was, well, she was patriotic and had all them movies. And not everyone knows it, but they done covered up all her freckles."

We all stared. After a pause, Shirley continued. "Well, I'da knowed it if she was a communist. She sang 'Kay Sarah Sarah,'." Help us, Lord, I thought.

"Okay," I said. "Doris Day. You're right. She's alive. Not a communist."

"How anyone could call her a communist, well, that's the craziest thing I ever heard. Everybody loved her. And I don't think she was ever in your church neither. She's a Christian." I lowered my head to the table, for just a moment, then got up with Thomas to start clearing the dishes.

When I returned with the pies, Ben began playing air guitar. He and Alison sang "She's My Cherry Pie." Joe joined the conversation for the first time by singing "Bye, Bye, Miss American Pie," and Shirley warbled "Can she bake a cherry pie, charming Billy."

When they institutionalize me, I hope I remember it was Dorothea Dix who advocated for my rights, that she never sang "Que Sera Sera," and she really was a Unitarian Universalist. After we had eaten dessert, I left the dishes in the sink and joined Thomas under the gray skies of early spring to hide plastic eggs for our annual hunt. They were filled with dollar bills to keep the kids and any of their friends that might stop by interested in finding them, extending this childhood tradition one more year.

52

BONERS

Along with other residents at Cedar Hills, Shirley took pride in the fact that there were no "assisted living" services offered in the facility. If you were living at Cedar, it meant you could still paddle your own canoe when it came to basic needs in the areas of communication and mobility. Some remained past this point by hiring people to stay with them in their apartments. But when a person walked into the dining room without their pants on, the women at Shirley's table would cluck their tongues and say, "Looks like it's time for assisted living."

"What is it with the pants?" I asked Thomas. "You never hear about someone coming to dinner without a shirt. It's always the pants." Noting his attire of tee-shirt and underwear as he watched TV, the answer to my question began to come into view.

Shirley was disdainful of people in need of assistance. For this reason, when her osteoporosis limited her mobility and signs of dementia began to appear, we were careful not to talk about moving right away. She didn't want to go. As much as she complained about various managers or the food or the cleaning service, this had been her home for nine years since her arrival in 2000. She was 89 years old.

"I wonder if anyone else has been here that long," I said to Thomas. "How many month-long leases has she had for nine years? More than a hundred!"

"There's a few," Thomas said, "but not many. I guess we need to start thinking about where she's going to go."

"Have you brought it up with her?"

"No, and I don't want to either. Let's look for someone who can stay with her part time," he said.

So we put off broaching the subject of moving by talking

to her about someone who could keep her company a few hours each day. Someone who could do her laundry and help her keep the place picked up. "Well, who're you going to find to do that? That sounds expensive," was Shirley's response. "And what if I don't like them?"

Neither Thomas nor I wish to be credited with this brainstorm in hindsight, but Ben became our first candidate. He had been laid off at the university Psych Department workshop when research funding was cut, then had worked on a construction crew for a few months, but was now between jobs. He still liked to hang out at his grandmother's apartment occasionally, so why not get paid for it? As soon as the idea was hatched, I latched on to it, thinking about what buddies they had been all his life and how much they still enjoyed each other's company. I was relieved that he had quit working construction, given his stories about some of the workers showing up to the site stoned or drunk. This was not something I wanted to hear when thinking about my son perched on an upper story beam and relying on fellow crew members.

I was surprised that Ben seemed reticent when presented with the opportunity. "Can't you find somebody else?" he said.

"Well, probably, but we thought you'd like to have some income while you're looking for another job. And Grandma is more comfortable with you than she would be with someone else."

His expressions of doubt intensified, and my encouragement turned to insistence. Not the best start for something that was doomed regardless. He relented however, and we agreed to pay him for four hours a day, several days a week. After the first day, I called Ben to ask how it went. "I don't know, Mom. We just sat around and watched *America's Funniest Home Videos*. I took care of her laundry like you said. When I asked her if she wanted me to put it away, she seemed kind of mad."

"What do you mean?"

"Well, first she was mad because she thought she could do it. Then she was having trouble with the hangers and got mad that I wasn't helping her. And, Mom, I don't want to fold her underwear."

From the beginning, it didn't look like it was going to work out. It was alarming to see the relationship quickly deteriorating with Shirley complaining about Ben for the first time in his life and Ben barely tolerating the situation. After a few days, I stopped by to check on her and found Shirley agitated. She looked up at me from her stooped position and pointed to the television. "Well," she fairly shouted, "there's another one of Ben's boners."

This was an expression I hadn't heard in a while. "Excuse me?"

"I told him to turn the television around and he turned it the wrong way!"

"Oh," I said as I moved to the TV to turn it around. "I'm sure it was a misunderstanding, Shirley."

"Well, I can't explain everything just so. I tried to tell him but he got it all wrong."

Later, Thomas and I gave Ben a call and asked him how it was going. He was adamant. "Not good. She's mad at me all the time."

"Yeah," Thomas said, trying to maintain a neutral tone. "She told Mom about your boners."

Ben raised his voice. "What *is* that? I hate it when she says that."

"Oh, Ben," I said, "you know that just means mistakes. It's kind of an old-fashioned term."

"Well, that isn't what it means now, and I don't want to tell her about it. I just said I didn't like it when she said that and that made her say it more, like when Dad said he hated it when anyone says Walgreen's and then we said it around him all the time."

I laughed. "I doubt it's the same. We did that on purpose." I was surprised Ben remembered that. He must have been about five when Thomas proclaimed his personal dislike for the name of our drug store, Walgreen's. I suspect the real problem was that he was sick of hearing *me* say it, as in, "Did you pick that up at Walgreens?" or, "You know, I think you can get that at Walgreens," or, "I can't believe we forgot to stop by Walgreens." Ben had confessed he didn't like the way Terri Gross said "Fresh Air" on NPR, emphasis on the sh- sound, and I complained about the sound Thomas made whenever there was an unpleasant smell. If Shirley had reacted the way we did when hearing the source of each other's idiosyncratic irritations, she would have walked around saying, "Boner, boner, boner."

Ben continued his lament. "Yesterday, she said it when Dylan was on the phone and he *heard* her say it. And he's telling people. I don't want to go anymore."

With the best of intentions, we were paving the road to hell for Shirley and Ben. The good news was that it didn't take long after the arrangement ended for Ben to resume his visits as a grandson, rather than an employee. I admitted the idea had been one big boner and apologized to Ben, then promised not to say boner anymore.

53

GIVING UP THE FIGHT

"Well, I done give up fighting. If I have to go to assisted living, okay, then. I know I need more help, but it isn't what I want." Shirley collapsed on her couch after taking down the My Little Pony computer printouts she'd displayed for Alison years ago. A good first step toward cleaning out her place, but hardly a dent in this overwhelming task.

I sighed and nodded my head. This was not the mother-in-law with whom I'd bickered for 25 years. Some days, the cruel curvature of osteoporosis that forced her to face the ground and look up at me from a bowed head had knocked the sass right out of her. She was confused most of the time now, taking a lot of morphine for pain. At some point when I was at home and wondering what it would be like to never stand or sit up straight, I bent over and tried to go about my business for about fifteen minutes. It was enlightening, like when Ben was a baby and I once spent a few minutes of his nap time crawling around the house to see what the world looked like from his knee-high perspective. But this was worse because it was degenerative, rather than a normal stage of development. I noticed that I couldn't take a deep breath when I was stooped and shuddered to think of Shirley's inability to breathe deeply for more than a year at this point.

It hadn't been that long ago when Shirley had called to me in the parking lot of Cedar Hills, "Melissa, get me a book on All-timers. I'm gonna read it and do everything the opposite." Now she didn't seem to care about holding on to her independence. She was throwing in the towel.

Shirley had been uncooperative when we took her to Deer Park Home, an assisted living facility with an excellent reputation.

She snapped at the director who had asked her a few simple questions and snubbed the lovely woman we'd met when she had opened her apartment for us to see. At least Shirley was showing some spunk that day. On the way home, she had said about the woman whose apartment we'd seen, "She's a retired professor. Like Melissa." Clearly, this was not a compliment.

"I'm not retired, Shirley," I said, "and you shouldn't hold it against her if I were. She was really nice."

Thomas was annoyed with his mother. "You can't say mean things to people in the new place. It was embarrassing. And don't fart. I couldn't believe you farted in that woman's home."

"Well, what was I supposed to do?"

"Not that."

I wondered if the dread Shirley felt was familiar. She didn't want to move to the Home in 1928, but there was no point in fighting then, too. It was the only place to go. Here she was, a lifetime later, not even 100 miles away, dreading entry into another unfamiliar institution. "Shirley, I think where you're going is going to be better. I really think it's going to be okay," I said, back in her apartment.

"Well, you don't really know that, do you?"

I paused to take this in. "You're right. I guess I don't." I missed the retort that always followed such admissions.

That evening, I talked with Thomas about an 89th birthday party for his mother that could be planned in the next few weeks. "We shouldn't wait until she's 90?" he asked. He knew I could be superstitious about such things, but it wasn't about that this time. It was questionable that his mother would make it to her 90th birthday.

The whole family came to Cedar Hills for Shirley's birthday party in May of 2009. Four children, three accompanied by spouses, six grandchildren and three spouses, and four great-grandchildren. The weather was beautiful, and we were able to take family pictures outside.

After about an hour of celebrating, it was easy to see that Shirley was worn out. As she and I walked slowly back to her apartment, we encountered another resident named Vi, whose vim and vigor rubbed us both the wrong way. But I couldn't help doing a bit of bragging, which I saw in hindsight as opening a door I regretted. "It's nice to see you, Vi. Shirley's had quite a birthday party with 20 family members who came into town to celebrate with her."

"Is that all?" Vi said in a saccharine voice. "Well, I had 34 family here for my ninetieth last month! Do you remember that, Shirley? It was really something!" She was starting to question Shirley's age, saying she hadn't known it was her 90th, all a bit suspiciously, while Shirley and I kept putting one foot in front of the other, like the turtle determined to outrun that annoyingly spry rabbit. Finally, we made it to her apartment, closing the door on all the over-stimulation.

Shirley fell on the couch in a heap and started to take her pants off. I stared for a moment, then kicked into gear when she said, "Help me get these off. My butt's hot."

Once this was accomplished and her rear end was cooling down, Shirley said, "Do I have to go back out there? Do I have to put my pants back on? I'm tired."

"I think everyone is leaving now, and you already said your goodbyes."

"Good," she sighed with relief, then laughed. "Maybe I should go to the dining room like this, just to let everyone know I'm on my way out." There was a pause before she looked up at me from the couch. "What was Vi saying?"

"Nothing important," I said.

"She brags all the time," Shirley said. "I do not care for her."

"Yeah," I said, "me neither."

54

LAST ROAD TRIP

Thomas's oldest brother, Lee, was scheduled for surgery near his home in Ohio. Shirley wanted to see him and Thomas agreed to take her there. This turned out to be a bigger undertaking than he realized at the time. A five-hour drive with his mother on oxygen and bent into a position that caused relentless discomfort in the car was a tall order.

The plan was to drive to Columbus in time to visit Lee at the hospital, check into a hotel for the night, then leave in the morning to return home. I helped Thomas load the car before they left. The back seat was filled with a dozen canisters of oxygen, with more loaded in the trunk. "Whoa," I said. "Do people do this? I mean, is this done? Looks like the two of you would be blown to high heaven if you encountered an open flame."

"Yeah, well, I guess we'll just have to avoid that," Thomas said, his voice a little tense.

Around 9:00 that night, Thomas called me. "I don't know what I was thinking," he said.

"Pretty bad?" I asked.

"I'm wiped out."

I heard some curious background noise. "Where are you?"

"In the hotel bar."

"Where's your mom?"

"Well, I left her in the room, so I guess that's where she is. I couldn't take listening to her anymore."

"Maybe she feels the same way about you," I teased, but I knew it wasn't true. "I hope she's okay by herself."

Thomas acted like he hadn't heard me. "Maybe I won't go back. Maybe I'll just leave," he said. "She had a lot to say about

Katy getting pregnant and not using Cameron's 'seed.' This was at Burger King, thinking she was whispering when she really wasn't." Katy was a great niece recently impregnated by a sperm donor, since her husband's sperm wasn't viable anymore, according to what we'd been told. "Ha!" I said, "I remember when you and I were at the center of the conversation about seeds. Better them than us. How is Lee?"

"Okay, I guess," Thomas said. "By the time we got there, we were both too tired to focus, and he was kind of out of it." There was a pause in the conversation. I heard the sound of ice tinkling in a glass.

"So," I said, "how much have you had to drink?"

"Not enough. I need another drink before I go back. It's gonna be another long drive in the morning. After I drag out and load the oxygen tanks she doesn't use."

This turned out to be the last time Shirley saw her oldest son. Lee recovered after his surgery and accompanying treatment, but didn't make it to Bloomington to say goodbye before she died.

55

MOVING ON

Shirley was indignant. "That girl took my monkey!"

"What are you talking about?" I said.

"That girl you and Tom brung over. Jesseeca. She wasn't supposed to take anything away I still wanted."

"What monkey?"

"The one on my door. I kept it on there the whole time I been here."

I sighed. The Beanie Baby had hung by its neck on a spiraling plastic, green key chain on Shirley's door at Cedar Hills in the nine years she had lived there. All the other seniors had less startling decorations on their doors, such as seasonal wreaths or plaques that said, "Grandma's Place." But not Shirley. "I like being different," she said when four-year-old Alison stuck it there and she decided to keep it. Over the years, I heard people walking down the quiet halls and gasping at the sight of the hanging monkey when they saw it for the first time. They would whisper, "What in the world?" and laugh surreptitiously as they moved on. "Jessica would never have gotten rid of it unless you said it was okay. She's been really careful before she takes anything to Goodwill."

Jessica was a lovely young woman we knew, someone Thomas had befriended through his continued participation in Landmark seminars, this being the current iteration of the est® training where we'd met 25 years before. We had hired her to spend time with Shirley and help her get ready to move, but I always got the impression she would have done it without a fee. Jessica was the perfect person to fill this need of ours, developing compassion for and a fierce protectiveness of Shirley right from the start of their relationship, in spite of Shirley's prickly disposition at the time.

"You don't know," Shirley's rant continued. "You wasn't here. She's taking everything and I don't know what she's doing with it. Now I done lost it and I want it back."

"I can try to find you another one if you want to decorate your door the same way at the new place."

"I do. And this was a special one. It squeaked when you squeezed its belly."

I looked at Shirley, trying to appraise the situation. "It was a Beanie Baby and it didn't do that. I think you're angling for an upgrade."

Shirley laughed. "Not really. But I sure liked that monkey. Seems like I been losing everything I love."

I knew the move to Montgomery House was going to be a tough one, with losses on multiple levels. There would be a loss of independence, loss of friends, and loss of possessions that needed to be downsized since Shirley was moving to a smaller space. She already had too much furniture and clutter crammed into her larger one-bedroom apartment. Surfaces always had to be cleared to put down a cup of coffee or sit on the couch. It seemed like Shirley stopped talking as much about Patsy, likely distancing herself in preparation for her departure. I doubted this was intentional, more like a survival skill honed many years before.

When I inquired about the monkey, Jessica shook her head solemnly. "It was too soon. I should have held on to it longer. But she said she was finished with it. I asked her a couple of times before putting it in the box to go. I remember because she was preoccupied with finding the booties of that doll of Alison's that she keeps on her bed. She kept saying they were expensive. We turned the place upside down and never found them."

I rolled my eyes. "That puppet of the little old lady that swallowed the fly? I can tell you those booties weren't expensive." I shook my head. "It's hard to know what's important and what isn't these days. The other day, when I was going through a box of memorabilia with her, she told me to pitch the yearbook of her high school at the Soldiers' and Sailors' Home. I couldn't believe it and said, 'No way.' She said she didn't care about it and I should just take it."

Jessica nodded. "Well, I hate that she's upset about the monkey. Do you want me to look for another one?"

"No, I've got it. You're already helping us out by staying with Shirley when we can't be around."

"I like being over there and I think she's getting used to me. It helps that we have something to do now that I'm helping her get ready for the move. The other day when I was leaving, she said, 'I guess I love you, you little Jew.' And she doesn't talk to me about Jesus so much anymore."

I kept forgetting to look for a monkey as the moving day approached. There were so many things to take care of. It was astounding how much clutter Shirley had accumulated over the years, and I was sure I was responsible for it, at least in part. Shirley's home had been a roach motel for Ben and Alison's never-ending piles of stuff. Everything that was checked in never quite got checked out. Everywhere you looked was chaos resulting from nine years of indecision and disorganization. There were boxes, baskets, and plastic containers spilling their contents of costume jewelry, dress up clothes, video tapes, books, important papers, timeline markers of *Happy Meal toys – Sponge Bob, the Little Mermaid, Ice Age II* – headless dolls, pill bottles, photographs, magazines, bills, greeting cards, Beanie Babies, and Kleenex, so much Kleenex wadded up everywhere, even when I placed wastebaskets next to where Shirley sat.

More than once, I stood before the colossal mess of junk and tried to psych myself into taking it on by thinking about what could be worse. I had cleaned a nacho cheese machine at a Little League ball field on a cold and rainy day, without hot water. I had directed traffic at the county fair in 90 degree heat. I had fished my keys out of a gas station toilet when Alison dropped them in. Even when I imagined terrible things I hadn't experienced, like picking up roadside garbage in an orange jumpsuit, or being elected to the local school board, I kept looking at the flotsam and jetsam in all directions and walking away thinking, I'll work on it tomorrow.

Now we were left with this chore at a time when Shirley was most vulnerable and confused. When she rejected all the photographs and other documents from her childhood, I began to fill my own boxes to take all of it home to sort through once everything settled down.

We had to get rid of furniture, too, to fit Shirley into her new one-room apartment. It helped that she no longer needed her double bed, which took up a lot of room. She hadn't slept in a bed in a couple of years now, preferring her recliner as her body bent to the stern curves of osteoporosis. Other than the recliner, we needed to fit in a couple of dressers, a book shelf, and a television on the floor where Shirley could see it.

Whenever I was at Montgomery House, using a tape measure to figure out how everything might fit, a handsome older man kept stopping by to introduce himself. Edgar was his name and I couldn't help but think I might go for him if I were single and closer to his age. He was tall, impeccably dressed, had a sunny disposition, and was exquisitely polite. The only problem was that he never knocked. He would walk in quietly, peek around the corner of the entryway, and say, "Everything okay in there?" He seemed eager to meet Shirley, which made me uneasy, knowing that her disposition was mostly cloudy with a chance of rain these days. When I asked the aids about Edgar, they laughed and told me he used to be a night watchman. "Edgar checks on everyone," they said.

"My mother-in-law won't like that," I said. I wouldn't have liked it either, regardless of his looks. The night before moving day, Thomas put a big sign on the door that said, "PLEASE KNOCK." Looking it over, I gasped. "Oh, no! I forgot the monkey. And I told your mom I'd find one."

I ran all over town: Target, K-Mart, Wal-Mart. Finally, at Kohl's, I found a small, stuffed, purple gorilla in a display by the cash registers, only five dollars. It would have to do. I drove to Montgomery House to hang it by its thick neck on a piece of rope, which I fastened to the door just above the "PLEASE KNOCK" sign. Thomas and I stood before the entrance, briefly assessing the first impression everyone would have of the new resident, then moved inside to place pictures on the wall and set up the bathroom with all of Shirley's toiletries.

The next day, I waited in the new apartment for Thomas to deliver his mom. I spotted the high school yearbook from the orphanage in a bag of things I had meant to take home. It reminded me of a conversation she and I had had while looking through The Retrospect from 1938. There were pictures of various students, like Eula and Iola Woodworth, the twins with the long, shiny curls. Shirley said they were everyone's favorites and "got pushed ahead." Next to Eula's senior picture, it said, "lovely and laughing" – to which Shirley had said, "Bull." Next to Iola's picture, "dimples, the other half," and both had countless accomplishments and activities listed. Mavis Rose Redding was another favorite apparently. Next to her name, it said, "charming, poised, and talented." The caption by Shirley's picture read, "a lover of sports."

The seniors also had their nicknames listed. Eula Woodworth was Buzzy and Mavis Rose Redding was Minnie.

Out of 28 seniors, Shirley was the only one without a nickname. Next to her name, it said, "none yet." Shirley had shrugged her shoulders. "I wish my name was in there more. I wasn't popular and I wasn't active. I guess I was kind of shy, and, well, they sorted you out. Some of us got pushed ahead and some didn't."

In fact, in the Soldiers' and Sailors' Home 1938 Senior High School Report to the Governor was the following acknowledgement of academic tracking:

Under teacher guidance the pupils investigate their own abilities in the various fields. Certain prognostic tests given by the administrative staff gave the pupils a fair idea of their probable success in certain subject matter fields. This project definitely reduced the number who desired to follow the academic (college preparatory) curriculum.

What a life-altering decision this must have been for each pupil, I thought, pupils that were often referred to as inmates in these reports. Again I was reminded that there was no one, no parent or special guardian, there to advocate for them. No one to help them establish their individuality, anything that would help them stand out among their peers, all dressed in one of the three outfits allotted to them. Personal charm likely propelled individual children down a path to success, but a sparkling personality would have been hard to realize if you believed you'd been abandoned by everyone you had loved and trusted.

Shirley studied the pictures some more. "I would have liked to have an affair with Chuck Foley. He was real cute. Cecil Wiggins, too."

"Did you ever tell them?" I asked.

"No. Chuck liked me okay, but I was real shy and stupid."

"Did you ever tell anyone you liked Chuck or Cecil?"

"I guess not. I wouldn't have told anything to those

women about myself. They'd just go tell everybody." She had been a loner all those years at the home, in spite of having four younger siblings there. She often summed up her experience there by saying, "I was nobody's favorite." Every child should be somebody's favorite, I thought.

Shirley also had things to say about the adults at the Home. Next to the picture of Oda P. Jensen, an unsmiling older woman, the caption read, "for years an outstanding governess." Shirley said, "We called her Odie P. behind her back. She hated that." She jabbed her finger at pictures of a couple of teachers. "He got her pregnant. She got fired. He got to stay."

The 1938 senior class was the largest to date in the history of the orphanage. Their senior play that year was *Smilin' Through*, a popular story of a man communing with the spirit of his dead fiancée, killed by a jealous ex-boyfriend on their wedding day, and of his niece, orphaned when her parents drowned and in love with the son of the fiancée's killer, her uncle opposing the relationship, of course. Lots to smile through. When I asked Shirley what she remembered about the play, she just said, "Not much. Some people played two parts, but I wasn't in it."

The description next to the senior picture of Shirley Peacock in 1938 said, "Glee Club, Rifle Club, Dramatics, Athletic Club, and Young People's Society." I remembered Shirley talking about how you could pursue just about any hobby at the home. The problem was that if you felt like quitting, no one encouraged you to stay with it. She'd never become skillful at any of the pastimes listed by her name. Her weakness listed was basketball; her favorite food, celery; favorite tune, "Stardust." Her ambition was "to be a hair dresser," which she had indeed become, years of perms and pin curls before getting work at the commercial bakery where she stayed until she retired.

I stared at the picture of Shirley as a teenager. A few short months after the picture was taken, she would be expected to take care of herself for the rest of her days, following a childhood without parents. I closed my eyes and tried to imagine the bleak routine of Shirley's days at the orphanage, her anonymity among all those children. At the Home, Shirley had survived by not being seen. No wonder she wanted to be different now, even if it meant decorating your door with a hanging monkey. Her desire for individuality, some form of distinction, moved me. I realized I was proud of her.

Thomas called to say they were pulling into the parking lot and he could use some help, especially since he hadn't memorized the code he had to punch into the keypad at the front door. I walked the two of them inside. Shirley stopped before her door and backed up enough so that she could see it without lifting her head too high. "I know it isn't like the monkey you wanted," I said. "If you don't like it, I'll get you another one."

Shirley's eyes flashed up. "Well. It is my least favorite of all the monkeys. But I guess it will do."

56

NEW PRIORITIES

I took a deep breath. How was Shirley going to adjust to this new place? There was a big difference between a senior residence center and an assisted living facility. Like being locked in the building 24/7. And having someone come into your apartment to check on you every two hours throughout the night. The manager of the place, Jeannette, lovely and twenty-five if she was a day, had assured Shirley that it would feel just like home before she knew it. She'd even baked cookies just for her while we were shopping around for the right place. "Look," Shirley had said. "That sure is nice. She's a cute girl." I would have preferred staff credentials over baked goods to be the deciding factor to come here, but Thomas and I had decided it was Shirley's choice.

The dementia test had been interesting. "Shirley," Jeannette said, "do you know the name of this place?"

"Monster House."

"Oh. That's a new one."

Shirley sighed. "I know it's Montgomery House. I'm just kiddin'."

"What is your religious affiliation?"

"Who wants to know?"

"I do."

"Well, why does anyone need to know that?"

"It's one of the questions that helps me know how your mind is working."

"I'm a witcom."

"A what?"

I shot Shirley a look that said I was on to her. "She wants you to believe she's a wiccan, which she is not."

Shirley began to laugh. "Yeah, that's Melissa. She's a

whatever-you-call-it."

"Shirley," I said, "I am not a wiccan."

"Thomas says you is."

"Thomas says a lot of things to get a rise out of you." I noticed Jeannette was writing this conversation down.

Shirley looked disappointed. "So you isn't one of them? Well, do you know any witcoms?"

Then she remembered Jeannette was still sitting there. "The witcoms worship with feathers and rocks and stuff you find on the sidewalk. Or in the grass."

Jeannette turned to me with a puzzled expression on her face. I wasn't sure what I thought of her yet. "That about sums it up," I said with a smile and a shrug.

Two days after she moved in, I hurried from work to accompany Shirley on her first trip to the dining room. When she had refused to go the day before, they brought her a tray because it was her first day. I was nervous for her. It wouldn't be easy to make friends with a bent back that forced her to face the ground. When Shirley had moved to Cedar Hills nine years ago, it was hard to be the new person in the dining room, but this was harder. It was different then. She could stand up straight. She wore nice clothes and jewelry. She had her hair styled. Not like now. Shirley didn't want to face all those new people. I wondered if I'd get there in time to prevent a meltdown.

Hurriedly punching in the code that opened the door to the building, I walked briskly to the dining room and was struck by an unsettling quiet. There were thirty people sitting at their tables, but you could hear a pin drop. I saw Shirley's bag on a chair and asked Jeannette, who had donned a hairnet as she filled in for a server, where she might be.

"She had to go to the bathroom."

That's probably what I'd say, too, I thought, and I'd stay

there a long, long time. I smiled at Jeannette. "Thanks. I wonder if she knows where it is." But Jeannette was being summoned by Norma, who had dropped her fork, and she didn't respond.

I found Shirley coming out of the bathroom and heading the wrong way, clinging to her walker as she moved at a snail's pace. Her sigh of relief was audible. As we turned around and headed back, I asked her, "How do you feel?" She replied without hesitation, "Like I'm living in a nightmare."

Elaine was the one person sitting at Shirley's table when we got there. She was smartly dressed and her smile was engaging. I began a conversation with her and was fascinated by how clear her thinking seemed. She seemed physically able and was so lucid that I began to wonder if she was merely visiting someone who lived there. It was a sticky situation to explore. I settled on asking Elaine where she lived, hoping the answer would indicate resident or non-resident. "Well," Elaine said when I asked, "I live in the general vicinity. It's very hard to remember my street name when I spend so much time here." Ah. And now I saw her in a new frame, and was thankful that Shirley wasn't paying attention, given all the possible retorts she could come up with about that.

Suddenly, I remembered Elaine from the previous summer, when Thomas and I had been at the Farmer's Market and encountered an acquaintance with this woman who was introduced to us as the man's mother. She had seemed lovely then, too. Her oaf of a son had put his arm around her, saying loudly, "Yeah, Mom has Alzheimer's now, so we had to move her to a home here in Bloomington." Elaine had smiled without comment, while I fumed. Thomas was in full agreement about the guy's insensitivity, and later said, "I thought about saying you had a raging yeast infection, just to make a point."

So here is where Elaine lives, I thought. She really does have dementia. Jeannette had said that she'd placed Shirley next to Elaine because she was one of the few residents that didn't eat in silence as a rule. But Shirley was having none of it. She stared at her plate of food as if making decisions about where to begin, and acted like she was sitting all by herself.

Like a parent who brings a toy to help her child make friends, I pulled from my purse a DVD I had found on a sale table at the drug store and presented it to Shirley and Elaine. It was "These Old Broads," a truly awful made-for-TV movie about a show business comeback of characters played by Debbie Reynolds, Liz Taylor, and Shirley MacLaine. There was a magical moment. Elaine and Shirley got excited and started to talk about old movies they had seen starring these women.

"Maybe we could watch this together, Shirley," Elaine said.

Shirley hesitated. "Maybe I'll loan it to you after I watch it."

Good one, Shirley, I thought, mentally rolling my eyes as I beamed at them both.

I was astounded that Shirley ultimately liked the dining room experience. She loved the food, which I would never have predicted. And the quiet. "Nobody bothers me and that's how I like it," she said. There was a sad satisfaction in that moment.

57

HORSING AROUND

Overall, Shirley adjusted well to her new apartment after the first week. We did our best to keep Edgar from walking in during his daily rounds. Once, Thomas even closed the door in the poor man's face as he tried to enter. "He has to learn," he said when he saw my shocked expression.

Shirley seemed happy with the arrangement of her things. Although she had to step away from the walls to see the pictures we'd hung, she was pleased to know that others who came in would see them. She even said it felt roomier in this tiny efficiency, obviously because mountains of clutter had been removed. "Thank you," she said repeatedly, and it seemed like she meant it. I was touched by this tenderness, even though I knew it wouldn't last.

Before long, she was back to her wisecracking self and began to offer us money to do things for her. Ben and Alison thought this was great fun whenever they were visiting, but I didn't always get the humor. "Melissa? Melissa! I'm talking to you!" she'd say.

"I'm right here, Shirley," I said one Saturday morning, trying to hide my exasperation after this had happened several times in the past half-hour. I had come from the Farmer's Market, bringing the usual sausage and fennel tart and chocolate cookie, items Shirley had come to expect. This time, I also brought apple cider and a beautiful, pale blue pumpkin, one of my favorite finds at the market in the fall. After she had pronounced it "sickly looking," but said she'd keep it anyway if I really wanted her to, I had given myself permission to become engrossed in the newspaper.

"What did you want to ask me?" I said.

"Well, now I don't remember." She paused for a moment. "This wasn't it, but it's the services around here that get ya. Tom was tellin' me how expensive everything is. I'm just gonna have to make do. I'll give you five bucks to scratch my arms."

After the free arm-scratching, she thought of something new. "How is Jesseeca? Give her some money. Like thirty dollars." I furrowed my brow in confusion and she said, "Okay, thirty-five."

I had seen Joe's truck parked in the parking lot, so he must have come from his apartment some time that morning. "Where did you say Joe went?" I asked.

"How should I know? Is he in the bathroom? He's comin' around here too much. I can't entertain him all day. He was sayin' somethin' about Salisbury steak. Maybe he went down the hall to eat."

Thomas walked in as we were talking. "He's in the dining room. Some of the servers know him from when they worked at Sunrise when Dorothy was there. I guess they all work the nursing homes circuit."

"Do they charge him for the meal?" I asked.

"So far, no," Shirley said. "He tells 'em I don't want it, so they can give it to him. Then they bring me somethin' else if they think I'm lookin' hungry."

I looked at Thomas. "So, he's okay with how quiet it is in there?"

"He don't care," Shirley said. "He just wants Salisbury steak."

Thomas had a glint in his eye I recognized as mischief. He was searching his phone for pictures of a sculpture kit Alison had been working with. It was a horse's head that started as a skull, with directions for how to apply the clay musculature, eyeballs, skin, and hair. At this point, it was looking pretty scary with only one eye fitted loosely in its socket and no skin covering the red, striated muscles. Thomas had been documenting the work in progress and saw an opportunity unfolding to use the photographs, not for good. "Joe just learned how to get messages on the phone we got him. I'm gonna send him this picture of Alison's horse head."

"What?" I attempted a protest while laughing in spite of myself. "Why would you do that? It will scare him. Like a high tech version of leaving a horsehead on his bed."

"I know!" Thomas said with glee.

"Well, lemme see it," Shirley said. She studied it for a moment. "Yeah, that'll scare him, all right. If he really knows how to use that phone. He's the only person in there that's got one, I'll tell you that."

Thomas looked thoughtful. "I wonder what it will be like when we're old and trying to use our cell phones in the dining room. Maybe our grandchildren will set up farts for ring tones without telling us." He and Shirley began to laugh, especially when Thomas made flatulent sounds to act out our future progeny's tomfoolery, and Shirley emitted an actual fart for good measure.

"That'll be great," he continued. "This fart sound will come from our side of the table and we'll be thinking, 'Wow, I did not see that coming. Was that me?'"

"Okay, I gotta go," I said, laughing and shaking my head at how juvenile the conversation became whenever Thomas was hanging out with his mother. I had to admit that we were all feeling better with Shirley settled. Thomas had a spring in his step that an old man sitting on a bench outside had told him was a "young man's walk."

I passed the dining room as I headed for the front door, and there was Joe, with a forkful of meat halted in mid-air while he stared at his phone. His eyes were wide and his jaw hung open. Well, Thomas is missing it, I thought. Likely, he was still effecting rude ring tones for his mother's benefit, free of charge, as the soundtrack for meals we'd be taking someday. Life is just one big whoopee cushion for that guy, I thought. I punched in the code and opened the door to the world of more serious pursuits.

58

DIRTY LAUNDRY

The phone rang at half past midnight. A moment went by before Thomas got up to answer it. We weren't alarmed, though we expected alarming news. We had become jaded by the late night calls coming four or five times a week to report emergencies large and small. Sometimes Shirley had fallen. Sometimes she was short of breath. Sometimes she was confused and frightened and needed us to reassure her that she was okay. Thomas groaned as he reached for the phone. He soon began to pace. I could hear the nurse on the other end of the line in the dark stillness of our bedroom.

"Mr. Kuhn? I'm sorry to bother you so late, but your mother has fallen."

Facing another late night trip across town, Thomas closed his eyes and took a deep breath. "How did she fall?"

"Well, she's not really sure, but she fell backwards into her laundry basket."

I knew I was going to hell as I buried my head beneath my pillow to mute my laughter. Heaven knows I should have been more sensitive to this embarrassment, given my own inelegant falls in recent years, including breaking my ankle after slipping on ice. But the thought of being caught in your laundry basket was too much. To be cushioned and contained in one's unmentionables — yet another example of the humiliations of old age, which struck me as hilarious in that short-sighted moment.

Thomas was talking to Shirley now. "Mom, do you think you broke anything? I can come now if you need me to – or…first thing in the morning." Anyone could hear the hope in his voice. "Okay, I'll get there early tomorrow."

The x-ray taken the next day showed two fractures in her

arm, her one good arm, since the removal of lymph nodes on her other side still caused her pain. I felt a wave of nausea at the thought of Shirley suffering this pain through the night as we joked about laundry baskets and the constancy of her needs.

When Thomas called from Shirley's place to report the details, I could hear her talking in the background. "Tell Melissa."

"Okay," he said.

"Grandmas and grandpas is a drag on they's kids these days."

"Grandmas and grandpas are a drag on their kids these days."

"I know because I read it in the paper."

"She knows because she read it in the paper."

"And I'm livin' it."

"And she's livin' it."

"And shut up."

"And shut up."

I decided to shake off the guilt while coming up with strategies to help Shirley manage without her good arm. Death, taxes, and loss of control. And so it was.

A couple of days later, Shirley was back to her old self, offering me some Oxycontin, to which she was clearly addicted. This was something she liked to do for anyone who looked like they were feeling low, including her teenage grandchildren. "Want a pain pill?" she'd say. "I take 'em. I'm feelin' good."

She was refreshingly sarcastic about becoming the subject of her caretakers' scrutiny. "They know me through and through. They wash my face, my hind end, it's all true. And I can't find my lipsticks. None of 'em. And they's gonna say, 'She's lost her will to live. She's showin' up in the dining room with no lipstick, and she don't care about her looks no more.' Melissa, you better find 'em or get me some more."

I was happy to go to Target to find red lipsticks that

weren't too purpley, grateful for a small task that could make a big difference.

59

NOVEMBER IN PARIS

By mid-November, Shirley was as settled into Montgomery House as she was going to be. We were not happy with her care, but had been trying to fill in the gaps wherever we could between regular visits and Thomas's vigilance about her medical needs. It had been summertime when we decided to take a trip for our 25th anniversary on November 17th. Although Shirley had been fragile, she seemed strong enough for us to be away a short while. We probably wouldn't have decided to go if we'd known how rapidly she would decline in the months between making and carrying out our plans.

I took charge of the planning after observing how tired and stressed Thomas was at work that summer. We decided to go to Quebec City, just for a few days, and stay in Chateau Frontenac, a place I'd only heard about and wanted to experience. Sitting in front of my computer screen in July, I was dismayed by the high cost of the plane fare and found myself thinking, gosh, we might as well be going to Paris. This led me to check out flights to Paris and, finding the prices comparable, I hatched a plan for a surprise. A friend recommended an inexpensive place to stay near the Louvre and I made reservations for four nights.

Spending five days away from Shirley, Alison, and our home was going to be a tall order, but we were in full agreement about taking time for this anniversary. Thomas assembled a small village to care for his mother, writing pages of notes about medication, various contacts, and contingency plans for whatever might happen. Friends were scheduled each day to go to Montgomery House and keep Shirley company. Everyone knew that if she were to die while we were gone, Thomas didn't want to be contacted during our trip. He had made arrangements for everything so that we could enjoy this time together and face whatever needed to be faced upon our return.

Shirley was all for us taking time away. "Tom says you's goin' to some fancy place in Canada where they's French. How long will you be gone?"

"Five days," I told her, "We'll be back two days before Thanksgiving, so we'll still have dinner at our house. And I have a secret to tell you. Something Thomas doesn't know." I couldn't believe I was taking this risk. "We're really going to Paris, but it's a surprise. I'm going to tell him at the airport." It took a minute for Shirley to comprehend what I was saying. "Paris? They's a Paris in Canada? Where they talk in French?"

"No, we're going to Paris, France, in Europe, but Thomas doesn't know, so don't tell him."

"Ha!" she said. "He don't pay attention to anything I say anyway. If I forget, just tell him I'm crazy. It's probably what you say all the time anyway." Good plan, I thought, while chastising Shirley for thinking such a thing.

"He said he's goin' skiing," Shirley said. "Can you do that in Paris?"

This got me worrying, but things being as chaotic as they were, I soon forgot about it.

We were matter-of-fact in our goodbyes to Shirley, intent on not borrowing trouble. "We'll see you in a few days, Mom," Thomas said. "Don't forget that people will be coming by each day. And you have the numbers you need to call if you need anything."

"Have fun in gay Par-ee!" she said. "Don't forget to bring me a new body."

Thomas laughed. "Not Paris, Mom. Canada. I told you they speak French there. That's probably what made you think Paris."

Late into the night before our departure, we were still making arrangements and packing. I saw Thomas get out some ski gear and worry about what he could check on the plane. "This is going to be a blast!" he said. "I checked the weather in Quebec; it's going to be great for skiing." It dawned on me that this may not have been the best time to live out some romantic fantasy, and that Thomas might even be unhappy about the change. Four months before, he'd never heard of Chateau Frontenac, but now he was talking about it all the time.

I didn't know how to tell him about the change, so I left the boarding passes for our flight next to the bathroom sink for him to discover. He went to the bathroom to pack his toiletries. After a moment of hearing him rattling around in there, there was a pause. "Melissa?" He came to the doorway. "What is this?"

"Surprise!" I said. It was pretty weak. "We're going to Paris!"

"We're going to Paris? France? Why?"

"I thought it would be a fun surprise!"

"We're not going to Quebec City? What about Chateau Frontenac?"

"Well, we're not going there. We'll go there some other time." I hated that moments like this never worked out the way I planned.

"Oh," he said. "So, we're not going to Chateau Frontenac."

Damn it all if I didn't hear myself apologizing. "I'm sorry. I just thought it would be fun to surprise you. I'm telling you now instead of at the airport because I didn't want you packing ski gear, you know?"

"Well," he said. "Okay," and he slowly began to return his heavy sweaters to the closet. "Why didn't you tell me? I've been pretty excited about our plans."

"I know."

"Were we ever going to go to Chateau Frontenac? Was it

always just some scheme? I have to say I'm a little disappointed."

Happy flipping anniversary was what I thought.

By the next morning, Thomas woke up fully engaged in the new program. I think he'd made a decision to let go of his disenchantment and be happy about my surprise – and I was grateful. We boarded the plane, laughing that we'd avoided killing each other in our quarter century together, and I pulled out tourist books to make plans as we crossed the ocean. Thomas turned to me. "So, did Mom know we were really going to Paris? I thought she was just mixed up, as usual." He paused and looked at me. "What was it you said about that after we left her place? I don't think it was very nice."

"Yeah," I said. "She took one for the team."

We decided not to push ourselves, even though we were in the City of Light, a place we hadn't seen for many years, and never together. If the lines were too long to visit places like Notre Dame, we'd just move on; that was the deal. Truth be told, we slept a lot, in our tiny pension where our bed took up the whole room. We ventured out for long walks and meals in cafes, but much of our time was spent napping. Although this could have happened almost anywhere, say, Indianapolis, we were thrilled to do something this decadent when life had been about work and parenting and care of Shirley for so long. We drank champagne at the top of the Eiffel Tower at night, wrapped in scarves we'd bought on the street by day. It was a great celebration after all.

Changing planes in Philadelphia on the way home, Thomas used the layover to get on the phone and find out how his mother was. I watched his facial expressions as he spoke to the nurses and his assistant who was overseeing the coordination of friends helping out. First he was smiling, saying what fun we'd had. Then I saw his face change and he said, "Uh-huh," over and over again.

We were back. It had been fun, but now it was time to face the hard stuff again. I started to make a grocery list for Thanksgiving dinner, grocery shopping being the last thing I wanted to do upon our return. It was good to have taken this time away. I knew we were approaching the last chapter of Shirley's life.

60

FINAL BLESSINGS

We got home late from our trip, but rose early, Thomas to see his mother and check on work at his office, me to prepare for Thanksgiving the next day. I pulled out recipes and went to the grocery store while Alison made her way home from the friend's house where she had been staying. Thomas collected Shirley from Montgomery House and brought her home to our place to spend the night.

Shirley was full of tales about her adventures while we were gone. "One girl come over with her guitar. She played *Moon River*. She sung pretty good." This was our friend, Carrie, who had recorded more than a dozen albums. I was touched that Carrie knew to play songs Shirley would enjoy.

Thomas set up a baby monitor where his mother was sleeping. She called out every half hour and he ended up sleeping on the couch in the same room with her. The morning of Thanksgiving, she was spent and confused. It was as if she had become a different person overnight. I found myself missing her energy from holidays past. How long had it been since she drove me crazy in the kitchen, cooking her traditional frozen noodle side dish? Now, it seemed her dementia had taken over. Thomas had been up all night attending to her needs. He was asleep on the couch as she watched television, and I tried to prepare a turkey.

"Melissa," she called. "I'm talking to you! You lost your baby. Do you hear me?" Her voice was stern. She had just finished watching the movie, "Juno," about a pregnant girl and an adoptive couple. "Uh-huh," I said. "It's okay, Shirley. I'm just working on dinner over here."

Her tone brightened. "Oh. Want some help?"

"No, thank you," I said. "I've got this."

"I suggest we get a whole new program and new socks and let it float off in the distance. Let the dog take over." She paused. "What's Tom doing? Why is he still asleep?"

"He didn't sleep well last night," I said

"Well, where's Peanut Butter?"

I sighed. Shirley had started calling Alison Peanut Butter when she began to lose her grip on reality. When Alison first told me about it, I assumed it was a new term of endearment. Observing its use in context, however, I understood what Alison had tried to tell me, that if anything, it was a term of reproach, and confusing when used in a demand, such as, "Peanut Butter! I told you to bring me a tissue!"

"If you mean Alison, she's upstairs in her room, but she'll be down soon."

Shirley shifted her gaze back to the TV. "What's this movie I'm watching?"

"'Mamma Mia'."

"I don't get it."

"Remember? The girl is trying to figure out which of her mom's old boyfriends is her father, so she's invited all of them to her wedding."

"Well, it's stupid."

"It's supposed to be silly. And Tom picked it out because it isn't scary. It probably won't give you nightmares."

"Well, what do I care how many guys she done screwed?"

I turned off the TV and handed her a book. "Here's one of the library books we were talking about. *A is for Alibi*."

Shirley began to chant. "A is for alibi. B is for butt. C is for crud. D is for dammit. I haven't read that one."

"Sounds to me like you could write that one. You're cussing up a storm these days," I said.

"Well, shit," she said. "Look who's talking." And so it went throughout the day.

That afternoon, Ben arrived with a new girlfriend named Honna, who was joining us for dinner. Of course, I thought. She was getting an eyeful. I tried to tell Honna that this was a different kind of Thanksgiving for us, but knew it sounded defensive and willed myself to stop. Besides, there was no way to explain Thomas and his mother going into the bathroom after he had donned a face mask and rubber gloves. He waved, then smiled with a hello and happy holidays for our stunned guest. Eventually, Shirley exited the bathroom with Thomas guiding her. "I believe in Santa," was all she said. "I really do." Thomas and I looked at each other and laughed. Days before, we had been walking along the Seine.

Shirley had one lucid moment as the family gathered and sat down to dinner. "Hey. I got somethin' to say." She had our full attention. "Every year, Melissa makes us say something we're grateful about. And I hate that. This time, let's all share something about somebody else that they should change, something that will make 'em more pleasant to be around, that'll improve theirselves."

After a long day of carping at each other, Thomas lit up and looked my way. "Let's start with Melissa."

Feeling game, I shot back, "Bring it on, big boy."

Joe was checked out and Alison observed the scene dispassionately, but Ben's eyes were as big as his girlfriend's. "I don't think this is a good idea for Thanksgiving," he said. "I don't want to play this game." We grudgingly accepted the wisdom of his plea since Shirley had fallen asleep anyway.

After dinner, I observed our deflated group and remembered last year when we played *Taboo* after dinner. The word Shirley had tried to get her team to say was "lasagna." "It's noodles," she had said. "Oh, you ain't supposed to say that. Okay. It's I-talian; oh, you can't say that neither. Well, this is crazy. Wait,

I know. Melissa used to make it for Christmas and we didn't like it." When her word was "download," she had said, "It's something you do with Melissa's dishwasher."

"Hey. Let's play a game," I said, back in the present. No one responded, so I drank my coffee and continued making conversation with Honna. Little did I know that she would one day be a member of our family, and that this fleeting encounter with Ben's grandmother would be similar to my meetings with Thomas's grandmother, Fay, only enough to leave a limited impression of the person beneath the untranslatable surface.

Alison and Thomas were washing dishes. Joe was mumbling to himself. Shirley was asleep again, her face dangerously close to the cranberries on her plate. Ben got up quietly and tiptoed over to her to move it out of the way. He whispered, "Grandma's cannula is only in one nostril. She's probably not getting enough oxygen." As he carefully adjusted it without waking her, he looked at me and smiled. "Look, Mom. We're playing *Operation*. And I'm winning."

61

DEMENTIA

"She keeps handin' me these bluebirds and I have to dip 'em!" Shirley related this to me in a panic.

"What?" I said, taking off my coat and gloves as I walked into her apartment with Carrie, who accompanied me that day to check on her. Carrie had brought her guitar, remembering how the music she played for Shirley in a recent visit had soothed her.

Shirley spoke in a loud, plaintive voice. "It's my job! Y'see, they's all these bluebirds! And I have to dip 'em!" I had begun to go along with these episodes after observing how much worse it was when I just said it wasn't happening. "What do you mean, dip 'em?" I said. "What are you dipping them in?"

"A bucket of water!"

"Why do you have to do that?"

"She won't tell me!"

"Is the bucket of water still here? I don't see a bucket."

"It's here somewheres, and I have to dip them bluebirds in the water! I hold 'em like this," and she pretended to hold a bird in her fist, "and I dip 'em by they's heads like this."

We paused for a moment as I put my hand on her shoulder bent so close to the ground. Shirley shook her head. "I don't want to do it no more, I told her! But they's so many!"

"Let's sit down, okay?"

"It sounds crazy, I know, like it ain't real!" She stopped and peered up at me. "It's not really happening?"

I tried to lead her to her chair. "No. It isn't happening. No bluebirds in your room. I'm just sorry it felt so bad."

Shirley sat down hard in her chair as Carrie and I sat on the floor in front of her. She was still shaken, but laughed a little. "Well, I know you're thinkin' I done lost it."

"I think you've had a bad scare," I said. "Do you remember Carrie? The one you said had a good singing voice? She's back for a visit and she's going to play some songs. What do you think?"

Shirley sighed and seemed relieved. "Okay. How about 'Moon River'? Some girl played that for me last time." We sang "Moon River," "Danny Boy," and "Love is a Many-Splendored Thing," the last one reminding me of soap operas from my ill-spent youth.

When we finished those songs, Shirley asked me, "Did you bring that hymnbook you keep at your house? See if you can find, 'Tell Me the Old, Old Story.'" We did and we sang it. Next was "Rock of Ages," "Onward Christian Soldiers," "Just As I Am," "Shall We Gather at the River?" and "The Old Rugged Cross." This had a calming effect on us all. I loved those old hymns from my childhood and listening to Shirley's tremulous voice brought to mind my grandmother from years long past. Whenever Shirley seemed startled and began to look around the room in a panic, her memory of lines from each hymn's multiple verses proved to be a good distraction. When Carrie and I would stop to check the words, we marveled at Shirley leading us through the stanzas. A couple of times, she seemed to drift off and Carrie and I would exchange questioning looks, wondering if she was going to sleep. Then she had rallied, but remained calm. By the time we were on the last verse of "What a Friend We Have in Jesus," it appeared the crisis had passed. But then we sang that last line, "take it to the Lord in prayer," and Shirley thundered, "Just like them bluebirds!"

Carrie and I sighed heavily, accepting defeat in distracting Shirley from the terrors that overpowered her sense of safety, despite our best efforts.

62

GOING HOME

Before long, Thomas and I became focused on the conditions of Montgomery House as much as we were focused on Shirley. We felt uneasy about the increasingly lax standards and understaffing, which hadn't been as apparent when we moved her there. Doors that were supposed to be locked were propped open most of the time, enabling patients with dementia to leave and wander outdoors. Shirley's room wasn't being cleaned regularly. It was hard to talk with the manager, Jeannette, about it, since she was always covering others' jobs. At any given moment, she might be donning rubber gloves for cleaning or a hairnet for slinging hash. She was a whirling dervish.

We regretted letting Shirley choose between Montgomery House and a similar alternative named Hillcrest, now that we knew Hillcrest was the better choice. Jeannette had been charming and had made Shirley those cookies. A friend of Thomas's who was a nurse at Hillcrest had expressed concern about Shirley's safety at Montgomery when he heard of her decision. It was making sense to us now, and we found Jeannette less charming in her multiple roles of activities director, cook, business manager, and custodian.

The day the power went out for six hours and no one checked on Shirley, who was on oxygen all the time now, was particularly alarming. We decided to make a change but didn't know what that would be yet. It pained us to think of putting her through another move, but two events happened the next week that necessitated an immediate adjustment.

A nurse's aide called Thomas in the middle of the night to say his mother had fallen when trying to go to the bathroom, but that she would be okay if he wanted to wait until morning to come by and check on her. He took her at her word. When Thomas called me at work the next day, I could feel the tension even before he spoke. He was almost shouting. "I'm picking up her teeth off the carpet!"

"Her teeth! What do you mean?"

"I mean she knocked out two teeth with the fall, and her mouth is bleeding. We're going to her dentist now."

"Oh, my God. How is she? Where is the staff?"

"She's pretty confused. I haven't seen any staff anywhere."

"Does Jeannette know?"

"I don't know, but it doesn't matter. She's worthless in this mess." From the sound of Thomas's voice, I could tell he wanted to kick a wall in, but was keeping it together for his mother's sake.

"Do you want me to meet you at the dentist?"

There was a pause. "No. It's okay. I'll tell you about it later."

"Thomas? We have to get her out of there. Like, now."

We breathed into the phone for a few seconds. I broke the silence.

"She should come home with us."

"How would that work?" Thomas said. "We're gone all day."

"I know, but we'll figure it out."

Shirley was shaken by the thought of moving and not ready to leave that day. We asked Ben to stay with her overnight, considering his ability to sleep on the floor greater than ours. Shirley no longer had a bed and slept in the one cushioned chair, so the floor was all that was left for anyone staying over.

The second event happened the next day, when the headlines of the local paper's front page told the story Shirley and other residents of the facility had been living. The conditions at Montgomery House were summarily denounced. The report described their failure to meet numerous standards in a recent inspection. Thomas and I looked at each other astonished and nodded our heads as we read each example, including the doors left propped open for the staff's convenience. We'd seen employees smoking in the parking lot and assumed they left the back door propped open so they wouldn't have to walk around the building to reenter. We'd also seen them come back in and leave it that way. According to the article, one resident had been missing when he walked out this same door, without a coat, into the cold December night. After a frantic search, the staff discovered him wandering around a small lake across a busy street, freezing and terrified until he was led back to his room.

That afternoon, I loaded my car with as many boxes as I could fit, relieved I hadn't thrown them out from Shirley's last move. I arrived at the front door, punched in the code, and walked into an environment that was significantly changed from the day before. The place was crawling with clean-cut young men and women in suits, all smiling and asking if I needed assistance with anything. Did I need help finding where I was going? Could they help me carry my boxes? After declining their offers, I put the boxes down outside Shirley's room and called Thomas. "Corporate's here!" I said. "You should see this place."

"Yeah, I'm sure they're scared of being closed down. Did you tell them we're taking Mom out of there?"

"No, I didn't know how you wanted to handle that, but anyone with half a brain would have noticed the moving boxes I'm carrying and connected the dots."

"Okay, why don't you get started packing her up and I'll be there soon. I just finished meeting with the person I know at Home Instead, and I think we've got this set up."

"Really? That's great!" Home Instead provided round-the-clock services.

"Don't get so excited. It costs $400 a day."

It took a moment to realize what he had said. "You're

shitting me," I said.

"I shit you not," Thomas replied, and we laughed for the first time in a couple of days.

"Well, how much do you think we'll need to supplement what she has? Will it be okay?"

"I don't know. Let's just say she can't afford this indefinitely." He sighed. "She isn't doing well, so it probably won't be an issue." We ended the call on that sobering note.

Thomas's assistant, Bonnie, met us after work at Shirley's apartment. Between her truck and Ben's, along with our two cars, we had enough vehicles to pack Shirley up and leave in a couple of hours. I noticed as we were getting started carrying her things out that the back door was still propped open. Unbelievable, I thought, and started to shut it as I came back in from carrying a load to the car. Thomas stopped me. "What are you doing?" he demanded.

"I'm shutting the door. All these suits running around and they still can't keep the door shut."

Thomas rolled his eyes. "So, *now* is when you take this on? When we're making trips to the cars parked in back?"

I laughed. "Okay, we'll keep it propped until we're done. I'll tell Alison to stand guard. Then I'm going to complain about it to one of those nice young executives." As I said this, I realized I probably wouldn't be saying anything at all. We were finished here.

Thomas nodded with approval. "Better them than Jeannette. I just met with her about Mom's rent for the rest of the month, and she isn't happy. And she isn't so cute anymore either. I almost asked if she'd done any baking for the new people running around." We'd switched attitudes about Jeannette. I had been the mean one up till then, with Thomas reminding me that she was very young for so much responsibility.

"Well, she's probably freaking out," I said.

"Not our problem," Thomas said. "I need a piece of paper to write a statement that we're moving Mom out tonight, and Mom's gotta sign it. Did you already pack up her little notebook?"

"Yes, but I'll go find a piece of paper."

Jeannette stopped me in the hallway. "Melissa?" she said. "Shirley's really moving out tonight?"

"She is."

"May I ask where you're taking her?"

I shrugged my shoulders. "Home."

In that moment, my heart went out to this young woman who had tried to keep the place running with little support from the corporate owners. She'd been in over her head all this time, and now she was probably in trouble. But I had no words of comfort, plus I knew we were probably going to be doing battle over the considerable rent we'd be trying to get back for the weeks after Shirley was gone. I nodded at her and kept moving.

Shirley was confused, but only mildly alarmed. She mustered the energy for a brief protest. "It was just a couple teeth! I don't get why we have to go crazy. I just got here, and now Tom says I gotta go." She paused. "Where am I going?"

"To our house," I said. Now Shirley was even more confused. "You mean just for tonight?"

"No, to stay. This place turned out to be a bad one."

Shirley considered this. "Well, the food's okay," she said. "I mean it's always hot." I couldn't tell whether this was bait, given all the times Shirley had complained about meals being cold by the time I got them to the table. I decided not to go there.

"Who's gonna take care of me?"

"Thomas and Jessica and me," I said. "And the people from Home Instead."

Shirley assumed I'd gotten this wrong. "Thomas told me I

can't afford them! He says they's too expensive!"

"I guess he's gotten it figured out because now he's saying it's going to be okay," I said.

Shirley let out a rueful laugh. "Well, I better stop messin' around and die soon! That's probably what he figures. Call Dr. Kevorkian, she's out of money!"

I laughed, too. "That's between you and Thomas. So, where are your pills?"

"Don't ask me. Everybody hides things from me now."

Thomas arrived at our house with Shirley in tow shortly after the last of her stuff had been unloaded by Bonnie, Ben, Alison, and me. He and Ben carried her down the stairs slowly and carefully to our family room in the basement. We had decided it would be quieter there and more spacious for her hospital bed and caretakers. Her transport wasn't easy. With her body turning in on itself, a broken arm, and the other arm the source of chronic pain for years now, maneuvering her was negotiated step by step. She was frightened when they started at the top of the stairwell. But she closed her eyes and seemed to relax while placing her trust in her son and grandson.

Shirley fell asleep almost as soon as we got her settled. Thomas and I were taking turns sitting with her and I was up first. As she slumbered, I lightly traced with my finger the circular shape she had become, her knees drawn up to her chin. She could have been a baby in her mother's womb, waiting to be delivered. She had become so small. Too small to contain her spirit any longer, I thought.

Before I fell into bed in a heap later that night, Thomas stopped back in to get his pillow for sleeping in the basement. "Hopefully, we'll get a lot settled tomorrow, and we won't have to keep doing this," he said.

"Okay," I said in the middle of a yawn. "Are you all right?"

He stopped and looked at me. "Yeah. Mom said something interesting on the way over here. I guess she thought you wouldn't have been okay with her staying with us."

"What did she say?" I asked.

"She said, 'I guess Melissa really does love me.'"

We smiled at each other for a moment before Thomas kissed me goodnight and left. I lay down and stared at the ceiling while thinking about the countless ways Shirley and I had annoyed each other the past 25 years. The thinly veiled slights. The passive aggression. The sabotage. I laughed and said to myself, I guess I really do.

Almost immediately after we moved Shirley out of Montgomery, our house became Grand Central Station. The colonization of our home by Home Instead had a dramatic impact. Our comings and goings to work and school blended with that of the various caretakers who came through the revolving door all day and night. One morning, I stood at the kitchen island with a cup of coffee before leaving for work. A person I hadn't seen before came walking through the room. She stopped and politely asked who I was and what I was doing there. "I live here," I said.

Jessica came on a regular basis, filling in some nights to save us from having to pay for the overnight service from Home Instead. Her presence was a comfort. Her love for Shirley was always apparent and her down-to-earth manner had a calming effect on everyone in this hectic scene. Nothing Shirley did or said bothered her. This couldn't be said for all of us.

I struggled with the harsh things she said at times, to Alison especially, who was present and attentive throughout the last weeks of her grandmother's life. On a regular basis, she'd admonish any one of us regarding her needs, often raising her voice in anger, but Alison was the only one of us whom she'd given a new name. "I told you to change the channel, Peanut Butter, and that ain't what I wanna see. Peanut Butter? Well, where did Peanut Butter go?"

"If you mean Alison," I'd say, "she stepped outside for a bit."

Then Shirley would return to herself, if only for a moment. "Oh. Okay. That sounds good."

Days passed in a kind of haze as my semester at work came to an end. I graded students' finals while sitting next to Shirley's bed. A student named Isabel, whose work had been spectacularly average, called me to negotiate her grade. I spoke softly since Shirley was sleeping, and eventually moved to another part of the room to continue the conversation. Isabel rattled on about an assignment she had meant to turn in weeks ago and would I accept it now, and I wondered if my circumstances would matter to her if she knew them. If Shirley had been awake, the woman I'd always known would have urged me to use the situation to my advantage. She would have said, "Why don't you say your old lady mother-in-law is about to die and you can't talk on the phone right now?" But Shirley was relinquishing her grip on this life and didn't have the energy to crack wise anymore.

Eventually, whenever Shirley awoke, she had the same frustrated reaction to being among the living. "I don't know why I'm still here," she'd say. "I made my peace with the Lord. But I'm still here." She also had to suffer various miseries such as an allergic reaction to one of her drugs and terrible difficulty with swallowing that developed over a few days. It frightened us to watch her struggling with this basic function. Thomas's friend, Bob Spicer, a cranial-sacral therapist who had done energy work on everyone in our family, called Thomas one day to see how his mother was faring. When he heard about this latest challenge, he came over and took Shirley's hand in his. He spoke gently, asking if she would allow him to try to help. With her permission, he placed his thumb against the roof of her mouth and held it there until she began to swallow again. It felt like we were witnessing a miracle, Bob being the angel passing by that day.

Small victories to make Shirley more comfortable were offset by occasional incongruous interruptions. There was the time when Shirley fell asleep peacefully after listening to Thomas read from the Psalms, and Joe walked in, cheerfully and loudly calling out, "Am I too late?" as if he had missed yelling surprise at a surprise party. "What is wrong with you?" Thomas hissed. "Lower your voice!"

"Well," Joe did his best to lower his voice. "I mean…am I too late? Is she still alive?" Noting the look of frustration on Thomas's face, I led Joe out of the room, offering to set him up in front of the television.

Friends were kind and supportive throughout these last weeks. People stopped in when they could. Brenda and Dennis came to say goodbye. A friend and colleague from work took Alison to the mall several days before Christmas, getting her out of the house while I ran some errands. As I pulled into the mall parking lot to pick up Alison, Thomas called to tell me his mother was gone. Sensing that he didn't want to be alone after he had sent the caretaker home, I called Carrie, knowing she was only a mile down the road and home today, and asked her to sit with Thomas until I got there. I went into the mall, wondering how I was going to break the news to Alison, even though Shirley's death had been expected since we brought her home three weeks earlier. Alison walked up to me wearing a hat she had bought. She had had the words, Peanut Butter, embroidered on it. Laughing, she said, "Maybe Grandma will wake up and see me wearing this when I get home." But her smile vanished when she saw the look on my face.

Carrie met us at the door when we came home. I had called Ben, who pulled into the driveway the same time Alison and I did. Downstairs, the four of us sat next to Shirley's body, holding each other's hands and hers. Thomas asked Carrie to sing "Amazing Grace," one of his mother's favorite hymns. We heard her voice as the accompaniment to Shirley's departure, the one she had longed for, and we wept quietly.

After a few minutes, Thomas asked me, "What day is this?" I thought for a moment. "December 22nd. And it's winter solstice, the day that marks the return of the light." Breathing in this realization, I thought of Shirley's soul ascending into the light she so richly deserved.

When the people from the funeral home arrived to collect Shirley's body, it was a surprise to meet the grandfather of Ben's girlfriend Honna as he stood on our front porch, and to learn that he worked at the mortuary. His kind and respectful manner comforted me and put my mind to rest about letting Shirley's physical self go after months of controlling what happened to her moment to moment. Thomas and Ben carried her out of our house with great care. From there, Ben's grandmother's remains were transported to the funeral home by Honna's grandfather. This could have been seen as an example of living in a small world, but it felt more meaningful than a coincidence. It felt like a promise of our family growing and connecting with other families even when facing profound loss. It felt like hope.

The funeral was the day after Christmas. We were touched by how many family and friends were able to attend at such a busy time of year. It was a simple service, a perfect fit for the person we were honoring. I sat next to Joe, who sniffled and blew his nose throughout the songs, prayers, and eulogy. When the service was over, he stood to leave, and I chuckled when I saw the pile of tissues he had thrown on the ground beneath his chair. He walked away as I gathered them and looked up at what I was sure was a wink from heaven.

NAOMI AND RUTH, REPRISE

It doesn't matter which you heard,
The holy or the broken Hallelujah.
                -Leonard Cohen

Once, after Thomas and I had been married for some time, Shirley and I were looking at old pictures and she commented about her mother-in-law who was shown in one of them. "There's little fat Marie," she said. "She didn't like me and I didn't like her. Nothing was ever said." If this was a hint about our relationship, I had missed it entirely. I told her about an old acquaintance who bragged on Facebook that she and her new daughter-in-law were so close that they called each other, "daughter- and mother-in-love."

"Well, that's just stupid," was Shirley's response.

"I know!" I said, "Bleh!"

We never behaved as a mother- and daughter-in-love, and there are things I wish I could have said despite my fear of her wisecracking rejoinders. I have often thought about how heartbroken I felt for Shirley when she had declared herself "nobody's favorite" as a child. But I never told her that in the end, she really was someone's favorite, that she was a beloved mother, grandmother, and mother-in-law.

As time passed, I realized Shirley would never express tender feelings for me, but I can see now that I wasn't always an easy daughter-in-law either. I thought I was right and fair at times when I was neither. I thought I understood what normal meant, but it turns out that I walked into this family with rigid notions of normality. I had a lot to learn and wasn't always my best self. Now I am a mother-in-law. Ben married Honna six years after she was introduced to our family on Thanksgiving Day in 2009, when Shirley suggested a new tradition of telling each other how to be a better person. I wish I could say I know what not to do as Honna and I build our relationship in the years to come. But given all the ways there are to screw it up, my plan is a simple one. I'll do the best I can.

The closest Shirley came to conveying her affection for me was about a year before her death when she gave me a birthday card that said:

If people could pick out their daughters-in-law,
They'd want someone special with scarcely a flaw!
They'd want someone practical, sensible, smart,
With a good sense of humor and a very kind heart.
They'd want someone perfect at making life great.
In fact, they'd want YOU.
Well, too bad! They're too late!
Happy Birthday

Below the message, Shirley had written, "This card expresses my feelings," which made me smile.

I had come a long way, my view of the sanctity of our relationship having undergone significant revision. It wasn't the paean I had bargained for. It wasn't the song I had heard so long ago when I was imagining all that my mother-in-law and I would share. What I heard was the broken hallelujah, but it was surrounded by the sacred all the same. In the end, our relationship wasn't so far removed from that of Naomi and Ruth, but ours was a kind of renegade rendering of their devotion. After all, whither one went, the other was always there. We took care of each other, but we didn't go on about it. Or Shirley didn't, anyhow. It wasn't her way.

Epilogue

A POUND OF FLESH

I never saw Shirley cry, not once, and often wondered if her childhood circumstances inured her to various forms of suffering and loss. When she left her home in Indianapolis after Walter died, knowing she would never eat meals in her own kitchen again, she said, "You can get used to anything, y'know." This was clearly a life philosophy, but when had she reached this conclusion? It could have been her move to the orphanage as an 8-year-old, but after Shirley died, Thomas and I learned of even earlier experiences that might have led to this ambivalence toward change. Shirley never spoke of these events, leading us to believe that she never knew or had long ago forgotten significant portions of her own story. There was also a revelation that helped me better understand the enormity of the cost Shirley's mother Fay paid for perceived incompetence, a debt she paid for the rest of her life.

The source of this new information was Dot. The middle child of five, she was the last surviving sibling in 2011. Thomas and I went to Indianapolis to visit her that spring. She asked us to take her out to Wendy's for a change of scenery, where we sat and shouted personal information at each other, due to Dot's significant hearing deficit.

We began to talk about Fay. Thomas and I acknowledged how hard it must have been for her without support from her husband or family, especially given that there were so few options for women without means and in crisis. Dot stared at us curiously. "Well, yeah, there was all that, but mostly it ended up being about Annie."

"Annie?" Thomas said. "Who's Annie?"

"You don't know about Annie?" Dot said. "She was the little girl that got killed when our mother was supposed to be taking care of her."

Thomas and I looked at each other in confusion. "What do you mean?" he said.

"Our little cousin," Dot continued. "Well, maybe she was a cousin, I don't really know. I think she was our Aunt Anna's little girl. Maybe Aunt Anna was our mom's dad's sister, I don't know. But Annie and I were the same age, four, going on five. We were playing in the alley even though my mother told us not to. We were playing in these cardboard boxes someone had left out there. I had to go to the bathroom, so I ran inside, and that's when the truck came along and ran over her in that box."

We gasped. "What?" I said. "Shirley never talked about this. Why wouldn't she have talked about it?"

"I don't know," Dot said. "Maybe nobody ever told her."

"And when did it happen?" I asked.

"I told you. I was going on five, so around 1928 or so. Right before we went to the Home. Right before our mother got sent to Central State."

We peppered Dot with more questions. Again, who was Annie? Who was Aunt Anna? Was Fay blamed for the child's death? Was there a funeral? But Dot didn't know any more than she had already shared.

"It was a long time ago. I'm almost 90! But it really did happen."

Soon after this visit, Thomas had an opportunity at a family picnic to question his cousins, the three daughters of Shirley's sister, Roberta. He relayed the information Dot had shared.

For a couple of seconds, everyone stared at us. Then Lois, the middle sister, said, "Well, that never happened. Dot's crazy."

All three women jumped in at once, saying you cannot believe a word Dot says. They seemed satisfied with this conclusion, but it bothered me for some time, even if it really was a figment of Dot's imagination. Over the next couple of years,

Thomas and I explored what we could about his grandparents, Fay and Morris, and found more than we would have imagined, including Morris's prison record and many pages of interview notes and medical records from Fay's years at Central State Hospital, mostly from the Indiana State Archives. We never saw anything about the death of a child and I began to think it probably didn't happen. But after another visit with Dot, who was unwavering in her certainty, I decided to enlist some help.

Dot wasn't sure whether her family was living in Terre Haute or Lafayette, Indiana when she and her siblings were sent to the orphanage in Knightstown, but she knew it was one of those places. I mentally flipped a coin and started by calling the Vigo County Public Library in Terre Haute. After I was directed to Sean Eisele in the Special Collections Department, I described the sketchy circumstances to him: no last name, just a little girl named Annie, who may have been the daughter of someone named Anna. It might have happened in Terre Haute; it might have been Lafayette. I was guessing it was in 1928, but it could have been 1927. Annie was probably four, but it could be plus or minus a year.

It was my good fortune that Sean was intrigued by the story and worked out various ways to approach it over the next few weeks. He also encouraged me to contact the Tippecanoe County Alameda McCollough Special Collections Library in Lafayette. This tip led me to providence again in the form of a volunteer named Amy Harbor.

Amy said that a child's fatal accident would have been important news in 1928. She began to look, and what she found astonished me. In addition to the death record of Shirley's father, Morris Peacock, who was buried in San Antonio in 1972, she discovered documentation of Morris with a wife and child when he was working on the Panama Canal. There were no records of him divorcing Fay, who had been in Central State for over a decade at that point and would remain there for decades more.

Amy also discovered the Tippecanoe County Children's Services handwritten log, documenting the affairs of children in homes deemed unsuitable for their care. She described it to me before sending it, including the fact that Fay and her children were listed in it a number of times, beginning in 1925, one year after Fay's father died. In the summer of that year, the log indicated the children were awarded to the Board of the Children's Home in Lafayette. Entries mentioned the comings and goings of each of the children to the Tippecanoe County Children's Home, though never as a full group. They were apparently separated earlier than I'd realized, and in an orphanage in Lafayette before being sent to the Soldiers' and Sailors' Children's Home in Knightstown.

Based on the information in the Children's Services log in Lafayette, Shirley would have been five or six the first time she was removed from her home and mother. A photograph shows her standing among several other children, all of whom were unknown to her by the time we looked at the photo together late in her life. A small, hand-drawn black arrow hovers above her head. She believed it was taken at the orphanage in Knightstown, but it had always bothered me that she looked younger than eight, which was her age at the time of enrollment. I remembered how Shirley used to say she was six or six-and-a-half when she went to Knightstown, and that they changed her name from Edith to Shirley because there were too many girls named Edith in the first grade. She would have been older than first grade when she went to Knightstown. This led me to believe her name was changed at the Tippecanoe County Children's Home, two years before she went to Knightstown to live for the rest of her childhood, and that in her memory, the first orphanage experience had been folded into the next as one.

Other entries in the Children's Services log in the years

leading up to Fay's commitment included reports of Morris's desertion and imprisonment, as well as calls to Children's Services from his mistress, Mrs. St. John, saying the children weren't being properly cared for. In the beginning of 1928, the log entries include questions about Fay's emotional stability, such as "Mrs. Peacock is losing her mind according to Dr. Laws." The children were individually farmed out to various relatives, but never for very long. This also appears to be when the first suggestions were made to permanently place them in an orphanage.

Throughout the time when Amy and I were examining the log, Sean had been painstakingly building a digital notebook of information, adding to the momentum building about this story. I had a sense that he and Amy, working separately but sharing their findings through me, were on the verge of a discovery.

A new clue came from Dot in one of our visits. "I know Annie's mom was at our mother's funeral. I think she may have been our dad's sister." Sean looked up the names of siblings listed on Morris's prison record, but there was no Anna.

When Thomas called his cousin, one of Roberta's daughters, to inquire about Dot's claim, she told him that it wasn't Morris's sister, but rather his sister-in-law who came to Fay's funeral in 1986. "Her name was Wanda Bible," she said. "Nobody knew why she came. I don't think anybody talked to her." No one else at the funeral had seen Morris or anyone from his family, except Aunt Jean, in almost sixty years. It seemed significant that Wanda Bible was there, whoever she was. There wasn't a Wanda Peacock listed as a sibling of Morris on his prison record. If she had been his sister-in-law, her different last name could be explained by a second marriage.

The next time I saw Dot, I tried to remember the questions Amy had asked me, such as whether Dot remembered if it was hot or cold at the time of the accident. This might have narrowed the search to a particular season. When I asked Dot if she remembered the weather when she and Annie were playing in the alley, she responded without hesitation. "Well, we had coats on, I know that. But I don't remember anything else."

After a pause, Dot said, "There was something else I was thinking. I don't know that the little girl's name was Annie. I called her Annie, but that might not have been her name." I kept my amused reaction to myself, thinking about what a wild goose chase it had been to look for a little girl without a last name. Had she been a complete Jane Doe, I might never have attempted to find out what happened.

"What do you remember happening when you were in the bathroom?" I asked.

"I heard a big commotion," Dot said. "Then someone came in and told me to be quiet. I didn't know what happened. They wouldn't let me go out."

"Do you remember where your mother was after the accident?"

"She locked herself in a room and wouldn't let anyone in. I don't think she took me home and I don't know where I went, but it wasn't with her."

"Did you go to the funeral?"

"No, they wouldn't have had a little kid like me there."

"Where would Shirley and Georgie and Roberta have been that day?" I asked. "And Don, too?"

"I don't know," Dot said. "I don't know where they were. I think we were separated a lot." She paused and tried to think. "Annie's mother wanted me, did I tell you that?"

"What do you mean?" I asked.

"She wanted to adopt me after Annie died. But Aunt Jean didn't let her do that, and then, well, she just erased us. Nobody saw her again, except for at our mother's funeral, I guess."

I asked Dot why Shirley wouldn't have known about Annie's death. "Well," she said, "maybe Jean told just me about it because she knew I was there and thought I might remember it. I hadn't remembered it, but as soon as she asked me about it, all the details came back to me, just like that."

"And why didn't you ever tell Shirley or anyone else about it?" I asked. Dot seemed to be at a loss when she tried to answer. "It was a story that hurt my heart," she said. "I guess I didn't want to talk about it."

Later she added, "Y'know, I never really talked to my mother about it either when I'd go visit her at the hospital or the old folks' home over the years. I thought it would be too painful. She was really fragile. But there was this one time when I was visiting her when she said something about a little girl, and she said, 'I guess I'll be paying for that the rest of my life.'"

That night, I found two email messages, one from Amy and one from Sean. "Annie" had been found by both of them at the same time, except her name wasn't Annie after all. It was Evelyn Peacock, who was a week shy of turning five years old when she was run over by a truck in the alley behind her home in Lafayette at 9:25 on a Friday morning, April 27, 1928. She was the daughter of Elmo Peacock, Morris Peacock's brother, and his wife, Wanda Peacock. The details of the article were graphic, typical of the time period. The neighbor children with whom Evelyn was playing "Indian," as it was described, were listed along with their nearby addresses, but Dot's name wasn't one of them, and there was no mention of Fay as the babysitter.

A powerful mix of sadness, relief, and vindication washed over me as I read the emails and attachments from Sean and Amy. The vindication was for Dot, the one that Thomas's cousins had assumed was crazy. Of course, Dot didn't care about being vindicated. She knew what she knew and didn't have anything to prove to anyone. But I felt victorious for her. I thought about little Evelyn, too, the child whose story had been unknown to Thomas's family all these years.

The Tippecanoe County Children's Services log indicated urgent activity about the fate of Fay's children two days after Evelyn Peacock's death. One relative from Fay's family, her stepmother's sister, had driven from Indianapolis and met with the Children's Services agent about one of the children. They met in his home, which made me think the meeting took place after office hours.

Weeks later, there was a report in the log about a new placement for the children, moving them from the Children's Home in Lafayette to the Soldiers' and Sailors' Orphans' Home in Knightstown. On July 5th, Jean Alberts (Aunt Jean), took Dora Fay (Dot), Donald, and Roberta to their new home. The log specifies that Shirley and Georgia would be similarly transferred after their eye infections had healed. I recalled Dot claiming this fact that Shirley flatly denied, saying this was just another example of things Dot made up. I wondered how she could have remembered her sisters' eye infections so many years later.

Fay was committed for life to Central State Hospital for the Insane on June 4, 1928, one month after Evelyn Peacock was buried at the Order of the Oddfellows Cemetery in Delphi, Indiana, north of Lafayette.

Morris's family was the only support Fay had after her father died. What had they thought about his wayward conduct – his petty crimes, his mistress, his absence from his family? Did they blame any of his choices on Fay? Perhaps they didn't know Morris's whereabouts since he had escaped from prison six months earlier. Maybe Fay and her children were considered a burden. Maybe her commitment was a way to remove them all in a single, swift action. I doubted Morris was aware of what happened, albeit from a distance, but it was certainly possible.

I kept thinking about Wanda Peacock Bible at Fay's funeral almost sixty years later and wondering what really happened when

Evelyn died. The article said that Wanda was cleaning house at the time of the accident. Maybe Fay was at the house with Dot when Wanda asked her to watch the children. Had Wanda blamed Fay for her little girl's terrible death? What had she wanted to see when Fay was laid to rest? Maybe she wanted to know what happened to the five children who were orphaned as a result of her own child's death, at least in part, so many years past. Had she wanted to adopt Dot? Was she unable to erase the family from her mind as Dot had claimed? Was this closure? Perhaps she had seen the dreadful price Fay had paid and felt something was owed after so many years. It appears to be a mystery that will remain unsolved.

Shirley once told me, "My mother said she woke up weeks after she was left at the hospital. She looked out the window and said, 'Where's my kids?'"

The kids had been scattered once again and remained unknown to each other, though housed in the same institution. Years later, their resemblance as adults was limited to their physical qualities. Shirley had never been on an airplane and never cared about that, but Georgia had flown across the ocean when she spent time in Europe. Shirley's grammar always gave away her origins, but Dot spoke with surprising eloquence. They were an interesting group of unrelated siblings. Each eventually represented a kind of archetype. Dot was the trickster, lively and fascinated by the hidden stories of daily life. Roberta was Mother Earth herself, kind, generous, and idealistic. I'm told that Don died a lost soul, alcoholic and destitute, and that Georgia was embittered and isolated until she died a brittle old woman. Shirley was the caregiver, caring for her mother and in-laws, as well as Joe and his elderly wife. She took care of my children, and in doing so, took care of me. She was also a survivor, emerging from the tragedy of her youth with a sideways sense of humor and a tendency not to cry over spilled milk. Against all odds, she put down roots in the shifting ground beneath her feet.

Questions linger about how the wheels of Shirley's life were set in motion. What if Fay's father, George, hadn't died so young, four years prior to Fay's commitment, and had continued to provide financial support for his daughter and grandchildren? What if little Evelyn hadn't been killed on that fateful April morning? Would Fay have been committed to Central State? Would Shirley and her siblings have grown up in an orphanage? If Shirley were here, she'd mock such questions while chastising me for dwelling on them. She'd say, "What difference does it make? I don't know why you worry about things that's already happened. Just leave it alone."

After all, as long as we are clothed and sheltered, we're taught a trade, and food is served piping hot at suppertime, who could ask for anything more?

Acknowledgements

I have written this book over many years, starting as family stories for my children, but eventually, and with help, fitting them together as one narrative. The first people I wish to thank are the women with whom I've shared countless drafts. Carrie Newcomer was the first person who listened to these stories. Her steadfast support over all this time has inspired me more than I'll ever be able to express. Thank you as well to Hester Hemmerling, Michelle Henderson, Faith Hawkins, Krista Detor, Angela Siffin, Cynthia Port, Kathy Hart, Anita Todd, Susan Schertzer, Mary McMullen, and my sister Lynne Anderson. Their willingness to roll up their sleeves and give me strong and useful feedback has been invaluable. Truly, they have been brilliant advocates.

Thank you to Cate Whetzel for editing much of the writing while it was in process and providing constructive advice. Thank you to my editor Julie Mosow for taking what I thought was a completed manuscript and showing me how it could be much better. She asked all the right questions, pointed out what was missing, and cushioned her critique with encouragement to continue this work to completion.

I'm grateful to Glenda Schulz for coming up with the book's title when nothing else would do.

Many thanks to Parker J. Palmer and James Alexander Thom for their support of *Crazy is Relative.* As a longtime teacher, I have drawn inspiration from their commitment to lifting up our society in hard times. Parker's dedication to education with heart reminds me that success in any calling is based on trusting relationships and a willingness to question what we believe to be true. James' stories of our country's history illuminate the origins of our societal values, and enable us to ask ourselves who we are and who we wish to be. I cannot imagine higher praise than their encouragement.

I owe considerable appreciation to Sean Eisele, Special Collections Department Librarian of the Indiana Vigo County Public Library, and to Amy Harbor from the Alameda McCollough Research Library of the Tippecanoe County Historical Association. Their tenacious search for a little girl who died in 1928 was extraordinary. They inspired me to complete the manuscript upon their discovery of Evelyn Peacock's tragic fate, along with other compelling information about my husband's family. I'm forever indebted to my husband's aunt, Dot Daugherty, for her candor, her astonishing memory, and the trust she placed in me with some of her most personal feelings as a child growing up in an orphanage.

I am at a loss for words to adequately express my gratitude to the publishing team that brought this project to print: Carrie Newcomer, Robert Meitus, Faith Hawkins, Michelle Henderson, and Krista Detor. Their generosity knew no bounds. Thank you to Hugh Syme for designing the book cover and inside photographs, and to Tim Gaskins for the internal design of the book.

Thank you to my mother, father, sisters, and brother for teaching me the importance of one's clan, by lineage or by choice, and for telling the stories that make up our family lore to this day. Thank you to Thomas's and my chosen family as well, including Carol and Jeff Stevens, Jaime Sweany, and other friends who lovingly cared for Thomas and me, our children, our pets, and our household throughout my illness and the completion of this manuscript in recent years. Thank you to Jaime for giving her blessing to the inclusion of stories about her personal life, and for remaining an essential member of the Kuhn family over the years, particularly in her caretaking of Joe Kuhn in recent times.

Thank you to my children, Ben Keller-Kuhn and Alison Keller-Kuhn, for their willingness to laugh at their childhood foibles, and for loving their grandmother in a way that I couldn't resist recording for posterity. Thank you to my daughter-in-law, Honna Keller-Kuhn, who recently came into the Keller and Kuhn fold, navigating the strange territory of a new family with grace and humor. It is my profound hope that she never feels moved to write a book about me.

Every account in this book was read and approved by my husband, Thomas Kuhn. Without his love, support, and sense of humor, the collection of these tales into one manuscript would have come to a halt before the wheels were set in motion. I am grateful to him for the stories he had to tell, his reading of the final manuscript and its earlier components, and the corrections he made along the way, e.g. "That was Joe's pot growing in the back yard, not mine." I am thankful to him for accompanying me on this journey of becoming part of his family at the same time that he embraced mine. I'm deeply grateful for his modeling of family caretaking that our children witnessed every day, as well as the incredible patience he modeled in response to his mother's mishaps and mayhem, and my itch to document it all.

And thank you to my utterly inimitable mother-in-law, Shirley Peacock Kuhn, for eventually accepting her nosy daughter-in-law who wouldn't leave her family stories and photographs alone. Thank you to Shirley for being the unassuming and remarkable kind of person any writer would be fortunate to write about. In our years together, I learned that love is simple, families are not, and that family love takes many forms, none more genuine or heartfelt than another.

About the Author

Melissa Keller is a professor at the Indiana University School of Education. She and her husband Thomas Kuhn live in their home surrounded by the beautiful woods of Bloomington, Indiana with their cat and a small pack of unruly dogs. Their favorite pastime is sitting on their screened-in porch and watching the dance of territorial hummingbirds around the birdfeeders, a far and welcome cry from the days when they endured the drama of their children fighting over the bathroom. They have recently welcomed their first grandchild Lyla Rose into the world, and have no plans to teach her how to open childproof caps, ever.

Made in the USA
Lexington, KY
27 November 2018